The Existence or Non-existence of Race?

The Existence or Non-existence of Race?

FORENSIC ANTHROPOLOGY, POPULATION ADMIXTURE,
AND THE FUTURE OF RACIAL CLASSIFICATION IN THE U.S.

CONRAD B. QUINTYN

<teneo>
// press

YOUNGSTOWN, NEW YORK

*To all of those good people on both sides of the race issue
who have worked tirelessly to delineate the problems of race*

TABLE OF CONTENTS

LIST OF FIGURES

LIST OF TABLES

FOREWORD

In this book, Conrad Quintyn takes on the thorny question of race, a question that seems to forever resonate in American culture. As a cultural anthropologist, I have for many years taught in my classes the official position of the American Anthropological Association that race has no biological meaning, that what we call "race" in America is really "ethnicity" (i.e., it is a cultural designation, not a biological one). I have pointed out to my students the variability of *Homo sapiens* physically and the overlapping of physical characteristics we popularly note as race. I have shown how different cultures define the same physical characteristics differently and that a person of color might well be regarded as "white" in one culture and "black" in another. I have noted that African Americans traveling to Africa to find their roots are often disillusioned by how little they have in common with Africans. And I have argued forcibly that no connections exist between issues such as race and intelligence except to the extent that individuals believe there to be a connection.

Yet at the same time, I have been uneasy with these perspectives, aware that they are not the whole story. Certainly my students, most of them anyway, do not believe race is simply ethnicity. I know that the physical traits we identify with race in American culture have evolutionary significance and are products of geographical isolation and genetic adaptations. I also know that throughout history, humans have categorized people by race and the same broad physical characteristics have been used in those categorizations, regardless of where specific cultural lines are drawn. Race is truly an anthropological conundrum!

Conrad Quintyn's book examines these questions from his perspective of a forensic anthropologist who is asked to identify the race of human physical remains. He knows that law enforcement officials expect him to make these identifications from skeletal evidence and that he is able to do so with a high degree of accuracy. In this book, he examines all sides of the race issue in detail, and he is not afraid to say that the use of race is practical in the cultural realm, as in finding missing persons, political redistricting, redressing civil rights abuses, and elsewhere. Simultaneously, he emphasizes that scholars should continue to teach the true complexity of human physical variation.

Anthropologists have long contended that their discipline takes a biosocial approach to humanity. That is, we believe we look at humans as complex blends of biology and learned behavior. To anthropologists, the answer to the question "Are humans products of their genes or their environment?" is "Yes." And yet for decades, anthropologists have clearly favored the environmental or cultural component in their understanding of human behavior. In this book, Conrad Quintyn returns anthropology to its philosophical origins by emphasizing the complex interaction of the two.

—Prof. David Minderhout
Department of Anthropology
Bloomsburg University
Emeritus

PREFACE

The motivation to write a book about race began in graduate school at the University of Michigan, Ann Arbor, where I met Prof. C. Loring Brace. In fact, Professor Brace was my graduate adviser and PhD dissertation chair. I took his graduate course entitled "Human Variation and Race," which was fondly referred to as "Brace on Race." This course gave me a biological-evolutionary perspective on race that I had never been exposed to in my previous education. In fact, my knowledge about race had been confined to the sociocultural aspects, that is, cultural and language differences, civil rights issues, discrimination, and slavery, to name a few. In this course, I gained knowledge of the evolution of modern human traits, such as skin color and craniofacial features. I also learned that these traits evolved over time as a result of evolutionary forces acting on our prehistoric ancestors who were living (directly) in the natural environment. Brace used the term "clines" to describe mere gradations in the distribution of individual biological traits (Brace, 2005, p. ix). And in dealing with human variation, Brace believed biological traits could best be understood by using the concept of clines and dispensing with the concept of race. I found this perspective fascinating and absorbed it with great enthusiasm. To me, Brace's perspective was quite logical, and it equipped me with scientific ammunition in the battle against race and racism.

For 7 years at the University of Michigan, this view permeated my thinking. I would regularly emphasize the aphorism "there are no races, there are only clines," when I lectured on human variation as a graduate student instructor and later as a university professor. Frank Livingstone (another of my teachers) first produced this aphorism, later adopted wholeheartedly by Brace. However, it was a tough sell to students because most could easily identify someone of European, African, or Asian ancestry in the classroom, and they could not grasp the abstraction of clines. Nonetheless, I soldiered on, disseminating the Brace perspective proudly. I still do the same today but with some modification.

When I began to assist law enforcement in identifying human skeletal remains, they wanted race. This is obvious because race is the only *practical* means by which they identify victims and fugitives. Like the students in the classroom, they could not grasp the evolutionary mechanisms behind human variation. Over time, I began to rethink race from my exalted position as a university professor and to take a more practical approach. This new approach was reinforced as racial tensions involving Rodney King, Reginald Denny, and O. J. Simpson dominated the public arena. It is easy for us in academia to say biological races do not exist. And I do agree that biologically (i.e., genetically) it is very difficult to put populations into neat categories. Recall instances where an individual from one race needs a kidney and an individual from another race is a perfect match. Yes, "there are no races, there are only clines." And yes, there is more variation within populations than between populations (Lewontin, 1972). But the person on the street neither understands nor cares about these statements. They cannot see genes or clines. What they see is dark versus light skin, straight versus curly hair, or "pointy" versus "flat" noses. In the social world, these phenotypic traits are important in everyday life, hence the cases of Rodney King, Reginald Denny, and O. J. Simpson. We don't live in a vacuum; we live in a social environment where race becomes critical for civil rights, economics, law enforcement, and politics.

We believe what we see, and on any street in America, we can see race. "We live in a virtual world where belief matters more than fact, and perception shapes reality…an eternal aspect of human nature" (Berreby, 2005, p. xix). In other words, we begin to classify individuals instantaneously because it is part of our evolutionary makeup. Although racial classification will never end, we must not look at it as good or bad. It is practical in the social environment. So let's deal with it and, at the same time, educate our students on the complexity of biological variation.

Acknowledgments

I would like to thank Prof. Robert Corruccini of Southern Illinois University, Prof. David Minderhout of Bloomsburg University, and Prof. Martha Rees of Agnes Scott College for their valuable comments, which improved the manuscript greatly. I would also like to thank Dr. Paul Richardson and the staff at Teneo Press for their support and patience in preparing the manuscript for publication.

The Existence
or Non-existence
of Race?

INTRODUCTION

The American Association of Physical Anthropologists' "Statement on Biological Aspects of Race" reads, "Humanity cannot be classified into discrete geographical categories with absolute boundaries" (American Association of Physical Anthropologists [AAPA], 1996, p. 569). Similarly, the American Anthropological Association's (1998) "Statement on Race" reads, "With the vast expansion of scientific knowledge in this century, it has become clear that human populations are not unambiguous, clearly demarcated, biologically distinct groups" (American Anthropological Association [AAA], p. 1). It is no coincidence both of these statements lead to the single idea that "there is no such thing as race." These statements are not made lightly; many highly regarded and reliable scholars and scientists within anthropology and human biology support them. But how do we reconcile these statements with the fact that, with close observation and metric analysis, forensic anthropologists have been successful in determining race for law enforcement using individual skulls? More to the point, we have no problem picking out Americans of European ancestry surrounded by African Americans in the Apollo Theatre in Harlem.

Of course, we can resurrect that tired explanation that humans try to make sense of nature by categorizing or ordering complex variations—a practice exemplified by Carolus Linnaeus and other Enlightenment figures. But this explanation, though perfectly valid, makes no sense to the average man or woman, politicians, or law enforcement officers in the real world. They see and use race in their respective day-to-day activities. For instance, government officials use race to address past and present discrimination. Furthermore, law enforcement will use social race, for example, "white female, 35 years old, 5 ft, 1 in.," to find a missing person or one who has committed a crime. Geneticists and human biologists state that skin color and stature are polygenic (coded by many genes) traits, which are measured on a continuum. But as these scientists attempt to understand polygenic, pleiotropic, or Mendelian traits, there seems to be confusion within the lay public and disagreement among scientists on how genotypic variation is related to phenotypic (visible) variation.

Adding to these problems is population admixture. The increased rate of immigrants from developing countries and subsequent growth in admixed populations in the last century has made America complicated. This has, in recent history, led to the proliferation of the racial categories and addition of a "choose more than one race" category on the 2000 Census, resulting from pressure from non-race activists and mixed-race individuals demanding visibility and acceptance. Will this significant change by the U.S. Census Bureau lead to confusion in the administration of day-to-day business or justice?

In this book, I will analyze the evidence from both sides in biological anthropology and human biology. But first, I want to begin with a history of the conflict in anthropology in general and biological anthropology in particular to give the reader some critical background information. In part 2, "Race in Contemporary Society," I will analyze the arguments on race as it pertains to forensic anthropology and law enforcement; human biology; federal and state government services; the U.S. Census; immigration; population admixture; and the fight for and against multiracialism. I'll also add results of my recent work in race and craniometrics and discuss the future of racial classification in America, noting forensic anthropology and human biology. Finally, I will propose a practical com-promise taking into account real-world problems. I do not take sides or generate solutions from an academic armchair. For example, it would be ridiculous for academic scholars to say to students in a classroom or to the general public, "there is no such thing as race." In many books, for instance, we see quotation marks around the word *race* on the cover or in the text, suggesting the concept is not real. This begs the question, if there is no such thing as race, what would it look like if it did exist (Sarich & Miele, 2004)? And where do we put multiracial individuals if race is real? Thus, we must end the tradition of taking sides in the race question or putting quotes around the word—it is very real to millions of people. In my opinion, both sides are right. We are all a part of the American culture, and we must deal with the race concept from a practi-cal point of view. I will show in my compromise that we can "have our cake and eat it too," so to speak.

PART I

THE RACE CONCEPT

HISTORY OF THE CONFLICT IN BIOLOGICAL ANTHROPOLOGY

CHAPTER 1

ANTHROPOLOGY AND RACE

Within the subfield of biological anthropology, there is significant disagreement on the race concept. A large percentage of anthropologists are conflicted as to whether human beings can be divided into discrete categories based on physical (and cultural) attributes. The complexity of molecular genetics adds to the confusion. For instance, it is widely known that there is more genetic variation within populations than between populations (Lewontin, 1972). Paradoxically, phenotypical traits such as skin color, hair form, and nose shape that are coded by genes clearly distinguish populations. This confusion prevented the immediate ratification of the "Statement on Biological Aspects of Race" by the American Association of Physical Anthropologists (AAPA, 1996). In 1993, for instance, voters rejected a draft statement presented for a vote at the AAPA meeting 43 to 35, with 4 abstentions (Sirianni, 1993; Cartmill, 1999). Not until December 1996 was the statement on race finally approved and published in the December 1996 issue of the *American Journal of Physical Anthropology*.

When asked in a 1985 survey whether they agreed with the statement "There are biological races within the species *Homo sapiens*," biological anthropologists' answers were quite interesting. Of the 365 biological anthropologists surveyed, nearly half ($N = 181$) said yes. A smaller number ($N = 148$) said they did not agree with the statement, and an even smaller number ($N = 36$) was neutral (Lieberman & Reynolds, 1996; Cartmill, 1999). Lieberman, Kirk, and Littlefield (2003) did a follow-up survey in 1999 because there had been complaints about the original survey, which only asked, "Are there biological races within the species *Homo sapiens*?" "It was widely felt that this was too vague a question, and professional biological anthropologists might feel they were saying there is not significant biological variation within the species (the source of their professional livelihood) if they said no" (R. Corruccini, personal communication, September 14, 2009). The follow-up survey asked respondents to agree or disagree with the following statement: "Human biological variation is best understood in terms of continuous gradations (clines) not races." Biological anthropologists agreed to a significantly higher degree than cultural anthropologists (Lieberman et al., 2003).

BACKGROUND

In animal taxonomy, the term *race* is used as a synonym for *subspecies*. Theodosius Dobzhansky (1962) attempted to deracialize human variation by using the subspecies designation, but it was later abandoned. If we, for example, dissected the term *Homo sapiens sapiens*, the taxonomic designation for humans, the genus would be *Homo*, the species would be *sapiens*, and the subspecies would be *sapiens*. The taxonomist might find it quite normal to say *Homo sapiens africanus* or *Homo sapiens europaeus*, but it would never catch on in the greater social environment. Whereas use of the subspecies designation is normal for the taxonomist in the study of animal populations, the human biologist finds it inappropriate when applied to human populations, simply because some in the public will more than likely get it wrong. They will consciously or subconsciously omit the prefix *sub* and emphasize the word *species*. One could imagine the following headline in newspapers: "A Majority of Americans Believe That the Human Races Are Different Species!"

A more compelling idea is the concept that a subspecies is most likely in the throes of evolutionary change. In other words, the population is in the process of becoming a new species. Non-racialists[1] use this argument to claim human populations are not in the process of becoming several different species; therefore, they are not subspecies or races. To support their position, they use the example of the three gorilla subspecies: *Gorilla beringei graueri* (eastern lowland), *Gorilla gorilla gorilla* (western lowland), and *Gorilla gorilla diehli* (cross river) (see figure 1.1).

FIGURE **1.1.** Gorilla species and subspecies, or examples of true races.

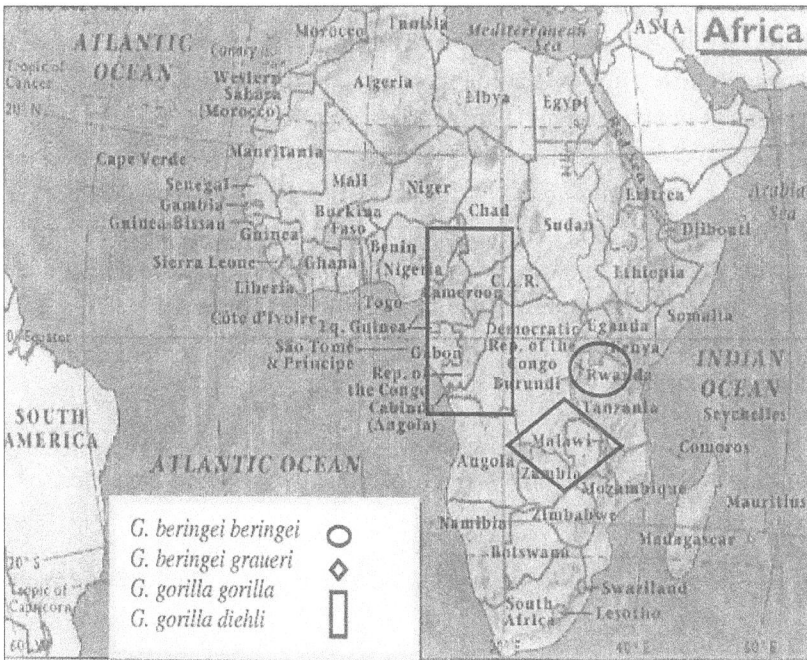

Source. Adapted from Code Network Media Group (©2006 Code Network Media Group).

Non-racialists, or opponents of the race concept, assert that these gorilla subspecies are the true races. We know that though these gorilla populations all belong to the same species, they are nonetheless physically and geographically distinct (Nystrom & Ashmore, 2008; Relethford, 2005). They do not cross each others' boundaries. Humans, in contrast, were and are constantly moving across population boundaries, resulting in a widespread geographical species. In short, non-racialists argue modern human populations have not been separated long enough to be classified as subspecies or races. However, later in this book, the molecular anthropologist Vincent Sarich, professor emeritus at the University of California, Berkeley, and Frank Miele, senior editor of *Skeptic* magazine, will find much greater racial morphological (cranial/facial) distance among human populations than among gorilla or chimpanzee subspecies. Interestingly, this is contrary to Lewontin's classic 1972 study; Fischer, Pollack, Thalmann, & Pääbo (2006); and Rosenberg et al. (2002), where there is much greater internal heterogeneity (F_{st}) and mean pairwise sequence difference (n_b) among gorillas and chimpanzees than among humans in genetic polymorphisms (see table 1).

Throughout the 20th century, several researchers—a few of whom would be considered racialists[2] today—did their best to define race. Stephen Molnar (2002) compiled the following samples of definitions of race in biology and anthropology. To these definitions, I have added a few more and placed all definitions in chronological order. It is interesting to read these definitions and, in particular, to see how some researchers changed their ideas over time.

HOOTON: A race is a great division of mankind, the members of which, though individually varying, are characterized as a group by a certain combination of morphological and metrical features, principally non-adaptive, which have been derived from their common descent (1926, p. 75);

HUXLEY
AND HADDON: Populations differed from one another, Huxley and Haddon stressed, only in the relative proportions of

TABLE 1. Internal genetic heterogeneity (F_{st}) and mean pairwise sequence difference (η_b) among chimpanzees, gorillas, and humans.

Chimpanzees F_{st}	Central	Eastern	Western	Gorillas	Eastern lowland/highland	Humans	Hausa	Chinese	Italians
Central		0.09	0.29*						
Eastern	0.20		0.32*						
Western	0.21	0.21							
Gorillas					0.12				
Eastern lowland/highland									
Humans									
Hausa								0.15*	0.14
Chinese							0.13		0.09
Italians							0.14	0.09*	

Sources. Adapted from Fischer et al. (2006); Guillén, Barrett, & Takenaka (2005).
Note. *Human populations are less differentiated than chimpanzee subspecies.

genes for given characters that they possessed. For existing populations the word *race* should be banished, and the descriptive and non-committed term *ethnic groups* should be substituted (1935; as cited in Kevles, 1995, p. 133; italics in the original);

BOAS: argued against the stability of many biological features. He examined head form, expressed by a simple index that was commonly used to distinguish races. He showed that it changed significantly in the first American-born generation of immigrants who came to America. Relatively long-headed people became broader, and relatively broad-headed people became longer. Because the change was rapid and converged on the same head form from different starting points, Boas argued it was environmentally induced—an important trait to distinguish races could easily change from one generation to the next. (1912; as cited in Wolpoff & Caspari, 1997, pp. 149–150);

DOBZHANSKY: Races are defined as populations differing in the incidence of certain genes, but actually exchanging or potentially able to exchange genes across whatever boundaries (usually geographic) separate them (1944, p. 252);

HOOTON: This insistence upon the use of "non-adaptive" characters in human taxonomy now seems to me to be impractical and erroneous (1946, p. 452);

W. C. BOYD: We may define a human race as a population which differs significantly from other human populations in regard to the frequency of one or more of the genes it possesses. It is an arbitrary matter which, and how many, gene loci we choose to consider as a significant "constellation" (1950, p. 207);

GARN: At the present time there is general agreement that a race is a breeding population, largely if not entirely isolated reproductively from other breeding populations. The measure of race is thus reproductive isolation, arising commonly but not exclusively from geographical isolation (1960, p. 7);

DOBZHANSKY: Race differences are objectively ascertainable facts; the number of races we choose to recognize is a matter of convenience (1962, p. 266);

COON: Race is a zoological concept meaning a division of species (1962, p. 5);

MONTAGU: An ethnic group represents one of a number of populations, comprising the single species *Homo sapiens*, which individually maintain their differences, physical and cultural, by means of isolating mechanisms such as geographic and social barriers. These differences will vary as the power of the geographic and social barriers acting upon the original genetic differences varies (1964, p. 317; italics in the original);

P. T. BAKER: It is concluded that race may be defined as a rough measure of genetic distance in human populations and as such may function as an informational construct in the multidisciplinary area of research in human biology (1967, p. 21);

HULSE: Races are populations which can be readily distinguished from one another on genetic grounds alone (1971, p. 262);

BRUES: A race is: a division of a species which differs from other divisions by the frequency with which certain hereditary traits appear among its members. Among these traits are features of external appearance that make it possible to recognize members of different populations by inspection with greater or less accuracy. Members of such a division of a species share ancestry with one another to a greater degree than they share it with individuals of other races. Finally, races are usually associated with particular geographic areas (1977, pp. 1–2);

MAYR: A subspecies is an aggregate of local populations of a species, inhabiting a geographic subdivision of the range of the species, and differing taxonomically from other populations of the species (1982, p. 289);

VOGEL
AND MOTULSKY: A race is a large population of individuals who have a significant fraction of their genes in common and can be distinguished from other races by their common gene pool (1986, p. 534);

BRUES: A race is a population that differs from others by the frequency of certain genes and the characters they produce. A more technical way of expressing it is to say that racially different populations have different gene pools. The existence of distinguishable gene pools within a species implies some mechanism of at least partial isolation, which in most cases is geographical in nature (1993, p. 77);

TEMPLETON: The word race is rarely used in the modern, nonhuman evolutionary literature because its meaning is so ambiguous. When it is used, it is traditionally a geographically circumscribed differentiated population (1999, p. 632);

MOLNAR: The term *race*, or *population*, will be used carefully to refer to that geographically and culturally determined collection of individuals who share a common gene pool. *Ethnic group* has some special meanings due to its various political and social *applications*; it may or may not affect genetic variability (2002, p. 33; italics in the original);

HAVILAND, PRINS,
WALRATH,
AND MCBRIDE: *race* In biology, the taxonomic category of subspecies that is not applicable to humans because the division of humans into discrete types does not represent the true nature of human biological variation. In some societies race is an important cultural category (***ethnic group***)...based on various cultural features such as shared ancestry and common origin, language, customs, and traditional beliefs (2005, pp. 323, 350; italics and bold in the original).

New knowledge—interpreted one way or another—cannot flourish without building upon the ideas of past scholars. The previous definitions show such a tradition. One can see the intellectual links between certain researchers and their predecessors on the race concept. Specifically, some researchers applied the relatively new science of genetics (which was a virtual black box until Watson and Crick unlocked the secrets of the genetic code in 1953) to their research and subsequent writings, indicated by the use of such words as *genes, gene pool, breeding population,* and so forth (particularly after Dobzhansky's 1944 writings). In contrast, one does not see morphological or phenotypical explanations, such as skin color, nose shape, and so forth, in these definitions. In a few instances, one sees the term *ethnic group* substituted for race. Moreover, the use of the terms *geographic subdivision, geographic isolation,* and any words indirectly referring to geography, such as *ancestry,* indicates that most of these researchers viewed geographical adaptation as an important factor in the formation of races. So let us agree for now that those individuals within a population who share more morphological features than other individuals are collectively called a race.

Knowledge also does not occur in a scientific vacuum; it is shaped by—and shapes—events in greater society. To appreciate the conflict within physical anthropology, I will, therefore, begin with the Enlightenment[3] figures Carolus Linnaeus, the father of animal taxonomy, who was responsible for applying scientific names to biological life forms and classifying them, *phenotypically,* according to similarities or differences; Johann Friedrich Blumenbach, who is recognized as the "father of biological anthropology," classified humanity into five "varieties": European, Asian, American, African, and Malay; and Stanhope Smith, the minister-scholar and president of Princeton University (1795–1812) who applied the Christian Common Sense position to the significance of human biological differences.

THE ENLIGHTENMENT ("AGE OF REASON"): LINNAEUS, BLUMENBACH, SMITH, AND THE MONOGENIST TRADITION

Loring Brace (2005) characterized it best when he discussed the genesis of the race concept. He stated, "If America was the workshop in which the concept of 'race' was to be cobbled together to resemble what is now accepted on a worldwide basis, the intellectual framework that served as a guide was entirely European" (p. 24). He added that the framework came from the traditions of Enlightenment scholarship.

Carolus Linnaeus' (1707–1778) work forms the basis for identifying and classifying biological species. We can praise or scorn Linnaeus for the establishment of the now universal tradition of referring to biological life forms by their generic and specific names. Some will definitely blame him for the present proliferation of species names. Nonetheless, Linnaeus believed it was his Christian duty to create order out of the chaos of the natural world. He really believed he was showing God's glory (Lindroth, 1983). And he emphasized this in the introduction to all the later editions of his *Systema Naturae*: "I saw the infinite, all-knowing and all-powerful God from behind as He went away and I grew dizzy. I followed His footsteps over nature's fields and saw everywhere an eternal wisdom and power, an inscrutable perfection" (as cited in Brace, 2005, p. 26). Like other great Enlightenment figures, for example, Sir Isaac Newton, Sir Francis Bacon, and Cotton Mather, Linnaeus was motivated to show God's glory. He was also inspired, according to some (Larson, 1971; Brace, 2005), by categories in Aristotelian hierarchy,[4] as his five categories—class, order, genus, species, and variety—were arranged in descending order of distinctiveness.

In the famous 10th edition of his 1758 *Systema Naturae* (1956), Linnaeus placed *Homo sapiens* in the order Primates (Brace, 2005). This was troubling and controversial for Linnaeus because 1) man was made in the image of God, yet man's skeleton was similar to that of Primates; and 2) the worldview of the 18th century was that man is on a pedestal just below angels and far removed from the animal world. Consequently, it was impossible for man to be in the order Primates or any classification with animals and plants. Thomas Pennant (1726–1798), a prominent English zoologist, indicated his displeasure of Linnaeus' classification of the human species as follows: "I REJECT his first division, which he calls *Primates*, or Chiefs of Creation; because my vanity will not suffer me to rank mankind with *Apes, Monkies, Maucaucos* and *Bats*, the companions LINNAEUS has allotted us" (as cited in Brace, 2005, p. 26; italics in the original).

When Linnaeus described human biological variation, he divided human populations into four "varieties" based on geographical regions. However, there are disagreements as to whether Linnaeus' model was cartographical (Gould, 1994) or hierarchical (Larson, 1971; Brace, 2005). For instance, Stephen J. Gould (1994) argued that Linnaeus divided the species *Homo sapiens* into four basic varieties, defined primarily by geography—*americanus* or Native American, *europaeus*, *asiaticus*, *afer* or African—and "interestingly not in the ranked order favored by most Europeans in the racist tradition" (p. 67). Gould continued by stating that Linnaeus merely mapped humans onto the four geographical regions: "In short, Linnaeus's primary ordering principle is cartographic; if he had wished to push hierarchy as the essential picture of human variety, he would surely have listed Europeans first and Africans last, but he started with native Americans instead" (p. 67). This is quite unusual because Linnaeus was raised, like most Europeans of his time, to believe in the *scala naturae* or Great Chain of Being, where God was on the top and angels just below. Then, following in specific order, ranked "man," animals, plants, and inorganic objects.

Indeed, it is hard to believe Linnaeus totally abandoned conventional beliefs about the superiority of his own European variety, given that he assigned behavioral characteristics to each human population, with Europeans, or *europaeus*, getting the most favorable characteristics— "albus, sanguineus, torosus" (white, sanguine or cheerful, muscular). For the *americanus* variety, Linnaeus wrote "rufus, cholericus, rectus" (red, choleric or prone to anger, upright); for *asiaticus*, "luridus, melancholicus, rigidus" (pale yellow, melancholy, stiff); and for *afer*, "niger, phlegmaticus, laxus" (black, phlegmatic or relaxed, lazy) (as cited in Sauer, 1993, p. 79; Gould, 1994, p. 67). One can argue that none of these categories explicitly implies ranking by worth; however, being cheerful and muscular does sound much better than phlegmatic or stiff.

Linnaeus' work on human biological variation would become the foundation on which future racial classification was built. Today Linnaeus is given some credit for his contribution to racial classification, but we credit his student Johann Blumenbach as the founder of racial classification.

Johann Friedrich Blumenbach (1752–1840) modified Carolus Linnaeus' model and added one more group, which he called Malay (Gould, 1994; Jurmain & Nelson, 1994; Molnar, 2002). This change was incorporated into the second edition (1781) of his *De Generis Humani Varietate Nativa* [On the natural variety of mankind]. By moving away from the Linnaean four-race system, which he still applied in the first edition (1775) of his treatise, Blumenbach radically changed the "geometry" of racial classification from a geographically based model akin to a rectangle—four corners of the globe—without explicit ranking to a hierarchy of worth, *curiously* based upon perceived beauty and fanning out in two directions from a *Caucasian* ideal (Gould, 1994, p. 66).

I have italicized the word *curiously* in the previous paragraph because Blumenbach was one of the greatest and most honored scientists of the Enlightenment and, based on his writings, the least racist of all Enlightenment thinkers. On further reflection, however, this break from the scientific method may not be so surprising. First, even the great Isaac Newton broke from the scientific method to incorporate religious faith. For instance, Newton had great anxiety that his new equations for gravity, which described the force of attraction between pairs of objects, might not maintain a stable system of orbits for several planets, causing them to crash into the sun or get ejected from the solar system (Tyson, 1999, p. 82; Tyson, 2005, pp. 28–29). Worried about the long-term fate of the Earth and the other planets, Newton invoked a Supreme Being as the force restoring order in this chaotic system. Second, Blumenbach was, unconsciously, presenting the worldview of his time. He lived in an age when European cultural and biological superiority dominated the world, and he was a product of this generation. Scientists are frequently unaware of (or sometimes do not care about) the impact of their ideas or substantive creations on the greater society.

I doubt, and many will agree, Blumenbach was actively encouraging racism (Gould, 1994 and 1996; Brace, 1996 and 2005; Molnar, 2002). His primary motivation was showing the glory of God; he accepted the biblical account of human origins and believed in the unity of man, or *monogenism*. The term *monogenism* originates in biology and is defined as a trait controlled by a single gene pair (*Merriam-Webster's Collegiate Dictionary*, 2003). The term has been adopted by religion, where the notion of "a single pair" now refers to one pair, Adam and Eve, as the origin of all humans. Blumenbach strongly opposed an alternate view, then growing in popularity, that each major race had been created separately. He ended his third edition (1795) by writing, "No doubt can any longer remain but that we are with great probability right in referring all...varieties of man...to one and the same species" (as cited in Gould, 1994, p. 68). This is certainly strong evidence indicating that Blumenbach's classification, where he depicts the European or Caucasian race at the pinnacle of a triangular model based on perceived beauty, had no malicious intent.

The most enduring of Blumenbach's contributions is the word *Caucasian*. The lay public more than likely does not know the origin of this word. Yet they know which population group it applies to. This term, which has no biological meaning, is entrenched in the American social, political, economic, and legal bureaucracy. Although the term continues to be the official label of one bureaucratic race in the United States, it was more than just a label of bureaucratic convenience for Blumenbach. In his own words:

> I have taken the name of this variety from Mount Caucasus, both because its neighborhood, and especially its southern slope, produces the most beautiful race of men, I mean the Georgian; and because all physiological reasons converge to this, that in that region, if anywhere, it seems we ought with the greatest probability to place the autochthones [original forms] of mankind. For in the first place, that stock displays...the most beautiful form of the skull, from which, as from a mean and primeval type, the others diverge by most easy gradations on both sides...white...we may fairly assume to have been the primitive colour of mankind. (translated by Bendyshe, 1865, p. 269)

The framework for Blumenbach's racial scheme was the Book of Genesis (Gould, 1996; Brace, 1996; Molnar, 2002). The reference to the "neighborhood" of Mount Caucasus in his previous statement supports this observation. According to the biblical account, Noah's ark landed on Mount Ararat. This region is bordered by the Black Sea in the west and the Caspian Sea in the east, and the peninsula that shares the name Caucasus extends toward Iraq in the southeast and Turkey in the southwest. Unlike Linnaeus, Blumenbach's monogenist tradition was an integral part of his explanation for human variation. It follows, in his mind, that the ancestors of all living people would have originated in this region. So, in Blumenbach's reasoning, Caucasians were the unchanged descendants of Adam and Eve. All other populations with different physical characteristics had "degenerated" (Bendyshe, 1865, p. 188).

Careful study indicates that Blumenbach did not mean degeneration in the modern definition of the word but modification in physical characteristics resulting from environmental change. Gould and Brace presented this in a slightly different way. Gould (1994) explained,

> Following the terminology of his time, Blumenbach referred to these changes as "degenerations"—not intending the modern sense of deterioration, but the literal meaning of departure from an initial form of humanity at the creation (*de* means "from," and *genus* refers to our original stock). (p. 68)

Similarly, Brace (2005) said,

> When Blumenbach stated that the differences visible between the various geographic populations of modern humans had occurred by "degeneration," all he meant was that distance and circumstances had combined to change their appearance from what it had been "in the beginning." (p. 46)

In essence, those who were physically very different—for example, Africans, Native Americans, Asians—had migrated farther away from this so-called "Garden of Eden" or Caucasian ideal and changed because of climate (e.g., dark skin) and culture (e.g., long skulls—cranial deformation). Several scholars have proposed that cranial deformation was a ritual performed in prehistoric and historical societies to achieve beauty (Romero, 1970; Schwartz, 1974; Burdeau, 1989; Dobson, 1994;

FitzSimmons, Prost, & Peniston, 1998). It is interesting that Blumenbach's worldview prevented him from realizing ideas of beauty are different from one culture to the next.

Blumenbach treated the idea of beauty like a quantifiable property, indicated in his description of a skull found close to Mount Caucasus:

> In the first place, that stock displays...the most beautiful form of the skull, from which, as from a mean and primeval type, the others diverge by most easy gradations.... Besides, it is white in color, which we may fairly assume to have been the primitive color of mankind, since...it is very easy for that to degenerate into brown, but very much more difficult for dark to become white. (translated by Gould, 1994, p. 69)

In his third (1795) edition, Blumenbach ended up with a model that placed Caucasians at the pinnacle, and then Asians (Mongolians) and Africans (Ethiopians) were presented on two symmetrical lines of departure from the Caucasian ideal (see figure 1.2). Blumenbach placed Native Americans between Caucasians and Asians because he wanted to designate intermediate forms between ideal and most degenerate; he believed all racial characteristics grade continuously from one people to another (today biological anthropologists call this clinal variation, or traits that

FIGURE 1.2. An illustration of Johann Blumenbach's racial classification, 1781.

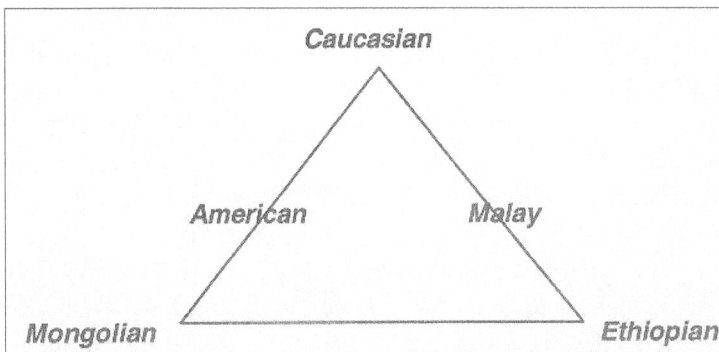

follow the intensity of the selective forces). The Malay race was placed between Caucasians and Africans.

Although Blumenbach's racial scheme has fostered many great social problems today, he embodied the monogenist movement in Europe. Another monogenist, Samuel Stanhope Smith, addressed similar issues on human variation in America.

Samuel Stanhope Smith (1751–1819), like any good Enlightenment scientist, believed scientific discoveries enhanced one's belief in God. There are a few who propose that Smith was America's first biological anthropologist and a staunch proponent of the Scottish "Philosophy of Common Sense," where each individual human being had the requisite common sense to understand the ways of God and the world (Hudnutt, 1956; Brace, 2005).[5] Smith adopted this Scottish philosophy as a student at Princeton University, known then as Princeton College, from 1767 to 1769 (Noll, 1989, p. 50). In the post-Revolutionary era of America, where ideas of monogenism and the Scottish philosophy were both at their zenith, Smith was elected president of Princeton in 1795. He instructed students in the Scottish philosophy with its teachings of "Christian Common Sense" as an approach in solving problems in society (P. Wood, 2000). An important component of this philosophy, or at least Smith's version, was the emphasis on science. Therefore, it did not take long for Smith to add a science component to Princeton by hiring the Scottish chemist John Maclean (1771–1814) in 1796 as the first professor of chemistry in an American college (Brace, 2005; Hudnutt, 1956). Smith did not stop there; he emphasized science in his own way by the application of the Christian Common Sense philosophy to the question of the significance of human biological differences.

Smith was elected to membership in the fledgling American Philosophical Society in Philadelphia in 1785 and, soon after, was invited to give a lecture on his work, entitled "An Essay on the Causes of the Variety of Complexion and Figure in the Human Species" (1787) (Noll, 1989, p. 118). In this lecture, Smith reasserted the writings in the Book of Genesis that all humans came from Adam and Eve—a single pair. He gathered supporting evidence to show that any male can mate with any female and produce a fertile offspring. He added that the visible differences in human populations were the result of different climates and social conditions.

Generally, Smith's monogenism was in the tradition of the European Enlightenment scholars, and it was quite similar to Blumenbach's assertions. In fact, Smith would later use Blumenbach's book to support his own book (1810) as a response to Lord Kames' publication *Sketches of the History of Man* (1774), in which Kames believed "there were different species of men, a phenomenon that came about by the action of God at the time of the legendary attempt to construct the Tower of Babel" (Brace, 2005, p. 54). Smith rebutted by advocating environment; that is, populations near the sun would be more pigmented and populations in cold climates would have shorter limbs to prevent frostbite. He added that if the "savage" was raised in a "civilized" environment, the "savage" would adopt intellectual and behavior refinements approaching "white" Europeans. And to Smith and Blumenbach, "white" Europeans were as close to what God wanted humans to be as was possible.

Although Blumenbach and Smith developed similar proposals independently, they were each working from a different frame of reference. For instance, it was easy to be a monogenist in Europe because the populations were mostly homogenous. As Winthrop Jordan (1965) put it, "Smith's book reveal[s] how very much more immediate the problem of human physical and cultural diversity had become for transplanted Europeans who lived with it than for those who sat reading about it in the comfortable home of civilization" (p. xli). Brace (2005) put it more directly: "Blumenbach's formulation was an abstract undertaking based largely on vicarious gleanings, whereas Smith's was stimulated by questions raised from the ongoing confrontation of three very different populations" (p. 52). In 19th-century America, there were three distinct populations (Native Americans,[6] European Americans, and African Americans) outside their ancestral regions (Native Americans' ancestry can be traced to North Asia) in constant conflict with each other because of cultural and visible differences. Modern societies put much value on the phenotypical (visible) traits of "the other."

It was no different in 19th-century America. The day-to-day interaction different cultures had with the accompanying smells, sights, and sounds was enough to make European Americans (who had political, economic, and military power at that time) rethink monogenism. It was by no means easy for monogenists to go against the Bible, but this "feeling" was quite powerful. In sociocultural history, some would call this Romanticism—feeling over reason (Brace, 1982 and 1997; Gould, 1994). Soon the shroud of polygenesis, which argued that separate pairs of Adam and Eves, one for each population, descended upon early America. At the same time, the American School of Biological Anthropology emerged from this muck to validate the differences among these populations in a very negative way.

"FEELING OVER REASON": THE FALL OF MONOGENISM

There may be myriad reasons why late-18th-century Christians slowly began to reject the biblical assertion of the "unity of mankind" despite the presence of mulattoes or biracial men and women who produced biracial offspring. One philosophical reason, still debated today, is Romanticism or "feeling over reason." The late historians Will and Ariel Durant (1967) give the best assessment of the changes that occurred at the end of the Enlightenment period:

> But what shall we mean by the Romantic movement? The rebellion of feeling against reason, of instinct against intellect, of sentiment against judgment, of the subject against the object, of subjectivism against objectivity, of solitude against society, of imagination against reality, of myth and legend against history, of religion against science, of mysticism, against ritual, of poetry and poetic prose against prose and prosaic poetry, of neo-Gothic against neo-classical art, of the feminine against the masculine, of romantic love against the marriage of convenience, of "Nature" and the "natural" against civilization and artifice, of emotional expression against conventional restraints, of individual freedom against social order, of youth against authority, of democracy against aristocracy, of man versus the state—in short, the revolt of nineteenth century

against the eighteenth…all these waves of the great Romantic tide that swept Europe between Rousseau and Darwin. (p. 887)

Another, simpler reason could have been "culture shock" after seeing "the other." In the average European explorer's mind, the natives of America, Africa, Melanesia, Polynesia, and so forth were so different in appearance and culture that they could not have come from the same Adam and Eve. The reader must understand that the average 18th-century European explorer was illiterate; and the educated naval officers and naturalists did not understand biological variation (not until Charles Darwin and Alfred Russell Wallace's work on natural selection did other biologists begin to slowly understand the importance of variation). The literate people spread the word of the naturalists' accounts that presented descriptions of many different biological life forms not mentioned in the Bible.

For instance, in 1735 the British naval surgeon John Atkins wrote, "tho' it be a little Heterodox, I am persuaded that the black and white Race have, *ab origine*, sprung from different-coloured first Parents" (as cited in Brace, 2005, p. 40; italics in the original). Atkins traveled from England to sub-Saharan Africa without stopping at any ports as his ship moved to the lower latitudes near the equator. Consequently, he (and everyone aboard) did not see the gradations in skin pigmentation as one travels from higher latitudes to latitudes near the equator. Atkins perceived distinctions in a discrete and categorical fashion, that is, "white" and "black." Brace (2005) calls this the "peasant perspective."[7] Another example from the clash of cultures is Edward Long (1734–1813), an English plantation owner in Jamaica. In *The History of Jamaica* (1774), Long stated that blacks and whites were different species and their offspring or "hybrids" were infertile and would eventually die out. Long wrote down what most Europeans were beginning to feel—that blacks were closer to apes, mentally inferior to whites, inherently bloody, brutish, idle, and superstitious (Long, 1774). The perceptions of human variations by Atkins and Long have not died with time. Today we still categorize complex variation. For example, we label people in three simple height categories of "short," "medium," "tall," even though a person can be 5 ft, 1 in.; 5 ft, 1¼ in.; 5 ft,

1 ½ in.; and so forth. And there are still some who believe blacks are mentally inferior to whites. As recently as 1994, for instance, late Harvard psychologist Richard J. Herrnstein and right-wing "political analyst" Charles Murray, in their book *The Bell Curve: Intelligence and Class Structure in American Life*, presented an assessment of the intellectual limitations conferred by an African ancestry. The conclusions the authors articulated were provocative, and a large percentage of those who read this book accepted these conclusions because they were supported by "irrefutable stats"—which most of the readership could not understand regardless.

In essence, Atkins, Long, and—let us not forget—Lord Kames and his *Sketches of the History of Man* (1774), treated in the previous section, are key among those whose views ushered in the era of polygenism, although monogenism didn't go down without a fight with John Bachman carrying the colors.

John Bachman (1790–1874), although pastor of St. John's Lutheran Church in Charleston, South Carolina, was not an average Southern clergyman. He had made the acquaintance of Blumenbach's protégé Baron Alexander von Humboldt (1769–1859) in Philadelphia in 1804 and again on visits to Berlin and Paris in 1838 (Brace, 2005). More important, he was a long-term collaborator of famous artist-naturalist John James Audubon (1785–1851) and even did most of the writing for the Audubon text *The Viviparous Quadrupeds of North America* (Elman, 1976, p. 17). One could speculate that because of his interest in natural history and the time spent on the *Quadrupeds* text—today in academia we would view this as time devoted to research and writing—he was appointed professor of natural history at the College of Charleston (Neuffer, 1960, p. 81). In short, Bachman had the requisite scientific qualifications to speak with authority on the rectitude of monogenism.

But Bachman was not a monogenist in the tradition of Enlightenment figures Blumenbach and Smith. As discussed earlier in this chapter, those two men, particularly Smith, believed the "savage" could be brought up to the level of whites if placed in "civilized" circumstances. As examples, Smith offered the case of the differences in appearance between the African Americans serving as "house" slaves and those used as "field" slaves.

He added that as African Americans and European Americans worked side by side, they would come to resemble each other over the course of several generations (Brace, 2005, p. 53). Bachman, in contrast, did not have this vision of racial admixture and equality. His support for monogenism was strictly based on his desire to stay true to the Holy Scriptures because to go against the Bible would be outright heresy. Bachman did not believe African Americans (or Native Americans) could be improved, even if placed in "civilized" circumstances. In response to Louis Agassiz's and Samuel George Morton's writings supporting polygenism using hybrid-sterility and separate-species arguments, Bachman's (1854) position was clear:

> The following are our views. That all the races of men, including the negro, are of one species and one origin. That the negro is a striking and now permanent variety, like the numerous varieties in domesticated animals. That varieties having become permanent, possess an organization that prevents them from returning to the original species, although other varieties may spring up among them. Thus the many breeds of domesticated animals that have arisen, some only within a few years, would never return to the form of the wild species without an intermixture. That the negro will remain as he is, unless his form is changed by amalgamation—which latter is revolting to us. That his intellect, although underrated, is greatly inferior to that of the Caucasian, and that he is therefore, as far as our experience goes, incapable of self-government. That he is thrown on our protection. That our defense of slavery is contained in the holy scriptures. That the scriptures teach the rights and duties of masters, to…rule their servants with justice and kindness, and enjoin the obedience of servants. (p. 657)

In 19th-century America, Bachman may have been one of less than a handful of monogenists. Polygenism, which rode the wave of Romanticism, gained momentum and strength in the mid-19th century and engulfed monogenism. Simultaneously, the Enlightenment belief in a rational world and use of the scientific method to deal with the nature of human biological difference disappeared.

CHAPTER 2

THE RISE OF POLYGENISM

RACE AND THE FOUNDING OF THE AMERICAN SCHOOL OF BIOLOGICAL ANTHROPOLOGY

NINETEENTH-CENTURY SCIENTIFIC POLYGENISM: SAMUEL GEORGE MORTON, LOUIS AGASSIZ, AND PAUL BROCA (IN FRANCE)

Very few biological anthropologists would recognize the name Samuel George Morton (1799–1851) or give him the title of "father of American biological anthropology." Aleš Hrdlička (1869–1943), founder and editor of the *American Journal of Physical Anthropology* and instrumental in the founding of the American Association of Physical Anthropologists in 1930, was one of the few people familiar with Morton's work and afforded him his lofty title. In his book *Physical Anthropology, Its Scope and Aims; Its History and Present Status in the United States* (1919), Hrdlička stated, "It is plain that Morton may justly and with pride be termed the father of American anthropology" (p. 41). Brace (2005), one of the few anthropologists who sees no racial bias in Morton's crani-ometrics, goes even further:

> [T]he original and enduring contribution that Morton made was in the invention and application of a battery of measurements that he used to compare large numbers of specimens from many parts of the world. Morton devised more than a dozen cranial mea-surements and basically initiated the use of metrics in compar-ing human biological forms. Many of the measurements Morton devised continue to be used for comparative purposes in biologi-cal anthropology today.... Morton, then, deserves recognition as one of the founders of the field of biological anthropology as a whole and not just its American manifestation. (p. 82)

So why are Samuel George Morton and his contributions to biologi-cal anthropology forgotten? Gould claims it was his "racial bias" that permeated his work (1981 and 1996). Others have argued that it was his tentative support of phrenology that accounted for his obscurity (Erick-son, 1977; Hrdlička, 1919). Further, Brace has argued that Morton's sup-port for polygenism and his association with outspoken proponents of slavery doomed his reputation and contributions to biological anthropol-ogy (Brace, 2005). These issues will be addressed in turn as we study the environment that gave birth to Morton's work.

In chapter 1, I noted that 19th-century America was composed mainly of three visibly and culturally distinct populations—African Americans, European Americans, and Native Americans—outside of their ances-tral homes in constant conflict with each other.[8] Their differences were exaggerated simply because most Americans at that time were not world travelers; consequently, they did not have a clinal view of the world's populations. The perception was of three distinct categories of humans—some more human than others, according to the dominant whites—who could not be part of the same species. On this fertile soil, biological anthropology established itself to prove "scientifically" that human pop-ulations had separate origins.

Morton obtained his medical degrees from the University of Pennsyl-vania Medical School in Philadelphia and the University of Edinburgh in Scotland between 1820 and 1823 (Brace, 2005, p. 79). Subsequently, he established a medical practice in Philadelphia, and its success allowed Morton to apply his considerable skills to research in academia. For instance, he conducted research in vertebrate paleontology and even identified a new species of hippopotamus. But the research that obliterated his legacy was his use of science to support the continued forced servitude of African Americans. Put another way, his research, like the Bible, was used to show that African Americans were suited for slavery. In addition, the dark skin—"a departure from an initial form of humanity" (Gould, 1994, p. 68)—was a strong argument for enslaving African Americans and propping up the political economy of slavery.

Morton was so preoccupied with race in America and, to a larger extent, the five major *races* of men (recasting Blumenbach's five *varieties* as five *races*) that he spent his life attempting to collect representative samples of all five races. Thanks to Morton's frequent procurement of skulls from within America and around the world, this collection still exists today at the University Museum in Philadelphia, where it is maintained by the Department of Anthropology at the University of Pennsylvania as part of one of the most important anthropological research resources in the world.

Morton expanded on the craniological approach started by Blumenbach in Morton's study of cranial form in the native populations of the Western Hemisphere. The result is his magnum opus, titled *Crania Americana; or, a Comparative View of the Skulls of Various Aboriginal Nations of North and South America; to which Is Prefixed an Essay on the Varieties of the Human Species* (1839). By now, most scholars in the biological sciences have highlighted the serious intellectual flaws in Morton's manuscript (Brace, 2005; Gould, 1981 and 1996; Wolpoff & Caspari, 1997), but it was an outstanding piece of scholarship for the 19th century, and his American and European colleagues praised Morton for this scholarship. Evidence of this praise can be found in a letter written to him by Blumenbach's protégé, von Humboldt: "Your work is equally remarkable for the profundity of its anatomical views, the numerical detail of the relations of organic conformation, and the absence of those poetical reveries which are the myths of modern physiology" (as cited in Brace, 2005, p. 82).

Morton opened his *Crania Americana* by discussing the major human classification schemes published in the literature. The great French naturalist Georges Cuvier (1769–1832) deserves mention here because his tripartite classification—Caucasian, Mongolian, and Ethiopian—was not adopted by Morton, even though, ironically, forensic anthropology and race classification by law enforcement still use this classification today—with slight modification.

But Morton went further than his peers. He believed the five races were indeed different species. Consequently, he placed race in a taxonomic context and subdivided each "race" into several "family" groups. For instance, his American race consisted of the American and the Toltecan families; his Malay race was made up of the Malay and Polynesian families; the Caucasian race had several families; the Ethiopian race had six families; and the Mongolian race, five (Brace, 2005, p. 83). This proliferation of racial categories was adopted by a subsequent generation of anthropologists and presented in the literature of the science (J. Baker, 1974; Coon, 1962; Coon, Garn, & Birdsell, 1950; Coon & Hunt, 1965). Interestingly, we have come full circle because today the number of categories one can choose for race has expanded, and there is again much anxiety about this. The topic will be treated further in chapter 6.

Morton's particular racial categories weren't used in the 1850 census (see figure 2.1) or any other later census. Nonetheless, he was correct in showing that individuals within one population group shared more features than they did with individuals from other groups. Non-racialists have argued that if Morton had used words like *regional groups* or *population groups* instead of *families*, he might have helped in a small way to take the sting out of the word *race*. But we will never know. As I have stated before, science does not occur in a vacuum. It is affected by the greater culture. Morton was a product of his generation. Despite the fact that he was "one of the most outstanding representatives of the first American generation of professional scientists" (Brace, 2005, p. 80), his racial bias may have seeped into his science.

FIGURE 2.1. Statistics of population of the United States decennially from 1790 to 1850.

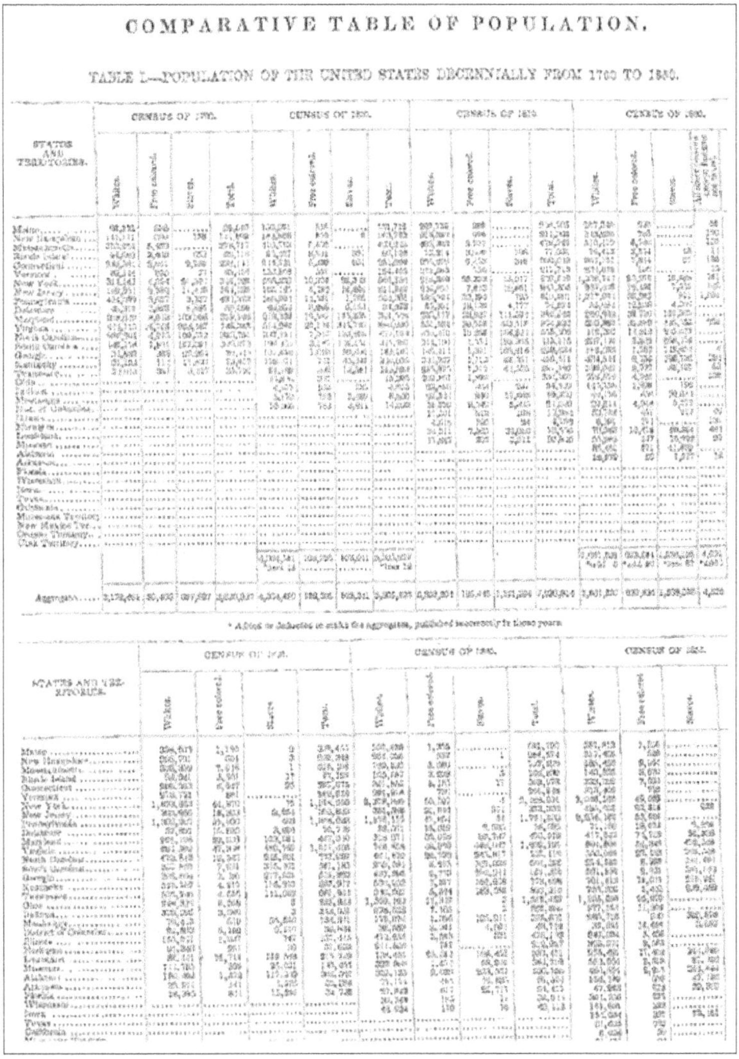
COMPARATIVE TABLE OF POPULATION.

TABLE I.—POPULATION OF THE UNITED STATES DECENNIALLY FROM 1790 TO 1850.

Source. U.S. Census Bureau (1850).
Note. This table has been reproduced as best as possible from the original scan.

Whereas Smith and Blumenbach believed the visible and behavioral differences among human varieties were the result of climate and custom, Morton (1839) felt "that the physical characteristics which distinguish the different Races...are independent of external causes" (p. 3). Like most great scientists of the 18th century and before, Morton then added a God component to his research: "Each Race was adapted *from the beginning* to its peculiar local destination by the agency of an all-wise Providence" (p. 3; italics added). This beginning involved the biblical Noah and his family. His reasoning is treated best by Brace (2005):

> Morton was brought to the conclusion that, since it was accepted to be some 4,179 years "since Noah and his family," assumed to be "Caucasian," "came out of the ark" and since Ethiopians, assumed to have been dark of skin, "were known to have existed" 3,445 years ago, if that latter were: "of the stock of Noah, the change must have been completed and a new race formed in seven hundred and thirty-three years, and probably in a much shorter period." (p. 83)

This reasoning was integral to Morton's other major anthropological work, *Crania Ægyptiaca* (1844). If one acknowledged the date for creation determined through the "begats" in the Bible as 4004 BC (as calculated by James Ussher, the Anglican Archbishop of Armagh), this put the ancient Egyptians close to the time of creation. By the mid-18th century, it was known that Egyptian written accounts went back to 3000 BC, based on information obtained from the Rosetta Stone, which Jean François Champollion deciphered in 1822.[9] In essence, Morton showed the races could not have come from a single pair as stated by monogenism. In his *Crania Ægyptiaca*, he identified Negroes and Caucasians of "modern type" both living in Egypt.

Morton's position is a lesson in contradiction for two reasons: first, he and other proponents of polygenism rejected monogenism because it was too tied to religion. But in his *Crania Ægyptiaca*, Morton had no problem using religion to establish an antiquity for modern racial variation that went back to near the purported time of creation. And second, Morton had no concept of the ancient age of Earth or "deep time," despite the fact that there was information on this subject available at the time.[10] Georges-Louis Leclerc, Comte de Buffon (1707–1788); James Hutton (1726–1797); and Cuvier all wrote about this perspective of infinite time, and Charles Lyell (1797–1875) provided the proof in his two volumes on the *Principles of Geology* (1830 and 1832). This is not so strange. Even today, the average student, despite the availability of information on geology and history, has no concept of deep time or history.

I have mentioned that most scholars in the modern biological sciences have noted serious intellectual flaws in Morton's research. One manuscript that still generates heated debate is his *Catalogue of Skulls of Man and the Inferior Animals*, published in 1849. Some have argued that Morton used his collection to arrange the races from the "original" (godly) to a "degraded" (ungodly) form (Gould, 1981 and 1996; Wolpoff & Caspari, 1997). In this view, Morton's critics claim Morton took Blumenbach's word "degeneration" as indicating degraded or of lesser worth. Furthermore, these writers argue that Morton used his collection to show this "lessening of worth":

> Morton used his collection to support the prevalent idea of a linear scale of increasing racial superiority: Africans were lowest, Aboriginal Americans and Asians were an intermediate level, and Europeans were of course on the top. Morton's cranial data reflected this by showing that nonwhite races had smaller heads than whites and of these, Africans had smaller heads than Indigenous Aboriginal Americans. (Wolpoff & Caspari, 1997, pp. 81–82)

Morton is accused of falsifying his results to support preconceived beliefs of a larger Caucasoid brain size—which, naturally, correlated with greater intelligence in the view of the 19th-century European American—compared to the other races. According to his critics (Gould, 1981 and 1996; Wolpoff & Caspari, 1997), Morton used the materials common during this time period—lead shot and seed—to estimate cranial volume. Cranial volume (measured in milliliters or cubic centimeters) can provide an approximation of brain size. Seed is compressible, and lead shot is not; consequently, one can pack more of the former than of the latter into a given cranium, which would result in a "difference" in cranial volume depending on the material used. Morton's detractors have suggested he packed Caucasoid skulls with seed to obtain larger cranial volumes, thus proving his preconceptions. In other words, Morton had a presumption (or worked with an *a priori* assumption) of white supremacy and endeavored to fit his data to his specific hypothesis. Today we call this inductive reasoning. In his book *The Mismeasure of Man* (1981 and 1996), the late Stephen J. Gould, a Harvard paleontologist, is quite candid concerning Morton's fraud:

> During the summer of 1977, I spent several weeks reanalyzing Morton's data. In short, and to put it bluntly, Morton's summaries are a patchwork of fudging and finagling in the clear interest of controlling *a priori* convictions…. Yet—and this is the most intriguing part of the case—I find no evidence of conscious fraud; indeed, had Morton been a conscious fudger, he would not have published his data so openly. (1981, p. 54; 1996, p. 86)

Alan Mann of Princeton University takes issue with this criticism. In an article entitled "The Origins of American Physical Anthropology in Philadelphia" (2009) published in the *Yearbook of Physical Anthropology*, Mann notes the following:

> Reading Gould's discussions of Morton's work, it is difficult not to come to the conclusion that his criticisms are based on actual examinations of Morton's collection (now housed at the University of Pennsylvania Museum in Philadelphia). There is no record at the University of Pennsylvania Museum of a visit by Gould for the purpose of examining the Morton Collection…. One would have to read carefully to realize he was not reporting his own work but was examining the two sets of data that Morton actually presented, which compared the use of seed and shot in the same skull. (p. 161)

Furthermore, Morton is accused of controlling the *average* cranial capacities of the races by, for example, choosing all the larger crania (and omitting the smaller crania) in Caucasoids and choosing all the smaller skulls (and omitting any larger ones) in the other races (Wolpoff & Caspari, 1997).

Emily Renschler of the University of Pennsylvania has studied the Morton Collection extensively. Concerning the African crania, she states:

> [A] letter to Morton that accompanied their shipping box described the crania as coming from Africans who had recently arrived in Havana, Cuba, as part of the slave trade.... Skeletal analysis of the crania indicates that *the majority of the individuals in the sample were adolescents and young adults* in their 20s at the time of death. (Renschler & Monge, 2008, p. 33; italics added)

Clearly several abnormally small and subadult crania were selected by Morton to make cranial capacity of Africans seem smaller. Because the statistical mean is very sensitive to large and small numbers, a sample consisting of a majority of crania with relatively large volumes will have a larger mean cranial capacity than a sample group with relatively small cranial volumes.

It would seem Morton's preconceived notions or unconscious bias did seep into his work; Brace, however, disagrees with the accusations leveled at Morton. He notes,

> Morton, of course, did live in a society that was racially biased, and some of his private correspondence makes his own acceptance of that bias quite clear. At the same time, Morton was an exemplary scientist, and a careful analysis of his work shows that his "racial" bias had no effect at all on the major pieces of anthropological investigation that he published. (2005, p. 90)

Results from a reanalysis of Morton's *Catalogue of Skulls of Man and the Inferior Animals* data support Brace's position. According to John S. Michael, the author of the reanalysis, Morton's "1849 data are *reasonably* accurate and there is no clear evidence that he doctored those tables for any reason" (1988, p. 354; italics added). I italicized the word "reasonably" because Michael did indeed find minor "miscalculations and omissions" (p. 354).

Morton turned his attention to the question of hybrid sterility because of the growing problem of mulattoes in an era when federal law prohibited sexual or social intercourse between the races. He mined the literature, using material from John Ray (1622–1705) and Georges-Louis Leclerc, to produce a paper entitled "Hybridity in Animals, Considered in Reference to the Question of the Unity of Human Species" (1847), which was published in the *American Journal of Science and Arts*. Paul Broca, the eminent French physiologist-anthropologist, would address hybridity in 1860. Moreover, the question of hybrids and speciation still plagues us today. Hybrids are selected against in nature because they are usually born sterile, for example, the mule resulting from the mating of a horse and a donkey. But nature is chaotic; in the past few years, biologists, primatologists, and others have seen sibling (i.e., closely related) species mate in the wild and produce viable offspring (Jolly, 1993). While this complicates the species question, it also has implications for human evolution.

However, Morton's argument was totally wrong. Like Bachman, he refused to accept the fact that if a black man and a white woman (or vice versa) mated and produced viable offspring (the 19th-century label for the offspring would be *mulatto*—Morton's "hybrid"), this indicates "Unity of the Human Species" or, more simply, that the parents belong to the same species. Morton created a complicated scheme of species ranging from those that never produce hybrids—"remote species"—through those that produce sterile offspring—"allied species"—to "proximate species," which produce fertile offspring (1850, p. 82; 1851, p. 276). As noted earlier, the problem of species is a complex issue simply because of, in the words of the great evolutionary biologist Ernst Mayr, "the leakage of genes" (1996, p. 265). This leakage of genes is hybridization. One must give Morton credit for raising this issue at such an early time, even though he was wrong in using human races as representatives of his species typology. In the end, Morton (1847) concluded that "the mere fact that the several races of mankind produce with each other, more or less *fertile progeny*, constitutes in itself, no proof of the unity of the human species" (p. 212; italics added). At this point, we see the "triumph of feeling over reason" or Romanticism (Brace, 2005, p. 57).[11]

Returning to the question posed earlier in this chapter, why are Samuel George Morton and his contributions to biological anthropology forgotten? One might argue it was guilt by association. In criminal law, for example, the individual who simply provided the vehicle to transport the corpse after a murder was committed is as guilty as the individual who pulled the trigger. Morton was associated with George Robins Gliddon (1809–1857) and Josiah Clark Nott (1804–1873), who publicly supported slavery, and his work was used by them, directly or indirectly and more so after his death, as scientific evidence for keeping men, women, and children of African ancestry in slavery.[12] In the court of public opinion, Morton's legacy was in serious jeopardy. When slavery was abolished and the Old South fell in 1865, his name and the American School of Biological Anthropology were buried beneath the rubble. Although the American School of Biological Anthropology disappeared as a recognizable entity, Morton's outlook on race lingered, kept alive by a monogenist-turned-polygenist named Louis Agassiz, a prominent Harvard paleontologist.

Louis Agassiz (1807–1873) was born in the French-speaking part of Switzerland and received his training in France and Germany, eventually earning his medical degree in Munich. Along the way, he was a student of Cuvier's and came to adopt the French naturalist's theoretical framework of "natural theology" as manifested in Catastrophism, Cuvier's explanation for evolution (Brace, 2005, p. 94; Lurie, 1960, p. 283; Rudwick, 1972, p. 153).[13] This early training rendered him forever immune to Darwinian evolution. He later declared, "The resources of the Deity cannot be so meager that in order to create a human being endowed with reason, He must change a monkey into a man" (as cited in McCullough, 1977, p. 14).

This theoretical framework of natural theology was a descendant of the Enlightenment, when scientists found evidence for the existence of God in nature and the purpose of science was to show God's glory. The doctrine that all humans were descended from Adam and Eve in the Garden of Eden was built into this traditional Christian view. In fact, a year before Agassiz came to America, he published a small volume entitled *Notice sur la Géographie des Animaux* (1845) in which he supported monogenism:

> Whilst the lower animals are of distinct species in different zoological provinces to which they belong; man, *notwithstanding the diversity of his races, constitutes only one, and the same over all the surface of the globe.* In this respect as well as in so many others, man seems to us to form an exception to the general rule in this creation, of which he is at the same time the object and the end. (translated by Bachman, 1855, p. 491; italics added)

Interestingly, this publication was later used against Agassiz by Bachman in their many debates on the origin of the races.

Money problems would force Agassiz to leave Europe in order to seek better opportunities in America. This move was profound because it exposed him to the multicultural American social environment, where his monogenist beliefs slowly changed. Agassiz had never been face to face with people of color in general or African Americans in particular until he was invited to meet Samuel George Morton in Philadelphia. In the dining room at his hotel, people of African ancestry served him. He later wrote to his mother in Switzerland, detailing his culture shock:

> I hardly dare to tell you the painful impression I received, so much are the feelings they give me contrary to all our ideas of the brotherhood of man and the unique origin of our species. But truth before all. The more pity I felt at the sight of this degraded and degenerate race, the more...impossible it becomes for me to repress the feeling that they are not of the same blood as we are. (letter of December 2, 1846, as cited in Gould, 1996, pp. 76–77)

It is interesting to speculate whether Blumenbach would have had the same reaction if he had come to America. Would he have maintained his monogenist orthodoxy? We will never know.

Agassiz's appealing personality and great public lecturing ability made him a favorite speaker at the Lowell Institute Lectures in Boston.[14] This led to a professorship in zoology and geology at Harvard University, which he accepted on October 3, 1847 (D. N. Livingstone, 1987, p. 26; Lurie, 1960, p. 138). Four years later, he was elected president of the newly established American Association for the Advancement of Science (AAAS). The AAAS would become the most prestigious American scientific organization in the latter half of the mid-19th century. The installment of Agassiz as president gave it the stature necessary to rival European scientific organizations.

The third annual meeting of the AAAS was held in Charleston, South Carolina, in March 1850, and during that event, Agassiz began to articulate his "feelings" against the Unity of Man based on the shock he experienced in the dining hall in Philadelphia (Lurie, 1960, p. 143). There was a session devoted to unity versus diversity in assessing the question of human origins, and outspoken racists like Josiah Clark Nott and George Robins Gliddon were given a large forum to show that the institution of slavery was "justified" by the findings of science. In short, the AAAS meeting of 1850 in Charleston saw "the injection of these views into mainstream American scientific thought as a result of the approval and support given by Louis Agassiz" (Brace, 2005, p. 101).

Agassiz's break from monogenism was very public, to the disappointment of the traditional Protestant New England establishment that had welcomed him into their community. He published several of his unscientific beliefs in the *Christian Examiner*, the voice of the Boston-Harvard Unitarian establishment (Brace, 2005, p. 101; Lurie, 1960, p. 259). In the March 1850 issue, he was explicit:

> That Adam and Eve were neither the only nor the first human beings created is intimated in the statement of Moses himself where Cain is represented to us as wandering among foreign nations after he was cursed, and taking a wife from the people of Nod.... it is not for us to inquire further into the full meaning of the statements of Moses. But we are satisfied that he never meant to say that all men originated from a single pair, Adam and Eve, nor that the animals had a similar origin from one common centre or from a single pair. (Agassiz, 1850a, pp. 184–185)

In the July issue of the *Christian Examiner*, Agassiz discussed rank-ing the "other" races based on features (particularly skin color) that were most similar to European Americans:

> So can we conceive, and so it seems to us to be indeed the fact, that those higher attributes which characterize man in his highest development are exhibited in the several races in very different proportions, giving, in the case of the inferior races, prominence to features which are more harmoniously combined in the white race. (Agassiz, 1850b, p. 135)

This statement reflected the worldview of all Europeans of that era, even Smith and Blumenbach.

Agassiz's conversion to polygenism and to the views of the Old South was complete when he discussed "separate and unequal":

> For our own part, we entertain not the slightest doubt that human affairs with reference to the colored races would be far more judiciously conducted, if, in our intercourse with them, we were guided by a full consciousness of the real difference existing between us and them, and a desire to foster those dispositions that are eminently marked in them, rather than by treating them on terms of equality.... *We conceive it to be our duty to study these peculiarities and to do all that is in our power to develop them to the greatest advantage of all parties.* (Agassiz 1850b, p. 144)

This view concerning the social intercourse between blacks and white is identical to Bachman's position. It is interesting how, despite their rather fundamental differences, 19th-century American monogenists and polygenists agreed on the rectitude of slavery.

In the end, Agassiz continued Morton's tradition of inductive "sci-ence" in questions of human origins. This becomes clear in the last two lines of the previous quote, where the *a priori* hypothesis of inferiority of the colored races is stated as fact and the suggestion is to find evi-dence to fit the respective hypothesis, then apply "appropriate" social solutions. In addition, Agassiz's name had become synonymous with science, and his views were carried by his students beyond the biological sciences and into the social realm. For instance, the Immigration Restriction League, which advocated the closing of America to eastern and southern Europeans and Asians, was founded by three wealthy graduates of the Harvard class of 1889; they persuaded a former Agassiz student, John Fiske (1842–1901), to head the organization (D. N. Livingstone, 1987, p. 154). Another of Agassiz's students, Nathaniel Southgate Shaler (1841–1906), became his successor as professor of zoology and geology at Harvard.[15] But Shaler did not make an impact on zoology or geology; his legacy—or Agassiz's legacy—was to:

> perpetuate the pre–Civil War stance of the American School of Biological Anthropology and ensure that this was an integral part of the knowledge of a generation of Harvard graduates, who were to play major roles in how America was run and what it was to contribute to the world in terms of attitudes and ideas. (Brace, 2005, p. 105)

Two of those graduates who had a notable impact were the American president Theodore Roosevelt (1858–1919) with his policy of intervention in Panama and the Philippines as the "white man's burden"[16] and U.S. senator Henry Cabot Lodge (1850–1924), who sponsored the Chinese Exclusion Act[17] and many other immigration restriction laws. But the pre–Civil War stance of the American School of Biological Anthropology was not restricted to Harvard graduates; it also found its way into Europe under the stewardship of Paul Broca and his Société d'Anthropologie de Paris in France.

Paul Broca (1824–1880) was one of the most distinguished biological anthropologists and medical doctors in France during the third quarter of the 19th century. He acquired his formal education in anatomy and pathology in Paris during the 1840s. A few years earlier, Morton's *Crania Americana* was published and praised internationally. Broca probably read this monumental piece of scholarship because he noted that "Morton was his hero and model" (Gould, 1981, p. 84). In addition, Broca took his views on polygenism and discussions on hybridity and race from Morton and his followers, repackaged them, and "sold" them as his own. Ironically, when we hear the name Broca, it is not polygenism or human origins we recall but his neuroanatomical work, where he demonstrated that the left parietal brain is important in controlling speech (Brace, 2005). In his honor, that area of the brain is called Broca's area.

Broca's first public presentation on race and hybridity to the Société de Biologie in 1858 was not well received by the membership because he was challenging the widely accepted theory of monogenism (Schiller, 1979, p. 129). It is still quite perplexing that Broca would readily accept polygenism when his interaction with people of color was almost non-existent compared to the American environment of Agassiz or Morton. Nonetheless, the controversy that followed his presentation prompted him in 1859 to found the Société d'Anthropologie de Paris, whose aim was the scientific study of human races (p. 135). This organization was Broca's "baby," so to speak—he moderated the discussions and retained control of its agenda and publications until his death.

Broca continued his discussions on the question of hybridity and, in 1860, published a volume entitled *Recherches sur l'hybridité animal en général et sur l'hybridité humaine en particulier, considérées dans leurs rapports avec la question de la pluralité des espèces humains* [Researches on animal hybridity in general and on human hybridity in particular, considered in reference to the question of the plurality of human species]. The English translation of the title is relevant because it bears a striking similarity to Morton's 1847 publication "Hybridity in Animals, Considered in Reference to the Question of the Unity of Human Species." This repackaging indicates the important influence Morton and the American School had on Broca.

Broca, more than likely, never saw a biracial individual. Nonetheless, he was fascinated by Morton's conclusion that, though the races might be able to produce offspring, that was not proof of the "Unity of Man." Broca modified Morton's categories of remote, allied, and proximate species using the terms *agenesic, dysgenesic, paragenesic,* and *eugenesic,* ranging from sterile in the first case and "partially fertile" in the second and third cases to fertile in the last case (Brace, 2005, p. 152).

In essence, Broca was a polygenist in the tradition of Morton and the American School of Biological Anthropology, and in the spirit of this tradition, he believed human races were created separate and unequal.

Whereas Broca is vilified for his refusal to look more closely at Darwinian selection—he closed his mind to the antiquity of human existence and the time needed for change but accepted biblical accounts instead—he is applauded for his administrative and organizational skills. In addition to founding the Société d'Anthropologie de Paris in 1859, he also established the Laboratoire d'Anthropologie in 1867 (Schiller, 1979, p. 135). In 1876 Broca founded his École d'Anthropologie, which is particularly important because it established the "four-field" approach—that is, biological anthropology, cultural anthropology, linguistic anthropology, and archaeological anthropology (each with its respective subspecialties)— which is the same structure used in most modern anthropology departments in the United States today. American anthropologists can thank Broca for this holistic view of the field. Unfortunately, this four-field method was dismantled four years after Broca's death, whereas his writings on hybridity and polygenism would shape biological anthropology in Germany, England, and, curiously, the United States—Morton's work repackaged and sent back to America.

TWENTIETH-CENTURY SCIENTIFIC POLYGENISM: WILLIAM RIPLEY, ALEŠ HRDLIČKA, EARNEST HOOTON, AND CARLETON COON

As the 19th century drew to a close, the legacy of the pre–Civil War stance of the American School of Biological Anthropology played an integral role in American domestic and international policy. In 1882 the Chinese Exclusion Act was passed, and later America began its quest to become a colonial power in Latin America and South Asia under the banner of the "white man's burden."

Around the same time, William Z. Ripley (1867–1941), assistant professor of sociology at the Massachusetts Institute of Technology in Cambridge and lecturer in anthropology at Columbia University in New York, delivered the Lowell Institute Lectures on "physical geography and anthropology" in Boston (Brace, 2005, p. 169). Subsequently, these lectures were compiled and published as a book entitled *The Races of Europe: A Sociological Study* (1899). Although Ripley's book had a powerful effect on European Americans, the framework for his study wasn't original but could be traced back to Paul Broca.

In *The Races of Europe*, Ripley divided the Europeans into three racial categories: "Nordic" (or Joseph-Arthur, Comte de Gobineau's Teutonic category[18]), "Alpine," and "Mediterranean," a system that included the thinly veiled idea that each race was endowed with different and unequal capabilities. Others, in the tradition of Linnaeus, were more direct in applying behavioral attributes, which helped shape American public policy after World War I and provided "scientific" justification for the racial policies of Adolf Hitler (Gobineau, 1853 and 1855; Grant, 1916, 1918, 1920, 1921, and 1933; Stoddard, 1920[19]).

Like Broca, Ripley had the political savvy to avoid controversy wherever possible. Furthermore, his assessment of the identity of each race depended on head shape, pigmentation, and stature. Writing about head shape, Ripley (1899) stated:

> The form of the head is for all racial purposes best measured by what is technically known as the cephalic index. This is simply the breadth of the head above the ears expressed as percentage of its length from forehead to back. (p. 37)

It must be noted, however, that the cephalic index did not originate with Ripley. It was formulated by Swedish anatomist Anders Retzius (1769–1860) in 1842. Retzius believed European populations could be divided into three *types* based on their head shapes: a long, narrow head was associated with the superior Indo-Aryans, and a round or short and broad head represented other Europeans (Molnar, 2002). Of course, Retzius described the Swedish skull as long-headed.

In choosing this index, Ripley believed it was immune to environmental effects. But Franz Boas (1858–1942), who was also a faculty member at Columbia University at the time, argued against stasis or the stability of complex traits. He used the cephalic index to show that it changed significantly in the first American-born generation of immigrants (Boas, 1912). Boas discovered that because the heads of long-headed people became broader and those of broad-headed people became longer from one generation to the next, head shape was susceptible to environmental effects and therefore not a good trait to use in distinguishing populations. Sixty years later, William W. Howells (1908–2005), professor of anthropology at Harvard University, provided extensive skeletal metric data in his monograph entitled *Cranial Variation in Man* (1973) (and later an updated version of that monograph entitled *Skull Shapes and the Map* [1989]) to show the variability of skull shapes within population groups.

When Ripley tried to explain his other key "racial" traits—pigmentation and stature—he made the situation even more difficult. In human adaptation, continuous traits or traits affected by the environment are often very difficult to explain. Ripley could only conclude, and with good reason, that the significance of skin color is unknown (Ripley, 1899). He tried to use the eyes and hair color as substitutes; however, his argument fell apart, as it did in the case of stature, where he simply stated that tall populations were innately superior to short ones, not realizing that many factors affect stature, including nutrition.

Ripley certainly believed in the race concept, as evidenced in his statement, "Three stages in the development of our proof must be noted: first the distribution of separate *traits*; second their association into *types*; and, lastly, the hereditary character of these types which alone justifies the term *races*" (Ripley, 1899, p. 105; italics in the original). But he found it very difficult to explain his "key" racial traits and acknowledged this in his writings. Yet despite evidence to the contrary, his "feeling" about the strength of his three-race model in identifying European races could not be overturned.

With behavioral characteristics directly tacked onto Ripley's three-race model, for instance, "Nordics," were said to be "natural rulers and administrators," which accounted for England's "extraordinary ability to govern justly and firmly the lower races"; the "Alpines" were always and everywhere a race of peasants" with a tendency toward "democracy,"

although "submissive to authority"; and the "Mediterraneans" were superior to Alpines in "intellectual attainments" but far behind Nordics "in
literature and in scientific research and discovery" (Grant, 1918, pp. 207,
227–229). The European environmental conditions were perfect to sustain the storm of World War I, which was on the horizon. In the meantime,
derogatory names, such as *sauerkrauts* (or *cabbage* [*head*] in English,
but it actually refers to pickled cabbage, which is served shredded) for
the broad-headed Germans, were hurled by members of one race at those
of another. These ideas found their way into human evolution, where
Cro-Magnon—the earliest modern European *Homo sapiens*, dated at
approximately 40,000 years—is described as upright, tall, and with a high
forehead, whereas the Neanderthal—the late archaic *Homo sapiens*—is
described as hairy and short, with a large brow ridge, large face, and bent
knee, and widely accepted among European biological anthropologists
(and a similar percentage of American biological anthropologists) as not
ancestral to modern humans. Many Neanderthal fossils were initially
found in the mid-19th century and early 20th century in western and eastern Europe (Wolpoff & Caspari, 1997). But the first complete analysis of a
Neanderthal skeleton was done in 1908 by Marcellin Boule (1861–1942),
a prominent French anthropologist.[20] Not understanding the pathology of
old age, he included in his description terms like "bent-knee," "long arms,"
"apelike gait," and so forth, in short: primitive. In a separate incident, a
Neanderthal skull in the Feldhofer Cave near Dusseldorf in the Neander
Valley of Germany in 1856 was labeled "the skull of a Russian Cossack
from the Napoleonic War of 1814" because the anatomist, August Franz
Joseph Karl Mayer (1787–1865), who analyzed the skull could not readily identify it (Stringer & Gamble, 1993; Wolpoff & Caspari, 1997). This
clash of race and human evolution will be addressed in the next chapter.
The point here is that the "Nordic" or northern Europeans were considered the "noble race," whereas the "Alpine" and "Mediterranean" varieties were deemed "primitive" and compared to Neanderthals.

Aleš Hrdlička (1869–1943) was born in what is now the Czech Republic, and he would be categorized as belonging to the "lower races" (Alpine)
based on the idea of hierarchy and worth implicit in Ripley's three-"race"

model. In the early 1880s his family moved to New York City, where he began his medical studies (Brace, 2005, p. 223; Spencer, 1979, p. 38). He graduated from the New York Homeopathic Medical College in 1894 and then became associate in anthropology at the Pathological Institute of New York State Hospitals. A few years later, he obtained the position of assistant curator in the Division of Physical Anthropology at the Smithsonian (where he would remain for the rest of his life) and became the founding editor of the *American Journal of Physical Anthropology* and one of the founders of the American Association of Physical Anthropologists.

Whether Hrdlička was a monogenist before he came to America is unknown. Nonetheless, his worldview about race may have been shaped to some extent by his four-month stay in Paris (1896) at the École and Laboratoire d'Anthropologie, initially established by Paul Broca and then run by his student and successor Léonce Manonuvrier (Spencer, 1979, p. 111). Here Hrdlička adopted Broca's outlook on human races. For instance, he believed blacks were "lower" in cognitive capacity than whites. Two others also influenced this outlook: the Frenchman Alphonse Bertillon (1853–1914), who used measurements of the head and face to identify criminals, and, particularly, Italian medical doctor Cesare Lombroso (1836–1909), who was convinced the presence of certain physical traits that were significantly different from the population norm were remnants of our "primitive" ape ancestry, indicating savage behavior in the carriers (Molnar, 2002; Spencer, 1979).

Hrdlička did not challenge Madison Grant when Grant asserted in his introduction to Lothrop Stoddard's book *The Rising Tide of Color Against White World Supremacy* (1920):

> [T]he more primitive a type is, the more potent it is. That is why crossings with the negro are uniformly fatal. Whites, Amerindians, or Asiatics—all are alike vanquished by the invincible prepotency of the more primitive, generalized and lower negro blood. (Grant, 1920, p. 301)

Franz Boas, reviewing Stoddard's book, wrote that there was no evidence to support Stoddard's "beliefs" and the principles of genetics would prove Stoddard wrong (Boas, 1920). However, Hrdlička did speak out against statements Grant, Stoddard, and their political sympathizers made that the average American's capacities were being diminished by the immigration of eastern and southern Europeans (Brace, 2005). He even went as far as signing a draft statement protesting the 1935 German program of racial hygiene written by Earnest Hooton (and initiated by Boas) (Wolpoff & Caspari, 1997, p. 150).

One will always be struck by Earnest A. Hooton's (1887–1954) ambivalence about race. On the one hand, he wrote the draft statement protesting Germany's racial hygiene program at the request of Boas, and on the other hand, racism and eugenics are apparent in his publications. For instance, he published this respective draft titled "Plain Statement About Race" (1936) in *Science*, the official voice of the American Association for the Advancement of Science (Barkan, 1988, p. 187; Brace, 2005, p. 235; Wolpoff & Caspari, 1997, p. 150), speaking out against the evils of discrimination, yet he was sympathetic to eugenic ideas. Specifically, Hooton believed individuals with physical deformities, mental retardation, and the like should be prevented from having children, or genetically transmitting their affliction. It is interesting that whereas Gregor Mendel's work on inheritance was rediscovered in 1900, most anthropologists and so-called "geneticists" 36 years later still did not understand that an individual could look perfectly normal but have a recessive trait (i.e., the individual inherited the respective "bad" gene from only one parent so it is not expressed) that would appear in a future generation.[21] Furthermore, in the last edition of his major text *Up From Ape* (1946), Hooton wrote, "we are fairly safe in assuming that the Australian is far less intelligent than the Englishman" (p. 158).

Hooton might be considered the "father of American physical anthropology in the 20th century" or, at least, an extremely influential figure in this field in the first half of the 20th century (Brace, 2005; Shapiro, 1981; Wolpoff & Caspari, 1997). He came to Harvard University in 1913 after completing his Rhodes scholarship obligations at Oxford University in England. From that point on, he was responsible for training virtually the entire second generation of American physical anthropologists at a time when physical anthropology was not offered at many universities (Wolpoff & Caspari, 1997). Curiously, his notable contemporaries—Aleš Hrdlička and Franz Weidenreich (1873–1948)— did not spawn any anthropology students even though they had museum and anatomy department positions. Beginning in the early 1920s and continuing for the following two decades, Hooton supervised more than two dozen PhD dissertations in biological anthropology (Brace, 2005). And most of his students went on to produce their own students, incorporating Hooton's scientific polygenism, more or less, into their thinking except for some, such as Sherwood Washburn (1911–2000), who ushered in the "new physical anthropology" (Washburn, 1951). This new physical anthropology was against racism and typology racial studies. In a publication entitled "The Study of Race" (1963) published in the *American Anthropologist*, Washburn emphasized the unimportance of race:

> Race, then, is a useful concept only if one is concerned with the kind of anatomical, genetical, and structural differences which were in time past important in the origin of races. Race in human thinking is a very minor concept. (p. 527)

Returning to Hooton, where did his racial outlook and scientific polygenism come from? Some tentatively point to Sir Arthur Keith (1866–1955), the British anatomist at the Royal College of Surgeons in London, where Hooton obtained his training in skeletal anatomy (Brace, 2005; Wolpoff & Caspari, 1997).[22] Although Hooton supported Keith as a mentor and a friend, he did not exhibit Keith's strong racial prejudice in advocating hostility (war) and competition between the races as positive/necessary factors in human evolution (Brace, 2005; Wolpoff & Caspari, 1997). This particular perspective can be traced back to Ernst Haeckel writing in pre– and post–World War I Germany. Interestingly, Hooton may have acquired his racial outlook from another Harvard anthropologist, Roland Dixon (1875–1934) (Wolpoff & Caspari, 1997). Dixon divided races into primary and secondary races, an approach Hooton adopted in his own classification. According to Dixon, primary races

date back to the divergence of humans from apes. Hooton (1931) modified Dixon's evolutionary polygenism to a model in which the human
races were derived from different fossil anthropoids and evolved along
parallel lines while maintaining species separation:

> During the Miocene period a family of giant generalized anthro-
> poid apes, the *Dryopithecus* family, which was spread over a wide
> zone in the Old World, evolved into the ancestors of the existing
> and extinct forms of anthropoid apes and those of several vari-
> eties of man.... Certain of the progressive *Dryopithecus* genera
> took to the ground in several parts of the anthropoid zone. Some
> of these became the ancestors of extinct human precursors, while
> others were the progenitors of the lines leading to present day
> races of man. (pp. 572–573)

In summary, Hooton's views on race were complex. In a paper entitled "Method of Racial Analysis" (1926) published in *Science*, Hooton
wrote that a race is "characterized as a group by a certain combination
of morphological and metrical features, primarily *nonadaptive*, which
have been derived from their common descent" (p. 75; italics added).
Twenty years later, he modified his views: "This insistence upon the use
of 'non-adaptive' characters in human taxonomy now seems to me to be
impractical and erroneous" (1946, p. 452; quotations marks in the original). Within that 20-year span, he once wrote,

> We have no proof that racial differences in psychology and
> behavior actually exist, but if they do they should be studied and
> explored so that each racial element could be taught to realize
> its fullest possibilities of success capitalizing its strength, and to
> avoid certain endeavors which through its peculiar weaknesses
> lead to failure. (1939a, p. 12; 1939b, p. 11)

Like proponents of the Great Chain of Being, Hooton believed each
race had its place in this great hierarchy. What Hooton implied in this
hierarchy is that his northwest European stocks were "a little lower
than angels" (Hooton, 1939a, pp. 19–29). One of his Harvard graduate students—Carleton Coon—took this view of race even further by

applying a human evolutionary spin to it, which Hooton was very careful not to do. Hooton (1946) made this absolutely clear:

> Bridging the gap in history [evolution] between dry bones and living persons is a very precarious business…. My long and extensive experience in the fields both of skeletal raciology and of the racial classifications of living peoples has made me very critical of my own efforts and those of other anthropologists. (p. 575)

Carleton S. Coon (1904–1981) argued that the five races evolved *separately* from five different *Homo erectus* (a prehistoric human ancestor dated at between 200,000 and 1.8 million years ago) species inhabiting the four large geographical regions, and each one evolved into *Homo sapiens* at different times. The race that crossed first was more evolved in biology and culture (Coon, 1962). "Caucasoids" and "Mongoloids" were first to cross the line into modernity (or the "*Homo sapiens* line"), and presumably, therefore, they were the most "advanced" (p. 482). The African and "Australoid" races crossed the *Homo sapiens* line late and were deemed the most "primitive." Coon believed this *Homo sapiens* line was identified by large brain size, which was set at approximately 1,250 cc to 1,300 cc, despite the fact that brain size is variable within as well as between populations. Again, in the framework of Romanticism, Eurocentrism had reared its ugly head.

However, Coon's polygenism theory is not original. The "evolving separately" component comes from Earnest Hooton (1931, pp. 572–573), which can be traced to Arthur Keith (1936, p. 194; 1950, p. 631). The evolutionary component, however, comes from Franz Weidenreich's polycentric (not polygenic) model, but it was misinterpreted by Coon. Weidenreich's populations were never "separate" or "isolated" when each crossed Coon's "Rubicon" or "*Homo sapiens* threshold." Weidenreich's polycentric model showed "gene flow" between populations in Africa, Europe, Asia, and Australia, preventing speciation and enabling any adaptively advantageous gene appearing in one population to spread throughout the species range (Brace, 2005, p. 237; Wolpoff & Caspari, 1997, p. 249). In short, if there was a *Homo sapiens* threshold, then the five races crossed it together.

Coon adopted his "scientific" polygenism from Hooton at Harvard. He earned his PhD under Hooton in 1928 and then became a colleague in Hooton's department in 1934. In the late 1930s Coon was contracted by the Macmillan Company to rewrite Ripley's *Races of Europe*—his version was published in 1939. By agreeing to rewrite this book, Coon supported Ripley's views about the inherent superiority of the Nordic "race." Even at this time, when World War II had already begun in Europe, Coon was not responsible enough to reject the offer, given that this type of book would likely increase hostilities on that continent. This particular behavioral trait would plague Coon for the rest of his life: he was oblivious to the social changes in his own environment and did not apply his anthropological skills to help the common man. Although the social environment was changing and the word *race* was regarded as anathema to most nations largely because of the extermination of 6 million European Jews perpetrated by the Nazi regime, Coon the detached anthropologist-adventurer never grasped the importance of these changes, even though he served as an intelligence officer in the OSS (the precursor to the Central Intelligence Agency) and probably had some knowledge of the Nazi atrocities.

Coon returned to Harvard after the war and was promoted to associate professor in 1945. Three years later, he left Harvard for the University of Pennsylvania. The physical location of the University of Pennsylvania in Philadelphia was quite different from Harvard's pristine Cambridge surroundings. Specifically, the University Museum bordered the neighborhood of West Philadelphia, which was inhabited by impoverished African Americans in decrepit housing. It's a safe assumption that institutional racial discrimination was a large factor in the plight of African Americans in West Philadelphia and in other cities in post–World War II America. But this was not how Coon saw it—he never questioned the plight of blacks or the domination of whites. In his worldview, it was as it should be, "everyone in their place." Nonetheless, changes in the relationship between the big three populations of the time—African Americans, European Americans, and Native Americans—were coming in the form of the civil rights movement. But Coon's naïveté kept him from understanding how civil rights could change the evolutionary fate of blacks (Coon, 1981). It appears, for instance, that Coon worked behind the scenes to undermine the desegregation that followed the *Brown v. Board of Education* decision of 1954 (Brace, 2005). This information is based on Coon's correspondence, housed at the Smithsonian, with Carleton Putnam (1901–1998), author of a book entitled *Race and Reason: A Yankee View* (1961).[23]

Despite a new social environment that was ripe for unity and equality, Coon continued to believe that the *European Homo erectus* crossed the *Homo sapiens* line first; therefore, the European race was culturally superior. This was a common theme in his most controversial book, *The Origin of Races* (1962). Most anthropologists who were in support of the civil rights movement and applied their skills to help the common man did not receive the tome well. In fact, Coon's *Origin of Races* and the rising civil rights movement were the last nails in the coffin of raciology. Regardless, Coon was articulating the old "separate and unequal" views of the Franco-American polygenism of the 19th century, applying a misinterpreted version of Weidenreich's evolutionary model combined with an ignorance of evolutionary mechanisms. Coon was a typologist; he extended race all the way back to the Plio-Pleistocene epoch (2.5 million years ago) and treated racial categories and evolutionary stages the same way, as concrete and meaningful (Wolpoff & Caspari, 1997).

Coon was out of touch; he was ignorant not only of the social revolution in the mid- to late 20th century but also of the modern evolutionary synthesis that unified Darwinian natural selection, biology, and Mendelian genetics into an edifice for understanding evolutionary change. Theodosius Dobzhansky (1900–1975), one of the architects of the Modern Synthesis,[24] noted this ignorance in his review of *The Origin of Races*:

> The specific unity of mankind was maintained throughout its history by gene flow due to migration…. Excepting through such gene flow, repeated origins of the same species are so improbable that this conjecture is not worthy of serious consideration; and given

gene flow, it becomes fallacious to say that a species has originated repeatedly, and even more fallacious to contend that it has originated five times, or any other number above one. (1963, p. 172)

Just like the incompatibility of the Modern Synthesis with any form of polygenism, Coon was incompatible with the new physical anthropology (in the Boasian tradition).[25] His beliefs, like those of many polygenists before him, were so powerful that they permeated his science. Jonathan Marks (1995) has stated, "Coon's mistakes were inferring race from fossils, using cultural criteria for ranking races, and ranking races on very poor evidence by inferring different times for becoming human" (p. 105). Unfortunately, inferring race from fossils continues to this day, as evidenced by the Kennewick Man controversy of the late 1990s, which I will discuss in some detail in chapter 5. Coon tried valiantly to extend race into prehistory, but the mixture of racial typology and human evolution proved to be volatile. But Coon's ideas did not die with him. Currently, the debates on race and human evolution have taken different forms with the addition of better technology.

In 1950 the United Nations Educational, Scientific and Cultural Organization (UNESCO) brought together several eminent scholars in biology, genetics, psychology, sociology, and economics to draft a "Statement on Race," partly because of the atrocities committed by both the Allies (represented by United States, England, and Russia) and the Axis powers (represented by Germany, Japan, and Italy) because of race (UNESCO, 1951). Ashley Montagu (1905–1999), one of those scholars, who had written a book entitled *Man's Most Dangerous Myth: The Fallacy of Race* (1942), wrote the statement. Since its original publication, the statement has been updated periodically and adapted and modified by the AAA and the AAPA. But if one skims small portions of each association's statements, they are all still very similar. For instance, UNESCO's 1950 "Statement on Race" reads as follows:

Human races can be and have been differently classified by different anthropologists, but at the present time most anthropologists agree in classifying the greater part of present-day mankind into three major divisions, as follows: The Mongoloid Division; the Negroid Division; and the Caucasoid Division. *The biological processes which the classifier has here embalmed, as it were, are dynamic, not static. These divisions were not the same in the past as they are at the present, and there is every reason to believe that they will change in the future.* (p. 13; italics added)

The AAPA's 1996 "Statement on Biological Aspects of Race" reads, "Humanity cannot be classified into discrete geographical categories with absolute boundaries" (p. 569). Finally, the AAA's 1998 "Statement on Race" reads, "With the vast expansion of scientific knowledge in this century, it has become clear that human populations are not unambiguous, clearly demarcated, biologically distinct groups" (p. 1). It is no coincidence that all of these statements lead to a single idea, which is that "there is no such thing as race." This statement has continued to fuel many debates. But some colleagues, especially the forensic anthropologists, counter this statement by asking, "If races don't exist, why are we so good at identifying them?" (Brues, 1993; El-Najjar & McWilliams, 1978; Gill, 1998; Gill & Gilbert, 1990; Gordon, 1993; Hinkes, 1993; Jantz & Moore-Jansen, 1988; Krogman, 1962; Ousley & Jantz, 1996; Rhine, 1990 and 1993; Sauer, 1992; Walker, 1993). I will treat this disagreement in greater detail later in the book.

CHAPTER 3

RACE AND HUMAN EVOLUTION

HUMAN EVOLUTION: RACE AND THE NEANDERTHAL QUESTION

In the previous chapter, I stated that the death of Samuel Morton and the outbreak of the American Civil War conspired to obliterate the American School of Biological Anthropology as a recognizable entity. But despite the publication of Charles Darwin's (1809–1882) *On the Origin of Species by Means of Natural Selection, or the Preservation of Favoured Races in the Struggle For Life* (1859),[26] which should have been the final stake in its coffin, the spirit of the American School lingered on in America and found its way overseas, nurtured by Paul Broca and his Société d'Anthropologie de Paris. Subsequently, Broca's treatise on "hybridity" (1860), which challenged traditional European doctrine of the "Unity of Man," was important to biological anthropology as it grew in England and Germany (Brace, 2005, p. 149). In this scientific environment, the clash of race and human evolution occurred, and the discovery of Neanderthal fossils (which was the key catalyst for this clash) forced the conflict into the social environment.

Neanderthal fossils were being discovered as early as 1829 (in Engis Cave, Belgium), although the 1856 discovery in the Neander Valley is the archetype that gave Neanderthals their name (Wolpoff & Caspari, 1997). The prevalent worldview at the time, despite the monogenism-versus-polygenism arguments, was that God created "man." It followed then that "man" could not have prehistoric ancestors. In short, no one knew what to make of these Neanderthal fossils. Their large face, large brow ridge, midfacial projection, missing chin, and occipital bun were traits not found in the Caucasian variety that Johann Blumenbach described as "really the most beautiful form of skull" (as cited in Gould, 1994, p. 69). Therefore, the only viable explanation to most 19th-century European naturalists was that these bones belonged to the "other" races. For instance, a friend of Broca's who presented himself in Paris as Dr. Franz Pruner-Bey applied racial labels when he published his "beliefs" about the famous Neanderthal skull (the Neander Valley discovery): The Neanderthal skull was "indubitably the skull of a Celt...corresponds nearest... to that of a modern Irishman" (Pruner-Bey, 1863, p. 319).

Unfortunately, Darwinian evolution (or the theory of natural selection)[27] did not end the monogenism-versus-polygenism debates. Instead, Darwinian evolution was corrupted by a new breed of polygenists who advocated the "best of both worlds." In essence, these "evolutionary polygenists" believed in a common descent of the human races, but they diverged from a prehuman ancestor (in pre-Darwinian polygenism, there was no prehuman ancestor; there was only God) and settled on a *parallel progression* that evolved to modern humans (Wolpoff & Caspari, 1997, p. 110). Because many 19th-century naturalists, biologists, anthropologists, and so-called "evolutionists" could not comprehend Darwinian evolution, many European scientists, including Broca and Keith, rejected his theory of natural selection. Broca did respect Darwin's intellectual achievement, but he was reluctant to cede to Darwin the title of "father of organic evolution." Broca would reserve this honor only for Jean-Baptiste Lamarck: "It was Lamarck, I think, in his *Philosophie zoologique*, who was the first to have clearly formulated this idea" (in 1809) (as cited in Brace, 2005, p. 157). And Keith, in his book entitled *Essays on Human Evolution* (1946), rejected the "randomness" of Darwinian selection: "I have just reaffirmed that there are evolutionary processes inherent in living things and therefore in Nature—trends of change which are akin to human purpose and human policy" (p. 218). This new goal-directed polygenism is a synthesis, in my view, of the new "evolutionary monogenism" (where God is replaced by Darwinian evolution) and "scientific" polygenism. However, I will continue to use the term "evolutionary polygenism" because the emphasis of its proponents was on *separate* and *parallel* evolution of the human races.

This new polygenism was a synthesis of polygenism and Darwinism resulting in the mongrelization of Darwinism and subsequent misinterpretation of human origins. For instance, Alfred Russell Wallace (1823–1913), the codiscoverer of the theory of natural selection, implied evolutionary polygenism in a paper he presented at the Anthropological Society of London in 1864 (Wolpoff & Caspari, 1997). His implication was that human races descended from a single ancestor but diverged and evolved separately into modern humans. In contrast, the minority view proposed several different prehistoric anthropoids[28] in different geographical regions, converging into a single species (Vogt, 1864). The evidence for this, according to Karl Vogt (1817–1895), was in the races. He applied Ernst Haeckel's (1834–1919) recapitulation theory (an evolution where the children of the descendant [advanced form] resemble the adults of the ancestor [primitive])[29] and concluded that as a "primitive" race, Africans are like the children of the "advanced" (Caucasian) form. It is important to note that Haeckel was a very strong proponent of evolutionary polygenism and applied progress to Darwinian evolution, suggesting that some races (or separate species, in Haeckel's view) evolved further and lost more apelike characters than others. Haeckel then creatively applied natural selection to the social world:

> That the immense superiority which the white race has won over other races in the struggle for existence is due to Natural Selection.... That superiority will, without doubt, become more and more marked in the future, so that still fewer races of many will

> be able, as time advances, to contend with the white in the strug-
> gle for existence. (as cited in Wolpoff & Caspari, 1997, p. 134)

Today many would call this social Darwinism.

Like Haeckel, most paleontologists in the second half of the 19th century established a hierarchy of living and fossil forms that represented
steps in evolution. However, some of them disagreed with Haeckel to
some extent. One of those scientists was Gustav Schwalbe (1844–1917),
a German anatomist and human paleontologist at Strasbourg. Although
he treated races and fossil humans together in his evolutionary schemes,
he did not believe Haeckel's recapitulation theory explained evolution
(Wolpoff & Caspari, 1997). Consequently, the most "primitive" human
form was not the most neotenic African Pygmies, as was the prominent
belief. In contrast, Schwalbe believed the Javan form *Pithecanthropus*[30]
(the first *Pithecanthropus*, now known as *Homo erectus*, dated at 1.9
million years ago) was primitive enough to form the "root" or the most
primitive ancestor of the human races. Then he hypothesized that Neanderthals or *Homo primigenius*—a name he borrowed from Haeckel—
evolved from *Pithecanthropus* and that *Homo primigenius* gave rise to
all human races. Subsequently, the races diverged. But throughout his
life, Schwalbe was ambivalent about the Neanderthal's place in human
evolution. In one of his other schemes, for instance, *Pithecanthropus* and
Neanderthals were not in the lineage leading to modern races. They were
simply side branches or different species.

Another German anatomist working at the same time had no ambivalence about Neanderthal evolution. In fact, Hermann Klaatsch (1863–
1916) accepted Schwalbe's latter scheme, albeit with modification, where
Neanderthals are depicted as totally distinct from the genus *Homo*. Like
Haeckel and Schwalbe, Klaatsch considered himself a Darwinian but did
not really grasp Darwinian evolutionary mechanisms. He extended race
all the way back into the Paleolithic period, arguing that Neanderthals
and the Aurignacians (an upper Paleolithic population living 100,000
years ago) were separate species that coexisted and that the "lower
races," in Klaatsch's view, evolved from the ape-like Neanderthals.

Klaatsch studied the Feldhofer Cave Neanderthal limb bones and interpreted the "curvature" of these bones as an arboreal (habitual tree-
climbing) adaptation. We know now that the curvature of the Neanderthal
limb bones is the result of large muscle pull during activity and not an
indication of climbing ability. Moreover, Klaatsch's scheme of evolutionary polygenism became quite complex as he incorporated different
ape species within human racial lineages. Wolpoff and Caspari (1997)
detail Klaatsch's scheme very well:

> Klaatsch contended that the human basal stem was to be found
> in Australia, a stem also giving rise to the other anthropoids. The
> great apes, he believed, derived from different human lineages
> in various areas. From the basal Australian stem branched the
> two main human lineages, an Asian one and a European one. The
> Asian branch gave rise to the orangutans and also the humans of
> Asia and later of Europe…. The earlier European lineage gave
> rise to the Neanderthals and the African races, whom Klaatsch
> argued, a number of degenerate characteristics. It also gave rise
> to the African apes. Thus, modern Europeans are actually more
> closely related to orangutans than they are to African people,
> according to Klaatsch. Australians are the little-modified descen-
> dants of the basal stem and are not associated with the degenerate
> lineage and thus were seen favorably, as ancestral to Europeans.
> (pp. 125–126)

Most would consider Klaatsch's polygenism scheme as tortured logic.
It was a synthesis of progressionism and "feeling," resulting from a positive experience with the natives during his three-year stay (1904–1097)
in Australia. What is perplexing is that most Europeans in the 18th,
19th, and 20th centuries believed that, based on their craniofacial features, the "Australoids" were the most "primitive" of the human races.
Predictably, the paleontological community did not accept Klaatsch's
progressive ideas of the Australoids. They were more sympathetic to the
Pithecanthropus→*Homo primigenius*→*Homo sapiens* scheme with divergence of the human races thrown in. Still, this first *Pithecanthropus* fossil
did complicate the human evolutionary picture. But the common-sense

approach which a close associate of Schwalbe's, Franz Weidenreich, applied would ignite a debate that still rages today.

MODERN HUMAN ORIGINS: WEIDENREICH, RACE, AND POLYCENTRIC EVOLUTION

In his own quiet way, Franz Weidenreich (1873–1948) was a controversial figure who lived during exciting times in paleoanthropology and during dangerous world events where race was a major factor. Information drawn from a book by Milford Wolpoff and Rachel Caspari (1997) entitled *Race and Human Evolution: A Fatal Attraction* supports this statement. This book is the most current and accurate treatment of Weidenreich and interpretation of his work.

Wolpoff and Caspari argued very strongly that Weidenreich's polycentric model was misinterpreted by Earnest Hooton and, later, by his students Carleton Coon and William W. Howells, whose conclusions about Weidenreich's work were totally different from his own. Wolpoff and Caspari added that by reading about polycentric evolution through Coon and Howells (two of the most influential anthropologists of the mid-20th century), subsequent generations of biological scientists have labeled Weidenreich a polygenist (Cavalli-Sforza, Menozzi, & Piazza, 1993; Howells, 1950, 1993; Lewin, 1993; Tattersall, 1995; B. A. Wood, 1994). Others have stated that Weidenreich's model "had the interesting effect of placing the origin of races and racial differences far back in time" (Shipman, 1994, p. 202). Wolpoff and Caspari (1997) strongly disagreed. They laid out their case in defense of Weidenreich by first detailing how his model was misinterpreted by Coon and Howells and then presenting their own interpretation.

In the case of Carleton Coon, he praised Weidenreich for constructing a model that was "compatible" with his own views on the origin of races. Coon even dedicated his book *The Origin of Races* to Weidenreich in the introduction:

> While I was writing *The Races of Europe* in Cambridge, Massachusetts, he was busy in New York studying the *Sinanthropus*

remains. At that time he concluded that the peculiarities that made *Sinanthropus* distinct from other fossil men were of two kinds, evolutionary and racial. *From the evolutionary point of view Sinanthropus was more primitive than any known living population. Racially he was Mongoloid.* (Coon, 1962, p. viii; italics added)

In essence, Coon had misunderstood Weidenreich's polycentric model. Chinese *Sinanthropus*[31] was not "Mongoloid." There was no Mongoloid population 600,000 years ago. Wolpoff and Caspari (1997) agreed,

> These past races were not the present ones. *Weidenreich took the persistence of certain traits to be evidence of genetic continuity, not racial identity…. Combinations of features were seen to persist for long periods of time, but the continuity was of features, not of populations.* (p. 199; italics added)

In short, Weidenreich believed that races bump into each other, interbreed, and separate so that over time they are not the same populations. In Coon's interpretation of Weidenreich's model, the Mongoloid race persisted for a half-million years and the characteristics of living East Asians were present in *Sinanthropus*—"an underlying, unchanging reality to the Mongoloid classification, a valid manifestation of essentialism or typology" (B. J. Williams, 1979, p. 216). Of course, this was not Weidenreich's belief. Coon's interpretation is similar to the present "Eve" hypothesis for modern human origins, where all races can trace their ancestry to a single female who lived in a population between 200,000 years and 150,000 years ago. This will be treated in some detail in the next section.

Furthermore, Coon tried to trace the human races all the way back to the Pleistocene epoch. As stated in the last chapter, he believed that the races evolved separately into modern humans. Weidenreich argued, based on his studies of the European, Javan, Chinese, and African fossils, that there may have been several geographical regions where human characteristics evolved and then spread out:

> *There must have been, not one, but several, centers where man developed.* But we should be completely at a loss if someone

should ask on which special spot the decisive step was made that led from a simian creature into man. There was not just one evolutionary step. Evolution went on wherever man may have lived, and *each place may have been a center of both general development and special racial strains.* (as cited in Wolpoff & Caspari, 1997, p. 195; italics added)

If we took this quote out of context, we can see how Weidenreich's polycentric model was associated with polygenism and Coon. But Weidenreich was not finished; critical to his model was interbreeding or gene flow between populations: "He contended that human evolution was best understood as a network of interconnected [migration and gene flow] populations that retained regional continuity for at least some features" (Wolpoff & Caspari, 1997, p. 199). Because Coon advocated races evolving parallel and separate toward the *Homo sapiens* line, regional continuity of traits and gene flow were evolutionary processes, a fact he did not grasp.

But there are other aspects of Weidenreich's polycentric model, such as the balance of natural selection and gene flow in wide, geographically separated populations, that still have not been resolved.

Howells was a strong critic of evolutionary polygenism in the origin of the races. He addressed this in his 1942 paper entitled "Fossil Man and the Origin of Races." Howells was well aware of the strong "scientific" polygenism in the writings of his teacher Earnest Hooton and his colleague Carleton Coon, but he did not criticize them—it would not have been proper professional etiquette for 1940s academia; he attacked Weidenreich instead. However, Howells misinterpreted Weidenreich's polycentric model as well. It's conceivable that he simply misinterpreted poly*centric* as meaning poly*genic*, in addition to the possibility that no one understood universal hybridization and persistent genic exchanges or Weidenreich's explanation of these complex processes.

Nonetheless, Howells (1942) launched his attack by accusing Weidenreich of proposing an evolutionary polygenism hypothesis that required "parallel evolution going through a series of stages in all regions of the Old World" (p. 182). Later, in a book entitled *Mankind in the Making*

(1959), Howells described Weidenreich's model as one of "races derived from parallel phyla...arisen from different strains of sub-*sapiens* species of the genus *Homo*, by a general process of convergence.... The central idea is the one I have described, of parallel evolution" (p. 244). Howells would later christen Weidenreich's polycentric model the "Candelabra Hypothesis," describing it as "an exaggerated mental diagram, in which populations of *Homo erectus* spread out widely at the base [convergence], as in a candelabrum, with separate local ascents from that point to the modern races of *Homo sapiens*" (1993, p. 124).

I must note, as I have in previous chapters, that in the 1940s and 1950s many scientists still did not understand the dynamics of hybridization and non-Darwinian evolutionary forces (i.e., gene flow, genetic drift, and mutation), despite the articulation of the new Modern Synthesis. More important, not many understood how these forces interacted. Consequently, it is not hard to understand why Howells was so ignorant about Weidenreich's gene flow and interconnections between widely separated populations. Conversely, Weidenreich may have not been able to properly articulate the dynamics of his complex model in English, leaving it open to misinterpretation (Wolpoff & Caspari, 1997). In fact, Weidenreich spent most of his adult life in Germany and wrote his manuscripts in German. When he left Germany for the United States in 1934, he was 61 years old. In essence, Weidenreich probably did not get extensive practice in the nuances of English grammar. Nonetheless, Weidenreich did have notions of populations hybridizing (exchanging genes in today's language) continuously without separation. Weidenreich believed interbreeding was all-pervasive. So how did he come to formulate such a complex concept as polycentric evolution? To answer this question, we must go back and study his background and intellectual development.

Franz Weidenreich received his formal education in anatomy and hematology and obtained a doctor of medicine degree from the University of Strasbourg in 1899. At Strasbourg, he worked under Gustav Schwalbe until he was forced to leave when the region came under French control after World War I (Wolpoff & Caspari, 1997). Weidenreich's linear model of human evolution reflected, to some extent, Schwalbe's influence.

(Remember, Weidenreich believed that *Pithecanthropus* evolved into Neanderthals and Neanderthals evolved into modern humans.) Furthermore, his interest during these early years was in functional anatomy in the framework of human evolution. During this time, the Krapina Neanderthals were being studied by Dragutin Gorjanović Kramberger (1856–1923).

In 1921 Weidenreich took a position at the University of Heidelberg and continued his work on functional morphology in the framework of evolution. But in 1927 he made a slight detour in his otherwise benign work. In the late 1920s Germany was secretly rearming in an effort to regain its pre–World War I status. Fueled by the Romantic ideas of *Naturphilosophie* and *Das Deutsche Volk*, which emphasized the natural racial superiority of the "Aryan" or German people, the National Socialist German Workers' Party began constructing racial hygiene programs. Weidenreich published a book entitled *Race and Body Form* (1927), in which he discussed race, variation, and the fossil record. He believed race was a phenomenon of geography and the traits used to identify race were arbitrary. In short, he did not accept the idea of "pure races": "Any search for stable archetypes…will be condemned to failure…. Crossing is not a late human acquisition which took place only when man had reached his modern phase, but must have been practiced ever since man began to evolve" (Weidenreich, 1946, p. 82). In addition, he showed that the concept of "constitutional types," or a correlated suite of features believed to characterize different races, such as long headed versus broad headed or tall stature versus short stature, was not exclusive to one race or another. Wolpoff and Caspari (1997) make note of this:

> In *Race and Body Form*, he had noted that the elongated head form that Nazis believed characterized the "Nordic type" their racial purification laws were aiming for did *not* characterize the greatest Germans, including Beethoven, Goethe, Kant, Leibnitz, and Schiller. (p. 185)

Moreover, it is very likely Weidenreich was thinking along the lines of individual variation based on his comparative analysis of the available *Pithecanthropine* and Neanderthal fossil materials.

In 1928 Weidenreich published a description of the European *Pith-ecanthropus* cranial remains found at Ehringsdorf and then placed it in an evolutionary context as it relates to the other known *Pithecanthropine* fossils, such as the Kabwe skull from Zambia found in 1921 and the Zut-tiyeh facial bones found in 1925 (Wolpoff & Caspari, 1997, p. 182). In addition to the Ehringsdorf description, Weidenreich published a 1928 paper entitled "The Evolution and Racial Types of *Homo primigenius*" (Haeckel's term for Neanderthals in early-20th-century central Europe). He articulated linear evolution with a "Neanderthal phase" as a transitional stage between *Pithecanthropus* and *Homo sapiens*.

Weidenreich's writings emphasizing the fact that there were no racial types were not consistent with the Nazi biopolicy. In addition, the university forced him to resign his professorship because he was considered Jewish. Consequently, he was forced to leave Germany for a professorship of anatomy at the University of Chicago. Soon he would leave Chicago for Beijing, China, for a visiting professorship at the Peking Union Medical College. There he studied the fossil materials from the Lower and Upper Cave at Zhoukoudian. He called the Lower Cave fossil materials *Sinanthropus pekinensis*, which is placed in the species *Homo erectus* today.

Weidenreich prepared a monograph on the Zhoukoudian materials, describing them as variable and archaic (dated at 400,000 to 600,000 years ago), with large faces accompanied by flat cheeks facing forward, low nasal bones, and a wide (broad) nasal opening. He compared these fossils with the Upper Cave or Shandingdong specimens and saw "certain common features...three different racial elements, best to be classified as primitive Mongoloid, Melanesoid, and Eskimoid" (1939, p. 165). In short, he saw *continuity* in Asian features, or similar features through time.

In addition to the European and East Asian fossil records, Weidenreich had an opportunity to study the Indonesian *Pithecanthropus erectus* materials. The skullcap found near the village of Trinil in 1891 was already controversial.[32] Additional fossil remains were found around the villages of Sangiran and Ngandong[33] by G. H. R. von Koenigswald (1904–1982), another German paleontologist. Subsequently, Weidenreich and von

Koenigswald published their comparative analyses of the Chinese (Lower Cave, Zhoukoudian) and Javan (Trinil, Sangiran, and Ngandong) fossil materials, suggesting that these sample groups were races of the same species. They believed the Ngandong remains were younger in time, basing their evidence on the larger average cranial capacity of Ngandong compared to the other sample groups (Von Koenigswald & Weidenreich, 1939). In addition, Weidenreich felt strongly that, based on many shared cranial features and possible ancestors of the Aboriginal Indigenous Australians, the Ngandong individuals were descendants of the earlier Trinil and Sangiran sample groups. But the Trinil and Sangiran populations, dated at 600,000 years ago, and the later Ngandong populations, dated at 250,000 years ago, were not the same race. This was an important component of polycentric evolution. Weidenreich (1943) noted,

> [A]t least one line leads from *Pithecanthropus* and *Homo soloensis* to the Australian Aborigines of today. This does not mean, of course, that I believe all the Australians of today can be traced back to *Pithecanthropus* or that they are the sole descendants of the *Pithecanthropus–Homo soloensis* line. (p. 249)

One can now see the complexity of Weidenreich's model of human evolution, which involved a pattern of interconnections—horizontal and vertical—between populations. And based on his experience of studying human fossils from four different geographical regions (Europe, Africa, East Asia, and Australasia), he was able to formulate a *polycentric* or multiregional model for human evolution. In his 1940 paper "Some Problems Dealing with Ancient Man," Weidenreich wrote:

> More and more I am coming to the impression that, just as mankind of today represents a morphologic and genetic unity in spite of being divided into manifold races, so has it been during the entire time of evolution. While man was passing through different phases, each one of which was characterized by certain features common to all individuals of the same stage, there existed…different types deviating from each other with regard to secondary features. These secondary divergences have to be races as regional

differentiations, and, therefore, as correspondent to the racial dis-similarities of present man. (p. 380)

Essentially, Weidenreich argued that the definition of "modern" was different in different geographical regions but not different enough to warrant a reference to different species. Wolpoff and Caspari (1997) explained,

> There were different ways of becoming human, different pathways and even different rates of change. Kawbe [archaic *Homo sapiens* fossil from Zambia found in 1921], he had realized a decade earlier, was vertically differentiated from the Neanderthals by being more archaic, but it was also horizontally differentiated by being more African. Zhoukoudian folk had distinctive Chinese features, some unique to the Chinese, and in aggregate the features made them more like North Asians than like any other living population. (pp. 194–195)

In the end, Weidenreich formulated a trellis diagram detailing a network of vertical, horizontal, and diagonal lines of evolutionary relations (see figure 3.1). Many believed the lines constituting this network were arbitrary. According to Weidenreich (1946), however, the vertical lines represented different stages of human evolution through time, the horizontal lines represented the different geographical regions, and the diagonal lines represented patterns of genetic exchanges between populations. It was the genetic exchanges (interconnections) that Howells, Coon, and other anthropologists omitted or misinterpreted. This model incorporated very complex evolutionary mechanisms, that is, universal hybridization, gene flow, and natural selection, at a time when the Modern Synthesis was just being formulated. Adding to the complexity is the fact that Weidenreich did not articulate how it was possible to maintain regional continuity when there is universal hybridization (Wolpoff & Caspari, 1997). In an environment of universal genetic exchanges, populations in different regions should become more similar. Yet we have geographic differentiation or races. Unfortunately, despite the application of molecular genetics and the addition of new and relevant fossils, this question has not been resolved to date.

FIGURE 3.1. Weidenreich's trellis: A network of populations connected by gene exchanges.

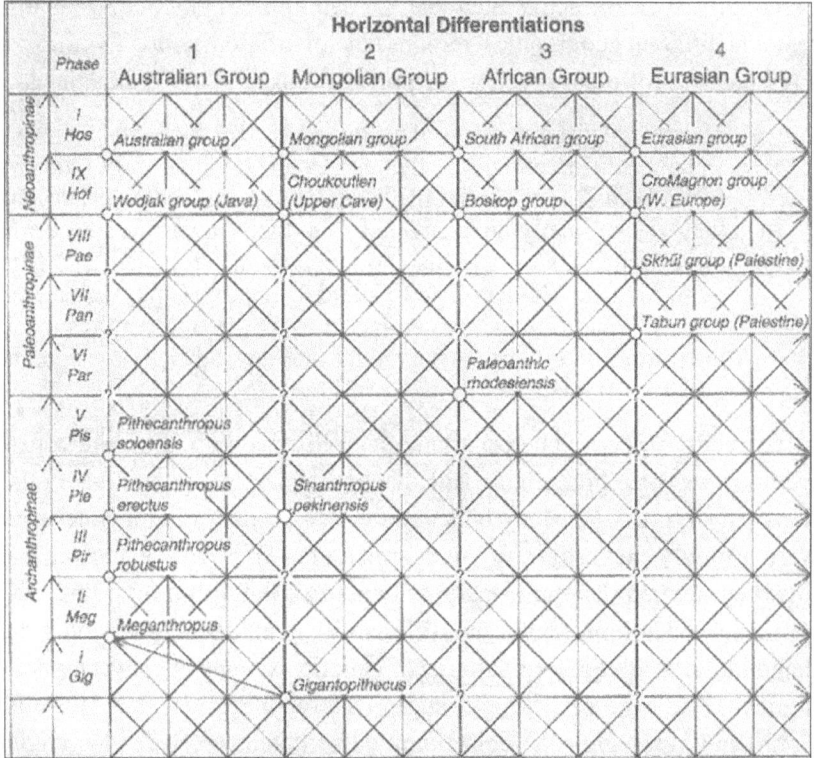

	Phase	Horizontal Differentiations			
		1 Australian Group	2 Mongolian Group	3 African Group	4 Eurasian Group
Neoanthropinae	i Hos	Australian group	Mongolian group	South African group	Eurasian group
	IX Hof	Wodjak group (Java)	Choukoutien (Upper Cave)	Boskop group	CroMagnon group (W. Europe)
Paleoanthropinae	VIII Pae				Skhūl group (Palestine)
	VII Pan				Tabun group (Palestine)
	VI Par			Paleoanthic rhodesiensis	
Archanthropinae	V Pis	Pithecanthropus soloensis			
	IV Pie	Pithecanthropus erectus	Sinanthropus pekinensis		
	III Pir	Pithecanthropus robustus			
	II Meg	Meganthropus			
	i Gig		Gigantopithecus		

RACE AND MODERN HUMAN ORIGINS: OUT OF AFRICA VERSUS MULTIREGIONAL EVOLUTION

It is quite amazing that the two major competing hypotheses in the current modern human origins debate can be traced back to the "Unity of Man" or the monogenism-versus-polygenism arguments of the 18th, 19th, and early to mid-20th centuries. The Out of Africa or "Eve" hypothesis is viewed as upholding the monogenist tradition in its supposition that mod-ern humans evolved from a single sub-Saharan African female who lived in a population approximately 200,000 years to 150,000 years ago. To the lay public, the "Eve" hypothesis implied the "Unity of Man," which is a positive message to combat chronic racism. To scientists, "Eve" indicated genetic unity of the human species. In fact, influential science writer Stephen J. Gould wrote, "Human unity is no idle political slogan…all modern humans form an entity united by physical bonds of descent from a recent African root" (1988, p. 21).

In contrast, the Multiregional Evolution hypothesis is viewed as up-holding the polygenist tradition, as in Weidenreich's polycentric model, advocating *multiple regions* for modern human origins. But let us first look at the Out of Africa hypothesis, which boasts "a recent African root" (Cann, 1987; Cann, Stoneking, & Wilson, 1987).

The Out of Africa hypothesis begins approximately 2 million years ago (as does the Multiregional Evolution hypothesis) with the initial migration of some *Homo erectus* populations to different parts of the Old World, that is, the Middle East, Europe, the Near East, Northeast Asia, and Indonesia. This assumption is based on the fact that *Homo erectus* fossils have been found in all these regions, with the oldest fossils from Indonesia dated at 1.8 and 1.6 million years ago. (Keep this in mind for the remainder of this section.) According to the proponents of the Out of Africa hypoth-esis, a modern population evolved in one place, Africa, approximately 200,000 to 150,000 years ago and left Africa over the course of several generations, "replacing" all existing populations in the Old World (i.e., other *Homo erectus* populations and their descendants, the Neanderthals, who did not evolve into modern humans) without interbreeding. The term *replacement* means that these modern populations probably out-competed *Homo erectus* and Neanderthals because they had better tools or were able to exploit the environment in a better way—in other words, because they were more intelligent. There is no evidence of a great cultural revolution, for example, brand-new tool technology, at this time in the fossil record.

The strongest evidence for this hypothesis comes from mitochondrial DNA (mtDNA), which was extracted from the placentas of females from the world's largest geographical areas (I will address this in more detail later in the chapter). The following branching diagram (figure 3.2), called a phenogram, is based on mtDNA. Figure 3.2 shows three large branches and many small ones. The most significant branching is the one showing how genetically distant modern Africans are to all other populations. So let us talk briefly on how the architects of the Out of Africa hypothesis obtained their data.

Mitochondria are organelles in the cytoplasm of the cell. They are interesting because they have their own DNA. We (males and females) inherit our mother's mtDNA unchanged—in fact, it is a clone of our

FIGURE 3.2. Phenogram showing genetic distances among a sample of human populations.

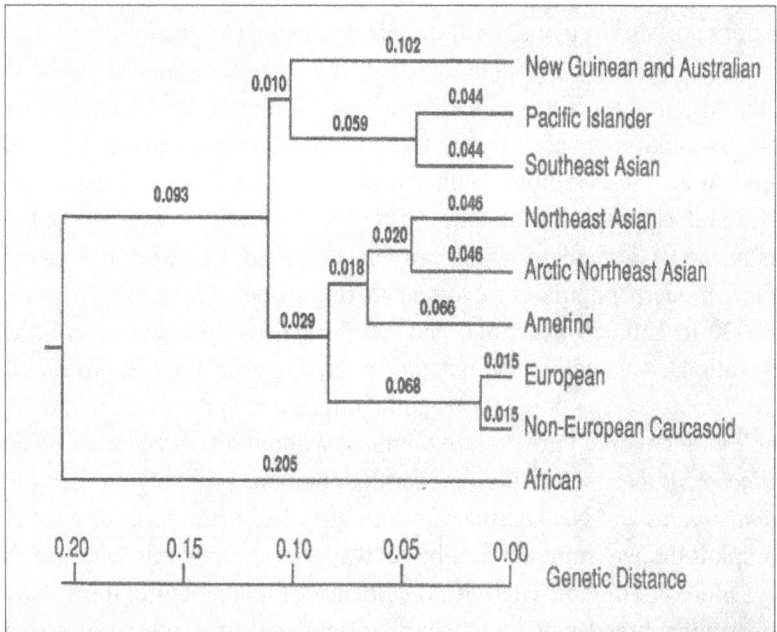

Source. Cavalli-Sforza et al. (©1993 Princeton University Press. Reprinted with the permission of Princeton University Press).

mother's mtDNA. But it is matrilineally preserved. It is believed that because the female egg has more cytoplasm than the sperm, the mitochondrion is able to be passed on. But there is some evidence of limited male transmission of spermal mtDNA (Danan et al., 1999; Houshmand, Holme, Hanson, Wennerholm, & Hamberger, 1997).

Now, if we have several generations of daughters and accumulated mutations are not affected by natural selection, mtDNA could be used as a clock to date the last common ancestor. In essence, maternal inheritance, rapid evolution, and small information content—only 37 genes or 16,500 base pairs in mtDNA, compared to 100,000 genes or 3 billion base pairs in nuclear DNA—make it possible to use mtDNA to reconstruct mitochondrial evolution. In essence, mtDNA transmission is the female analogue of "male surname transmission" in many human societies (Avise et al., 1987; R. Corruccini, personal communication, September 14, 2009; Gould, 1987). If all females took their husband's name, then purely by statistical chance (some families not having sons) over long periods, there would be deterioration to just one surname. So the mtDNA Eve is just a statistically certain eventuation.

In the late 1980s researchers collected the placentas of females from the world's large geographical areas (i.e., Europe, Africa, Asia, Indonesia, etc.) and then extracted mtDNA from these specimens (Cann, 1987; Cann et al., 1987; Wilson & Cann, 1992). Based on their analyses, they generated results similar to the phenogram depicted in figure 3.2. They found that the African mitochondria were more variable compared to those of the other populations. They then calculated mutation rates of the mtDNA in each population and found much more in the African mtDNA—hence the variability, according to these researchers. They then made the assumption that it would take a long time to accumulate those mutations. Therefore, they concluded the African mtDNA was the oldest and all other populations originated from a female (labeled "Eve") in a population in Africa who lived 200,000 to 150,000 years ago.

Opponents of the "Eve" hypothesis question the supposition that all mitochondrial lines lead to an African woman who lived that recently (Relethford & Harpending, 1994 and 1995; Templeton, 1993 and 1994;

Wolpoff & Caspari, 1997). What happened to the mitochondrial lines of the other women who were alive when "Eve" was? The "Eve" theorists argue that the name "Eve" is misleading—she was not the ultimate source of all the ordinary lineages as in the biblical Eve; she was simply lucky. A. C. Wilson and Cann (1992) argued that some maternal lineages proliferate and others become extinct in each generation, and eventually, by chance, one maternal lineage replaces all others (p. 71).

Opponents also question the supposition that greater genetic variability in Africans meant Africa was the place of origin for modern humans. They argue that the *Homo erectus* populations and their descendants who stayed in Africa after the initial migration (of other *Homo erectus* populations) to various regions of the Old World 2 million years ago were larger than the populations outside of Africa, and this would account for the greater African mtDNA variation. John Relethford and Henry Harpending (1995) explained,

> Our results support our earlier contention that regional differences in population size can explain the genetic evidence pertaining to modern human origins. Our work thus far has involved examination of the classic genetic markers and craniometrics, but it also has implications for mitochondrial DNA. *The greater mtDNA diversity in Sub-Saharan African populations could also be a reflection of a larger long-term African population.* (p. 672; italics added)

Opponents insist that how large or small populations were in the past and how much they fluctuated may have affected mtDNA evolution. Consequently, this leaves suspect the genetic evidence that modern humans descended from one population that replaced all others.

The competing theory is the Multiregional Evolution hypothesis. Proponents of this hypothesis argue that the *Homo erectus* populations that migrated out of Africa approximately 2 million years ago to different parts of the Old World evolved into modern humans in these regions. The Multiregional Evolution hypothesis is an elaboration of Weidenreich's polycentric model in conjunction with regional distinctions and universal hybridization between the races. But as stated in the last section, there were two problems with the polycentric model that Weidenreich could not solve: 1) the origin of geographic differences and the explanation of their continuity over time; and 2) how the contradictory elements of isolation (which is required to establish regional distinctions) and gene flow (which maintains the "unity" of the species) work together to produce *Homo sapiens* (Wolpoff & Caspari, 1997). The Multiregional Evolution theorists have provided solutions to these two problems while simultaneously vindicating polycentric evolution as the true model advocating the "Unity of Man."

Furthermore, Weidenreich (1947) regarded humanity past and present *as a single species that could potentially interbreed and have fertile offspring*, very few researchers in the late 1940s and early 1950s were sympathetic to Weidenreich's polycentric model. Theodosius Dobzhansky in his 1950 Cold Spring Harbor Symposium on "The Origin and Evolution of Man" was able to articulate the genetic elements of Weidenreich's polycentric evolution, but not many of his listeners could grasp the intricacies of the Modern Synthesis:

> In general the old anthropological alternative of monogenic versus polygenic descent of man ceased to exist when considered from the vantage point of the present evolution theory. Different populations (races) of a polytypic species may be descended largely from different races of the ancestral species and may differ in some genes in which these ancestral races differed. *And yet, a polytypic species may still evolve as a single genetic system. Favorable mutants or gene combinations arrived at in one part (race) of such a species may, under the influence of natural selection, eventually spread to all other parts and thus eventually become a common property of the entire species. Thus, local autonomy of gene pools of racial populations does not preclude retention of the basic unity of the species as a whole.* I would like to point out that this view agrees quite well with the conclusions reached by the late Weidenreich on the basis of purely morphological analysis of pre-human populations. This is worthwhile stressing because Dr. Weidenreich has sometimes used expressions that seemed to put him close to the old-fashioned polygenist camp, which he actually rejected absolutely. (pp. 106–107; italics added)

Although Weidenreich could not articulate some aspects of his model, "genetic species" played an important role in his thinking. And the Modern Synthesis provided a species concept that, to some extent, tied into evolutionary theory.

In more recent times, Multiregional Evolution proponents have proposed the "Center and Edge" explanation for the origin of regional variation and continuity over time.[34] They argue that in peripheral populations polymorphic traits[35] (i.e., nose shape, hair form, stature, skin color, etc.) could be reduced and become less variant in form and persist for long periods of time (Thorne & Wolpoff, 1992; Wolpoff & Caspari, 1997). For instance, they found, like Weidenreich, that crania from Indonesia, Australia, or Zhoukoudian were more homogenous within each group compared to the centrally located African crania, even though each region had different combinations of homogenous features. In addition, the early and late Croatian Neanderthals from Krapina and Vindija caves show continuity in features. This anatomical homogeneity, they argue, reflects a reduced number of genetic polymorphisms in nuclear (and mitochondrial) DNA. Wolpoff and Caspari (1997) explained, "More genetic variation has been lost because the characteristics of these gene pools were initially established by the partial isolation of numerous small populations with histories of drift and bottlenecking" (p. 262).

At the center, proponents argue, there were higher population numbers and therefore a higher frequency of contact where gene exchange could happen. According to Ernst Mayr (1963), increased gene flow elevates the frequency of anatomical variation because with more genes in the mix, more polymorphisms are found. In short, populations in the center should be heterogeneous because the effects of natural selection in weeding out variation should be less intense where humans are best adapted. But "Center and Edge" does not fully explain how populations retain geographical distinctions and yet evolve as a single species.

To tackle this problem, the Multiregional Evolution theorists discuss changes in human social behavior as an additional critical factor in the unity of the species. For instance, *Homo erectus'* Acheulean tool technology enabled him to exploit a wider range of habitats and brought groups into contact in regular ways. This probably led to alliances and exogamy or warfare (where there is a violent exchange of genes). In essence, when populations migrate, they take their culture and genes with them. In this process, advantageous gene combinations do "flow." Therefore, the exchanges of ideas, information, and technology explain how populations retain geographical distinctions and evolve as a single species (Wolpoff & Caspari, 1997).

The Out of Africa and Multiregional Evolution hypotheses are important in the arguments on the existence or non-existence of races. In their definition of "anatomically modern human," the Out of Africa proponents use the European *Cro-Magnon* traits (i.e., high forehead, rounded cranium, and reduced/absent brow ridges) as the standard; crania that were substantially different were considered archaic. This is reminiscent of the old racial typology; if it were applied to living Australian Aborigines, they would be considered archaic *Homo sapiens*. Similarly, the Multiregional Evolution hypothesis states that regional features (particularly nonadaptive features) can persist after they are established at high frequency when no evolutionary forces act to change them significantly. A good example is shovel-shaped incisors, which are found in high frequency in Asians. However, this trait is not exclusive to Asians; it is also found in other populations, albeit at lower frequencies. Consequently, Multiregional Evolution theorists emphasized that these regional features neither describe nor define races:

> While we view some characters differing between today's races as long-standing, we do not mean to imply that the races themselves are static, unchanging entities.... It is their combinations which exist in high enough frequencies, in certain regions, to support hypotheses of ancestry. (Wolpoff & Caspari, 1997, p. 357)

So could *ancestry* be a more accurate term than *race* or the term *clines* that came with Frank B. Livingstone (1928–2005) and the new anthropology?[36] Nonetheless, if examined closely, the Out of Africa and the Multiregional Evolution hypotheses both advocate the "Unity of Man."

CHAPTER 4

RACE AND HUMAN VARIATION

GENOTYPE: RACE AND GENETIC POLYMORPHISMS

The Multiregional Evolution and Out of Africa hypotheses attempt to explain human variation. The central theme of these hypotheses is the origin of modern humans, but to the greater social environment, these hypotheses speak to the origin of races or to how different races are related. Tradition dies hard. The public views race as a real, unchanging entity that can be traced into prehistoric times and can be divided into discrete categories based on specific features. This comes from the Platonic Essentialism outlook intrinsic to Western thinking, where objects in the environment are merely reflections of "ideal types" of the same objects that humans cannot perceive.[37] In essence, the race concept is based on typology—identifying a population based on a cluster of features found on the skeleton or soft tissue—and key figures, such as Samuel Morton, Paul Broca, William Ripley, Earnest Hooton, and Carleton Coon, used typology in their study of human variation. However, human variation is much more complex. For instance, Richard Lewontin (1972) analyzed the major genetic markers in the major geographical populations. He found that, with respect to those markers, there was more variation within populations than between populations. But to the average person, there is no "perception" of this in the real world. Why? Furthermore, many have seen people who resemble them more than their own siblings. Why? These are some examples of the complexities of race and human variation. We must discuss the underlying factors or genes that control the expression of these traits and then discuss the biological mechanisms behind those visible traits (skin color, hair form, or nose shape, to name just a few) that are so important to us and continue to be the source of tremendous conflict in America and around the world.

Charles Darwin knew variation was the raw material for natural selection. He also knew that this variation, in the form of traits, was passed from parent to offspring. What he did not know was the source of this variation or the mechanism of inheritance. It is interesting to note that mid-19th-century biology was moving in the right direction in its proposition that each body contained invisible particles called gemmules. Darwin went further by hypothesizing that representative gemmules for all body parts resided in the reproductive organs so that each parent contributed gemmules to the offspring (Larsen, 2008). According to Darwin, these gemmules "blended" to create the traits observed in the offspring. Over time, this explanation was proven wrong by three major events: Gregor Mendel's work on the mechanisms of inheritance, the articulation of the Modern Synthesis, and the discovery of DNA.

Gregor Johann Mendel (1822–1884), an Augustinian monk from what is now the Czech Republic, is recognized as the "father of genetics." Mendel's teachers recognized him as an extremely bright student, and he enrolled in the University of Vienna to study the natural sciences. While he was there, some of the scientific luminaries of Europe gave Mendel a first-class education. One of those luminaries was Franz Unger (1800–1870), a botanist whose hypothesis on the importance of varieties in natural populations was believed to be the stimulus for Mendel's work on the mechanisms of inheritance (R. Boyd & Silk, 2006; Mayr, 1982; Molnar, 2002).

Between 1856 and 1863, using the common edible pea plant, Mendel studied plant hybridization. He isolated a number of traits with only two forms, or variants. For example, he studied pea color, which had two variants, yellow or green, and pea texture, which was either wrinkled or smooth. Mendel was fortunate in his choice of characteristics because they happened to be traits of simple inheritance: the plants bred true, without intermediate traits—that is, each succeeding generation possessed the same traits as its parental generation (Molnar, 2002). For example, crosses (matings) between plants that bore green peas always produced offspring with green peas, and crosses between plants that bore yellow peas consistently produced offspring with yellow peas. Mendel then cross-pollinated these plants for color, shape, size, and form of seed pod.

In one set of Mendel's experiments with garden peas, a series of crosses between green and yellow variants yielded offspring that consistently bore yellow peas, matching only one of the parent plants. Modern geneticists refer to these hybrids as the F_1 generation (Molnar, 2002; Raven & Johnson, 2002). When members of the F_1 generation were crossed, some of their offspring produced yellow seeds and some produced green seeds. At this point, Mendel knew that, for color, yellow was the dominant trait and green was the nondominant trait. Similarly, in shape, smooth was dominant and wrinkled was nondominant. Later scientists determined that the unit of inheritance—a gene—has two alleles (or alternate form of a gene), one inherited from the mother and one from the father. Each allele is either dominant or nondominant (recessive). For a recessive trait to be expressed, the offspring must inherit a recessive allele from both parents. It is worth noting that Mendel's work—and subsequent studies based on his work—was well known during the American racial hygiene programs of the 1920s and 1930s. But the ignorance of the so-called racial hygiene "scientists," unable to grasp Mendelian genetics, led to the sterilization of hundreds of Americans because of a visible physical or behavioral deformity, whereas visibly "normal" Americans were viewed as healthy. As was the case in Mendel's breeding experiment just mentioned, some of these "normal" individuals could have been carriers of a recessive trait for a defect that would appear in a future generation.

Moreover, Mendel (unlike his predecessors) kept careful count of the numbers of each kind of individual that resulted. This was critical to the success of his experiment. These data showed that, in the F_2 generation, there were three individuals with yellow seeds for every one with green seeds. Mendel sought to explain these results by hypothesizing that these traits were determined by a pair of elements, or hereditary particles: one inherited from the mother and one from the father, which segregated independently in each generation. The American geneticist Thomas H. Morgan later named these particles genes (he derived it from the Greek root *gen*—to become or to grow out of). Moreover, modern geneticists call this segregation of particles the Law of Segregation (Molnar, 2002; Raven & Johnson, 2002).

Experiments crossing plants selected for a difference of two traits produced dihybrids with a certain ratio of these traits among the F_2 generation. These results demonstrated that traits such as seed shape and color were determined by paired elements that independently assorted in ovule (female sex organ) and pollen (male sex organ). Modern geneticists call this the Law of Independent Assortment. In summary, these principles, resulting from Mendel's breeding experiments, were key to understanding the mechanisms of inheritance and the source (and preservation) of variation.

In 1865, just 6 years after the publication of Darwin's *On the Origin of Species*, Mendel published the results of his work on inheritance, but no one grasped the significance of the results. In fact, Mendel sent a copy of his paper to prominent botanist Carl Wilhelm von Nägeli (1817–1891), who was studying inheritance and should have understood the importance of Mendel's experiments (R. Boyd & Silk, 2006). Instead, Nägeli dismissed Mendel's work, perhaps because it contradicted his own work or because Mendel was an obscure monk. It must be noted that at this time cellular structures and their functions were just being discovered, so most scientists did not have the knowledge to comprehend Mendel's results. Unfortunately, Mendel's work lay dormant until the dawn of the 20th century, when several botanists independently replicated Mendel's experiments and rediscovered the laws of inheritance.

In 1896 Dutch botanist Hugo de Vries (1848–1935) unknowingly repeated Mendel's experiments with poppies. Then in 1900, just as de Vries was ready to send off a manuscript describing his experiments, a colleague sent him a copy of Mendel's paper—de Vries was disappointed to find out that his "new" results were 30 years old. Around the same time, two other European botanists, Carl Erich Correns (1864–1933) and Erich Tschermak von Seysenegg (1871–1962), also duplicated Mendel's breeding experiments and derived similar conclusions (R. Boyd & Silk, 2006; Larsen, 2008; Molnar, 2002). Danish botanist Wilhelm Ludvig Johannsen (1857–1927) called the pair of alleles the *genotype* and the actual physical appearance (yellow or green, smooth or wrinkled) the *phenotype* (Larsen, 2008, p. 42). These studies and the thousands of experiments that followed during the early decades of the 20th century established the foundations for modern genetics.

By the time Mendel's experiments were rediscovered in 1900, it was well known that virtually all living organisms were built out of cells. Embryological work had shown that all cells of complex organisms arise from a single cell through the process of cell division. Moreover, between the initial discovery of the nature of inheritance and its rediscovery at the dawn of the 20th century, the chromosome was discovered. In 1902 Walter Sutton (1877–1916), a young graduate student at Columbia University, made the connection between chromosomes and the properties of inheritance revealed by Mendel's principles (R. Boyd & Silk, 2006). Mendel's first principle states that traits were determined by a pair of elements, or hereditary particles—one inherited from the mother and one from the father—that segregated independently in each generation. In other words, genes reside on chromosomes, and individuals inherit one copy of each chromosome from each parent. Furthermore, the proposition that observed characteristics (the phenotype) are determined by genes from both parents is consistent with the observation that mitosis, or body cell production, transmits a copy of both chromosomes to every daughter cell so that every cell contains copies of both maternal and paternal chromosomes (R. Boyd & Silk, 2006; Molnar, 2002). Mendel's second principle states that genes segregate independently of each other.

The observation that meiosis (sex cell production) involves the creation of gametes (egg or sperm) with only one of the two possible chromosomes from each homologous pair is consistent with the notion that each of these genes is equally likely to be transmitted to gametes. This is one of the sources of variation that Darwin would never know about. Variation in this case is produced by "crossing over," that is, the exchanging of chromosome strands in the first stage of meiosis. Because genes reside on chromosomes, exchange of chromosome strands recombines the genes, producing variations in observed characteristics. In addition, hidden variation accumulated because of low mutation rates is exposed to natural selection in subsequent generations. For example, a chromosome strand for the pea plant has a gene for smooth texture and a gene for yellow color (smooth/yellow). Because these genes are on the same chromosome, they will, more than likely, be inherited together. They are said to be linked. Furthermore, the other strand has a gene for wrinkled texture and a gene for green color (wrinkled/green). After crossing over occurs, the resulting observed characteristics are smooth/green and wrinkled/yellow. In essence, traits segregate independently of each other because the genes that code for them are on different chromosomes.

It is surprising that many scientists in the early 20th century did not accept Mendelian genetics or Darwinian selection. It follows that they did not agree with Walter Sutton's findings either. It would take many experiments by Thomas H. Morgan and his colleagues at Columbia to prove Sutton right.

In the meantime, blood grouping techniques were being developed. In the racist environment of 19th- and mid-20th-century America, terms such as "black blood" and "white blood" were normal. Mixing of blood, whether by sexual intercourse or blood transfusion, between different races was anathema (see chapter 2 for a full discussion). But prior to 1900 transfusions were used only as a last resort in an attempt to save a patient's life. If the patient was white and learned that the blood they would receive for the transfusion came from a black person, the white individual would often refuse the "black blood." This was the ignorance of racism. Nonetheless, it was the beginning of blood grouping, which would lead to the discovery of blood polymorphisms, knowledge on population history, and evidence for population admixture. But before all this, transfused blood would cause shock and even death because of agglutination of the incompatible antibodies and red cells (Molnar, 2002). It was by sheer dumb luck that some transfusions were successful because some mixtures of blood happened to be compatible. In 1900 Karl Landsteiner (1868–1943), an Austrian immunologist, began to systematically analyze the pattern of agglutination between blood donors and recipients by mixing the blood serum of one with red cells from another. Landsteiner discovered that agglutination occurred when serum from a type-A person was mixed with red blood cells from a type-B person and vice versa, and these results were consistent in thousands of tests (Molnar, 2002). Transfusions could now be done safely, but the ignorance of racism overshadowed this breakthrough in science. Several years later, the ABO system was defined, and other major blood groups were discovered.

In 1908, meanwhile, Thomas H. Morgan (1866–1945) and his associates bred the common fruit fly in experiments that built on Mendel's breeding experiments. They discovered that all genes are transmitted from parents to offspring in the ratios Mendel identified. They confirmed Sutton's findings that the hereditary material or genes are on chromosomes and both the hereditary material and chromosomes are transmitted during reproductive cell division.

As stated earlier in this book, the appearance of Darwin's *On the Origin of Species* was instrumental in demolishing Samuel Morton's American School of Biological Anthropology, which was devoted to scientific racism. In addition, Mendelian genetics proved that genes themselves remain distinct physical entities when the chromosome strands separate during both forms of cell division; they do not blend. Unfortunately, the fear in 19th-century America concerning the "blending" of the races or miscegenation carried into the 20th century despite the knowledge of Mendelian genetics. In 1913 American eugenicist Charles Davenport (1866–1944) investigated the genetics of "Negro-white crosses" (Wills, 1994, p. 78). He thought that only two genes controlled skin color and that each of them came in two forms, or alleles: a "white" allele and a "black" allele. Furthermore, how dark a person was was a function of how many of the four alleles inherited from the mother and father were "black." Another notable character who revealed his ignorance of Mendelian genetics is Madison Grant, discussed briefly in chapter 2. In his discussion of race crossing, he implied that any crossing with blacks would be fatal to the other races:

> The result of the mixture of two races, in the long run, gives us a race reverting to the more ancient generalized and lower type. The cross between a white man and an Indian is an Indian; the cross between a white man and a Negro is a Negro; the cross between any of the three European races and a Jew is a Jew. (Grant, 1918, p. 18)

In short, though there were slow advances in elucidating biological change and variation, the worldview was still 19th century. This certainly affected the pace of scientific advances in the early 20th century because most scientists were products of this culture. Remember, science does not operate in a vacuum; it is affected by the greater culture.

The inability of many scholars and scientists to grasp (or accept) the complexities of Mendelian genetics and Darwinian selection in the early 20th century perpetuated the racist philosophy of Madison Grant, Charles Davenport, and their students. Darwinian evolution advocated gradual accumulation of small changes, but it could not explain why Mendel generated only two pea colors—yellow and green—or two pea textures—smooth and wrinkled—and no intermediate types. This seemed to prove that inheritance was fundamentally discontinuous and could not be reconciled with Darwin's idea that adaptation occurs through the accumulation of small variations (R. Boyd & Silk, 2006). This "proof" supported the long-held 19th-century contention that skin color, nose shape, and hair form were discrete traits that were inherited together and fit into a neat little package.

In the early 1930s British biologists Ronald A. Fisher (1890–1962) and J. B. S. Haldane (1892–1964) along with American biologist Sewall Wright (1889–1988) showed how Mendelian genetics could be used to account for continuous variation (R. Boyd & Silk, 2006). They argued that traits controlled by a single locus explained the discontinuous variation in Mendel's peas. Environmental variation has little effect because allelic substitution at the single locus is large—the trait has a high genetic component. However, when there are many loci and each has a small effect on the phenotype, environmental variation has a major effect by blurring together the phenotypes associated with different genotypes. Subsequently, this theory was combined with Darwin's theory of natural selection, leading to the idea that Darwinian evolution was simply *changes in gene frequencies over time*. Through the modern field studies by biologists such as Theodosius Dobzhansky, Ernst Mayr (1904–2005), and George G. Simpson (1902–1984), Mendelian genetics and Darwinian evolution were eventually reconciled in a body of theory called the Modern Synthesis (R. Boyd & Silk, 2006). This new synthesis solved the problem of explaining how variation is maintained. Simply put, low mutation rates can maintain variation because much of the variation is protected from selection.

The Modern Synthesis did not convince those scientists who were entrenched in their beliefs and blinded to the fact that Darwinian selection or adaptation was a functional shift in gene frequencies over time. Consequently, mutationist arguments emerged to explain change beyond the initial range of variation, and Darwinian selection continued to get a lukewarm reception in some quarters. But by the middle of the 20th century it was known that chromosomes contain two structurally complex molecules: protein and deoxyribonucleic acid, or DNA (R. Boyd & Silk, 2006; Molnar, 2001). It had also been determined that the particle of heredity postulated by Mendel was DNA. In 1953 American geneticist James Watson (b. 1928) and British biophysicist Francis Crick (1916–2004) offered a model to explain the molecular structure of DNA: a ladder-like double-helix structure consisting of two long "backbones" made of alternating sequences of phosphate and sugar molecules. Attached to each sugar is one of four molecules, collectively called bases: adenine (A), thymine (T), guanine (G), or cytosine (C). Adenine bonds only with thymine, and guanine bonds only with cytosine. This bond is very weak, allowing the two strands of DNA to "unzip" themselves during both forms of cell division and for protein synthesis.

The model proved to be an accurate description of this complex structure. Crucial to Watson and Crick's discovery was the work of British X-ray crystallographer Rosalind Franklin (1920–1958), who used a special technique, X-ray diffraction, to produce high-quality images of DNA (Larsen, 2008). Ultimately, this major breakthrough in biology convinced the remaining dissenters of the beautiful compatibility of Darwinian natural selection and Mendelian genetics. Watson and Crick illuminated how DNA chromosomes are replicated, how heredity leads to the patterns Mendel described in pea plants, and why there are sometimes new variations. In addition, this revolution in biology began to shed light on traits of simple inheritance (or blood polymorphisms), traits of complex inheritance (or body form, head shape, skin color, nose shape, hair form), and how these traits relate to race and environmental adaptation.

A sequence of three DNA bases codes for a specific amino acid, and the amino acid connects to other amino acids, forming a polypeptide chain resulting in different proteins. In essence, genes translate into proteins or the phenotype, such as the skeleton in growth and development, hair, skin, and blood. Blood, as mentioned earlier in this chapter, was and still is integral to romantic ideas of kinship, nationalism, or "race" on the one hand and population history, relationship, and adaptation on the other.

The ABO blood group is the best known of a long list of red cell antigens. The antigens are under control of at least three alleles at a locus on chromosome 9 (Larsen, 2008; Molnar, 2002); the possible genotypes are AA, AO, BB, BO, AB, and OO. Each person has one A, B, or O allele on one chromosome of the homologous pair and another A, B, or O allele on the other chromosome pair, which determines the person's blood type: A, B, AB, or O (the alleles A and B are codominants, whereas the type O allele is recessive). The comparison of ABO types in families has shown that the blood type is passed on by Mendelian inheritance. For example, a man with blood type AB will pass on either an A or a B to his offspring, but not both. The other allele will come from the mother. This is, as the reader will recall, the Law of Independent Segregation.

Within the blood plasma of each person, there are antibodies related to the "type" of red blood cell antigen. For instance, individuals with genotypes AA and AO (or blood type A) have anti-B antibodies in their plasma, and individuals with genotypes BB and BO (or blood type B) have anti-A antibodies. Consequently, a type-A person cannot receive type-B blood, and a type-B person cannot receive type-A blood. Further-more, genotype AB (or blood type AB) has no antibodies and therefore can receive any blood type, and genotype OO (or blood type O) has anti-A and anti-B antibodies and can receive only type-O blood.

So what is the significance of the ABO blood group? How does it relate to race? For instance, type B is more prevalent in parts of Asia, whereas type A is more prevalent among northern Europeans. Can this data be used to categorize populations? Most researchers believe the ABO blood-group polymorphisms are more important in understanding the incidence of disease than in finding race (Mourant, Kopec, & Domaniewska-Sobczak, 1978; Roitt, 1988; Vogel, 1975; Vogel & Motulsky, 1986; C. S. Wood, 1974). Craniofacial traits such as shovel-shaped incisors (men-tioned in the previous chapter) and alveolar projection (projection of upper jaw) are found in high frequency—but not exclusively—in Asian and Native American populations. Consequently, they can be used to determine race in forensic anthropology. These traits and other traits in the skeleton will be addressed in detail in the next chapter. But blood type cannot be used the same way. Whereas 100% of native South Americans are blood type O and more than 80% of some native New World popula-tions are blood type O, more than 50% of Canadian Blackfoot Indians are type A (Kottak, 2006). More than 20% of populations in their ancestral region in Western Siberia are blood type B. The point here is that the ABO blood-group polymorphisms cross population lines. Nonetheless, allele O is most frequent overall, with a frequency of 62.5%. Allele A has a frequency of 21.5%, and allele B is the rarest, with a frequency of 16% (Molnar, 2002). This distribution may be related to the environment (i.e., diseases) in which the population lived and natural selection.

In a study of noninfectious diseases in England, there was a slight correlation between blood type A and gastrointestinal-type disorders, from duodenal ulcers to stomach, pancreatic, and colon cancers (Aird, Bentall, & Roberts, 1953). This could explain the mere 20% frequency of blood type A in Europe. In the study of infectious diseases, type-A individuals were more susceptible to smallpox than type-O or type-B individuals (Molnar, 2002). When India experienced the world's last smallpox epidemic, a mortality rate of 50% was found in type-A individuals—with much smaller numbers for types B and O. This could explain why the frequency of the A allele in India is even lower than in Europe.

Furthermore, type-O individuals may be susceptible to the plague bacterium. In Europe, the pandemics of 1345 and 1645 resulted in mortality rates of up to 50% (Molnar, 2002). Consequently, blood type O today has the lowest frequency in those regions of the world—Asia, India, Iran, and Iraq—where the plague has the longest history. The type-O allele was selected out over time because it did not promote survival. Smallpox was also prevalent in these areas, resulting in the death of type-A individuals and a reduction of the A allele. In these populations suffering the double threat of smallpox and plague, the type-B allele would occur in high frequency, as it does in India today (Molnar, 2002, p. 102).

The frequencies of the ABO blood may also correlate with the behavior of insect species, in that some insect vectors appear to prefer one blood type over another. Some studies have demonstrated that the most mosquito bites recorded were on test subjects with type O, leading to the hypothesis that mosquitoes prefer type-O blood (C. S. Wood, 1974). Consequently, one finds the A and B allele at frequencies of over 20% in West Africa, Mesopotamia, and India.

But we do find the highest type-A and type-O frequencies in less dense populations on the edges of the human species range. Infectious microbes cannot persist where there is no population density to spread their progeny; therefore, there can be no epidemics or pandemics in small populations. Groups such as northwest Europeans, the Basques of northern Spain, Lapps, Australian Aborigines, Blackfoot Indians, and Polynesians are some examples of populations on the edges of the species range (or isolates) with high A frequencies (Molnar, 2002).

There are some blood groups that have been used in the past to study population history and race. Today, with better technology, they give information about population migrations, admixture, and race. First, the Rhesus (Rh) system is often involved in the hemolytic blood disease of newborns called *erythroblastosis fetalis* (Molnar, 2002; Relethford, 2005; Bowman 1997). In this disease, the fetus's blood (Rh negative *d*) gets into the mother's bloodstream (Rh positive *D*). Antigens on the surface of the fetus's red cells cause an immune reaction in the mother's bloodstream, destroying the red cells of the developing fetus. Although there are drugs to prevent this immune reaction, there is no explanation of a selective value for the Rhesus negative. Frequencies of the Rhesus negative throughout the world suggest selection for the heterozygote (*D d*) in an environment of rheumatic fever.

Second, another blood group system called the Duffy blood group has three types of antiserum, designated anti-Fy^a, anti-Fy^b, and anti-Fy^4. An individual's type is determined by red blood cell reaction to the antiserum. Studies have demonstrated that most people will react to either anti-Fy^a or anti-Fy^b, and many react to both (Molnar, 2002). For example, Europeans or populations of European ancestry have frequencies of 90% and 9%, respectively, for Fy^a and Fy^b. Rarely have Fy^4 types been reported among that population. But this might be changing because of admixture. In contrast, sub-Saharan Africans (central and West Africa) and African Americans have frequencies of 100% for Fy^4 and 0% for Fy^a and Fy^b. Non-racialists argue that we might be tempted to use Fy^4 to categorize people of African ancestry; however, Fy^4 is also found in high frequency in populations on both sides of the Red Sea and among Kurds of Iran and Iraq.

The distribution of Fy^4 is believed to be related to survival in a malarial environment in the Western Hemisphere. The malarial infection in the Western Hemisphere is caused by the vivax parasite. The African slaves brought vivax to the Western Hemisphere, and their descendants possessed a degree of immunity to this form of malaria, compared to Native Americans and European Americans, who suffered the devastating effects of this malarial infection (Molnar, 2002). The female

Anopheles mosquito must first bite the individual for the parasite to get into the bloodstream. Once there, vivax must enter a blood cell to begin its life cycle. In laboratory experiments, the red-cell antigens of Fy^a and Fy^b provide attachment points for the vivax parasite that allow entry, but the Fy^4 does not.

Like Fy^4, the hemoglobin S (Hb^S) allele, commonly known as the sickle-cell gene, provides a degree of immunity to malaria in individuals who have this mutation (F. B. Livingstone, 1958 and 1971). Unlike Fy^4, the Hb^S allele is a random point mutation in the hemoglobin beta chain and is found in the highest frequencies in sub-Saharan Africa, northeast India, Arabia, Greece, and Turkey. In the past, there has been considerable ignorance about Hb^S in general and sickle-cell anemia in particular. It was categorized as "the black disease," meaning it was found solely in the black race, because, initially, sub-Saharan Africa was the focus of research, and the highest frequency of the disease was found there. This ignorance about sickle-cell anemia flourished in the fertile environment of racism in the United States. Approximately 10% of African Americans were carriers. Interestingly, it was believed that an individual with the trait or one copy of the gene (inherited from the mother or father, if one of them is a carrier) was at greater risk of death when exercising heavily or working at high altitude. Consequently, military recruits applying for airborne duties and commercial pilots were examined throughout the 1970s, and anyone found with the sickle-cell trait was rejected for airborne duties, grounded, or fired (Molnar, 2002). This could have been the excuse for rejecting blacks for the high-profile pilot training in the armed forces and commercial airlines. Since the 1970s much research has shown that the sickle-cell trait is also found in Greeks, Indians (of India), Arabs, and Turks. Despite this fact, sickle-cell anemia still has the stigma of being a "black disease."

Red blood cells contain a high share of the protein hemoglobin. Hemoglobin is a large, complex molecule composed of four long chains of amino acids (Molnar, 2002; Relethford, 2005). Each chain has a large molecule containing an atom of iron that can carry a molecule of oxygen (O_2), which gives blood its red color when oxygenated. Oxygenated blood is transported to all parts of the body in order to sustain life. If the red blood cell is damaged, its ability to carry oxygen may be negatively affected. In fact, this is what the sickle-cell disease is all about. A random point mutation in position 6 of the beta chain results in a sickle-shaped red blood cell. Specifically, the codon (or nucleotide triplet) that codes for the amino acid glutamic acid in normal DNA is CTC (cytosine-thymine-cytosine). A nitrogenous base substitution replaces thymine with adenine so that the codon becomes CAC. This simple point mutation changes everything because in protein synthesis, the anticodon is GUG, which codes for the protein valine. This change radically alters hemoglobin shape and interrupts the normal red blood cell function, hence the term sickle-cell anemia (Molnar, 2002). Subsequently, the distorted cells clog smaller blood vessels, leading to circulatory problems and, eventually, death.

The sickle-cell gene is inherited in Mendelian ratios. For instance, the probability of the offspring inheriting the trait from the mating of two parents who are both carriers (heterozygote dominant—$Hb^A\,Hb^S$) is 50%. The probability of the offspring inheriting sickle-cell anemia (homozygote recessive—$Hb^S\,Hb^S$) from the same parents who are both carriers is 25%. In the homozygote recessive individuals, all hemoglobin is of the Hb^S type (in contrast to heterozygote carriers, who have a majority of normal hemoglobin [$Hb^A\,Hb^S$] combined with some abnormal hemoglobin [$Hb^S\,Hb^S$]), which comes with a high mortality rate. The average life expectancy of individuals with sickle-cell anemia in first- and second-world countries is about 40 years (Molnar, 2002); it is much lower in third-world countries.

As mentioned earlier, the highest frequencies of the sickle-cell gene are found in sub-Saharan Africa, northeast India, Arabia, Greece, and Turkey. Non-racialists use this as an instrument to sever the historical link between the sickle-cell gene and blacks, as they do for many other medical anomalies, such as hypertension. This will be addressed in chapter 5. Nonetheless, it has been established that natural selection has kept this pernicious gene in high frequency because it promotes survival for heterozygote individuals in malarial environments (F. B. Livingstone, 1958 and 1971).

Malaria is caused by several protozoan species of the genus *Plasmodium*. Four of these species infect humans and cause different types of malaria. Two of the most lethal species are *Plasmodium vivax*, mentioned earlier, the most common form, which is also found in the Western Hemisphere, and *Plasmodium falciparum*, found in tropical regions such as sub-Saharan Africa, northeast India, Arabia, Greece, and Turkey (Harrison, 1978; Molnar, 2002). Like the vivax parasite, an infected female *Anopheles* mosquito bites a human, passing sporozoites to the host (Larsen, 2008). A sporozoite is a motile form of the parasite. Once inside the human, the sporozoites travel through the bloodstream to the liver. In the liver, they create thousands of merozoites. A merozoite is a daughter cell that results from asexual reproduction. The newly produced merozoites enter the bloodstream and infect the red blood cells. Within these cells, the merozoites continue to multiply, eventually causing the cells to rupture. Subsequently, the merozoites invade other red blood cells in the bloodstream and continue their destructive work. Some merozoites develop in male and female gametocytes (cells that can divide and produce sex cells), which may be transferred to another mosquito that bites this host. Finally, the male gamete fertilizes the female gamete, forming a zygote that releases sporozoites inside the mosquito, and the mosquito bites another host to begin the cycle again.

In geographical regions where malaria is found, the sickle-cell gene is in high frequency. Why? As just detailed, the malaria parasite depends on red blood cells for nutrients during part of its life cycle. It follows that red blood cells containing abnormal hemoglobin cannot support malarial parasite growth. The mutant red blood cells are more fragile as the hemoglobin molecule releases oxygen to the surrounding tissue, causing the hemoglobin chains to alter their spatial orientation and change to a series of helical-shaped fibers (Molnar, 2002). Eventually, the fibers stretch to deform the blood cells. These factors reduce multiplication of the parasites, and the individuals with the mutation (particularly, the heterozygotes) do not suffer the deleterious effect of the disease. In essence, it provides a natural immunity.

The spread of malaria (and other infectious diseases) began with the agricultural revolution 10,000 years ago. American physical anthropologist Frank B. Livingstone hypothesized that around 2000 BP the Bantu, a group of peoples who speak the Bantu languages, migrated from northwest Africa into the equatorial south, carrying the mutation with them (F. B. Livingstone, 1958 and 1971). Their iron-working technology made it possible for them to create tools for cutting down large trees, plowing fields, and planting crops. This enabled them to clear large areas of unbroken forest, unknowingly creating an environment for the *Anopheles* species. Furthermore, plant and animal domestication and the adoption of a sedentary lifestyle had a great impact on the environment. For instance, slash-and-burn agriculture altered the landscape radically. This style of agriculture involves the cutting and then burning of trees, which removes the forest canopy and exposes the thin tropical soils to rapid erosion in high rainfall areas (Molnar, 2002). Stagnant pools of water collect and provide a great environment for female mosquitoes to lay their eggs. Slash-and-burn agriculture has also reduced the number of wild mammals that might have been hosts for the various mosquito species.

Sickle-cell anemia is just one of a number of hemoglobinopathies that exist at polymorphic frequencies and provide a selective advantage in malarial environments. Type E hemoglobin, for instance, is also the result of a point mutation in the beta globin gene. It occurs in very high frequencies (greater than 15%) among populations extending from India through Southeast Asia to New Guinea (Molnar, 2002). In New Guinea, Hb^E is most frequent among populations living on the mosquito-infested, swampy, low-lying areas, in contrast to the highland areas, where the Hb^E frequency is close to zero.

Thalassemia, a genetic anemia found in Europe (particularly Greece and Italy), Asia, and the Pacific causes hemoglobin to be clumped inside the red blood cells, which are subsequently destroyed by the spleen, resulting in anemia (Larsen, 2008). The malaria parasite cannot survive in this environment; consequently, heterozygous individuals have a selective advantage.

Since the 1930s researchers recognized an association between the glucose-6-phosphate dehydrogenase (G6PD) enzyme and malaria. Deficiencies were found to occur more frequently in males than in females, indicating that G6PD synthesis is under control of an X-chromosome-linked locus (Molnar, 2002). Without the G6PD enzyme, a person who eats fava beans risks the destruction of red blood cells, severe anemia, and death. This hemolytic disease is called favism. The confounding factor is that fava beans have been a dietary staple of many populations in the Mediterranean region for centuries, yet these populations have the highest frequency of G6PD deficiency (70% among Kurdish Jews) (Molnar, 2002). Also, southern China, the largest producer of fava beans in the world, has populations with high frequencies (15–20%) of the more severe form of G6PD deficiencies (Larsen, 2008; Molnar, 2002). A natural compromise seems to have evolved over time, where red blood cell hemolysis resulting from infection reduces the number of parasites, and Mediterranean and Chinese populations have developed a taste sensitivity to fava beans that limits consumption, thereby reducing the hemolysis rate.

There are other diseases, not involving the red blood cells, that have been applied to race. Tay-Sachs disease, for example, occurs in high frequency (once in every 2,500 to 3,600 births) among the Ashkenazi Jewish populations of eastern Europe and the United States (Boaz & Almquist, 2002; Molnar, 2002). Worldwide averages for the occurrence of Tay-Sachs are about one in every 400,000 to 500,000 births. It is a disease caused by the accumulation of a lipid-sugar molecule ganglioside, an important constituent of cell membranes. Normally, ganglioside is broken down by the enzyme hexosaminidase A. In Tay-Sachs individuals (homozygotes—infants who inherit the gene from both parents), this enzyme is not produced in the body and excess ganglioside accumulates in neuronal cells. The infant fails to develop normal neurological responses, which leads to paralysis, followed by loss of hearing and sight by the end of the first year.

Like sickle-cell anemia, Tay-Sachs is associated with a racial group, in this case, the eastern European Jewish race (or ethnic group). Racialists note that the highest frequency of the Tay-Sachs gene is in eastern

European (Ashkenazi) Jews. Non-racialists counter that Tay-Sachs may be more a factor of population history, discrimination, and natural selection, as in the other diseases previously discussed. According to Jared Diamond (1991), Jews who originally settled in France and Germany during the 8th and 9th centuries were later persecuted during the period of the Crusades. Fleeing eastward into Lithuania and western Russia, they remained there until the 19th century, when anti-Semitic attacks drove millions of them out of eastern Europe. So for more than 1,000 years, European Jews were confined to crowded towns because most were forbidden to own land. Tuberculosis thrived in these crowded conditions. Similarly, tuberculosis (and typhoid) was also prevalent in the crowded ghettos of Poland during the forced internment of European Jews by the Nazis. Heterozygote individuals had lower mortality rates, survived longer, and had higher fertility rates that balanced out the loss of Tay-Sachs infants over time. Of course, homozygote individuals died in infancy.

The other disease associated with race is cystic fibrosis. As a matter of fact, some researchers have stated boldly that cystic fibrosis is the "most common, fatal, homozygous recessive disorder of the *Caucasian* population" (Gabriel, Brigman, Koller, Boucher, & Smuts, 1994, p. 107; italics added). In the late 19th century it was known as "consumption" by the medical establishment and generally labeled as the white plague by the general public. It is believed to have appeared in epidemic proportions in 16th-century England and spread with the movement of people into crowded urban centers during the Industrial Revolution (Molnar, 2002). This disease is a disorder of the pancreatic enzymes and parotid salivary glands, where the patient suffers from respiratory and digestive problems due to secretions of thick, viscous substances that block tubules and do irreversible damage to the lungs and pancreas (Boaz & Almquist, 2002; Molnar, 2002). Today median survival is 28 years of age. In the United States, 5% of people of European ancestry carry one gene, and 1 in every 2,400 to 3,800 live births are homozygous for the disease. It is extremely rare among African Americans (1 in 17,000 live births) and even rarer in Asians (1 in 90,000 live births of Asians in Hawaii) (Molnar, 2002).

The cystic fibrosis allele is correlated with the distribution of cholera (and tuberculosis). Heterozygotes (those who inherited the gene from one parent) are protected from the cholera toxin at a 50% level. One researcher has proposed that heterozygote individuals could more rapidly repair cellular tissue damage caused by the bacterial disease because they secrete highly viscous fluids containing large amounts of mucopolysaccharides in the lungs (Meindl, 1987).

In summary, these blood polymorphisms provide ammunition for non-racialists who seek to decouple the link between genes and race. Much of the evidence from blood types (red cell variants), Rhesus blood groups, abnormal hemoglobins, thalassemia, G6PD deficiency, Tay-Sachs, and cystic fibrosis show only a tenuous link between these red cell polymorphisms or metabolic disorders and race. Nonetheless, racialists note that in the public arena blood polymorphisms as indicators of race may be used for convenience—to accumulate statistical data for insurance purposes and medical research—similar to traits used to assign race to an individual using the skull. But non-racialists present several interesting counterarguments (Brace, 1996; Brace, 2005; Brace et al., 1993; Lewontin, 1972; F. Livingstone, 1962; Molnar, 2002; Relethford, 2005), beginning with blood type: if we used blood type to identify racial groups, for example, then we would have to put northwest Europeans, the Basques of northern Spain, Lapps, Australian Aborigines, Blackfoot Indians, and Polynesians in the same race because they all have high blood type-A frequencies. Also, we would have to put sub-Saharan Africans, northeast Indians (India), Arabs, Greeks, and Turks in the same race because these populations have high frequencies of the sickle-cell gene. This makes no sense. These polymorphisms are more useful in understanding population history and, to some extent, geography. As noted earlier in this chapter, American geneticist Richard Lewontin (b. 1930) in 1972 studied several of the same genetic polymorphisms discussed previously in the major geographic populations and posed this question: How much variation in the genetic polymorphisms was responsible for the differences between populations? He found only 15%, which meant that 85% of the difference or genetic variability was within populations. In essence, only 15% of the variance (6% variance between races but 9% for populations within the races) accounted for race. Based on this data, non-racialists believe that, biologically/genetically, race does not exist. Specifically, there is a complex of antigens on the surface of the white blood cells (whose function is to protect the body against infectious organisms) that process antibodies during the immune response. They are referred to as *Human Leukocyte Antigen* or HLA. This extremely complex system functions as a protective response to the introduction of foreign tissue in the body, such as a liver or skin. In essence, HLA decides whether a newly transplanted liver or skin graft is compatible with the system. The point here is that there are cases where two strangers from totally different populations are a better match in liver, kidney, heart, or cornea than their own, genetically related family members. Racialists counter by posing an important question: If race cannot be delineated genetically, then how do we explain the phenotypic traits (i.e., skin color, nose shape, hair form, etc.) that make it so easy to find an individual of European ancestry surrounded by individuals of African ancestry in a market in Nairobi? (Brues, 1993; Sarich & Miele, 2004). To answer the question, we must look at the complex interaction of genes, ancestry, and environment.

Phenotype: Race, Complex Traits, and the Environment

In the previous section, I discussed traits of simple inheritance, such as phenotypes of blood types, enzymes, and hemoglobin that are determined by single genes. Some of these simple traits cannot be used to identify races, but others (like the Tay-Sachs gene) have a high frequency in certain populations and have been applied as identity labels for ethnic groups or races. Ironically, the complex traits—traits that are affected by the environment, such as skin color, nose shape, hair form, and hypertension, to name a few—have been applied as identity labels for ethnic groups or races. An individual of European ancestry surrounded by individuals of African ancestry is easily identified by his skin color, hence the euphemism

FIGURE **4.1.** Sub-Saharan African and Australian Aborigine have dark skin.

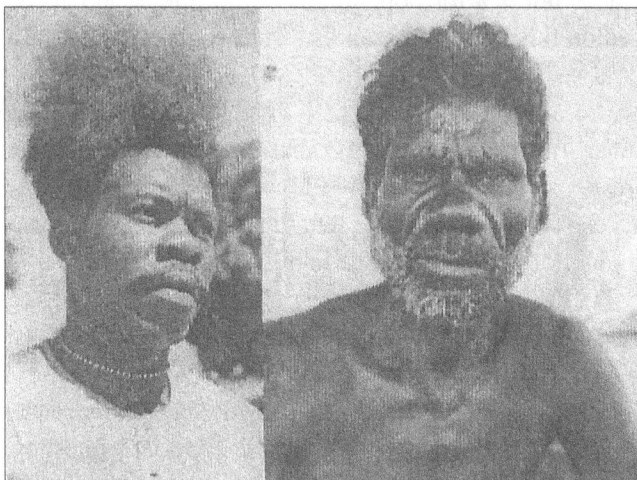

Source. Kottak (©2006 McGraw-Hill. Reprinted with the permission of McGraw-Hill Companies).

"white." Non-racialists emphasize that the use of easily perceived traits ignores the broad and continuous variability of complex traits that are strongly influenced by environmental factors (Brace, 2005; Relethford, 2005). They add that trying to group populations based on skin color or eyelid shape, for example, would lead to inaccuracies, such as putting Australian Aborigines and sub-Saharan Africans in the same group because of their dark skin (figure 4.1) or Asians and the !Kung San[38] in the same group because of similar eyelid shape (or epicanthic folds[39]) (figure 4.2). Nonetheless, traits such as skin color, face form, eyelid shape, nose shape, hair form, head shape and size, body form and weight, body size, and eye color continue to be used to classify populations into races.

Complex traits are polygenic, meaning they are coded by several genes or effects, and the environment affects the expression of these genes. Using skin color as an example, continuously varying or differing intensities of pigmentation and depigmentation (darkest→darker→dark→light

FIGURE **4.2.** Sub-Saharan African male and Northeast Asian female have similar eyelid shape.

Source. Kottak (©2006 McGraw-Hill. Reprinted with the permission of McGraw-Hill Companies).

→lighter→lightest) are produced under varying environmental influences (Molnar, 2002; Relethford, 2005). This is the same for body form and size. These and other phenotypes of complex inheritance vary over a continuous, broad range, and there is a great deal of overlap within and between populations. Non-racialists note that sub-Saharan Africans and Australian Aborigines (including populations from south India) have darkly pigmented skin but they are different populations.

Skin Pigmentation (Dark Skin), Depigmentation (Light Skin), and Current "Theories"
An important component of skin structure and color are specialized cells called melanocytes, located in the lowest level of the epidermis. The major function of these melanocytes is the synthesis of a substance called melanin. Melanin is a pigment responsible for the majority of variation in lightness and darkness in skin color (Molnar, 2002; Relethford, 2005). Much of the variation in melanin may be due to variation in two major

genes that affect the tyrosinase enzyme, which affects melanin production (Relethford, 2005).

Hemoglobin, in addition to its importance discussed in the previous section, is another pigment affecting skin color. Hemoglobin gives oxygenated blood cells their red color, and this red color shows through the skin. Consequently, light-skinned people, those commonly described as "white," who generally have little melanin near the surface of the skin, appear "pink."

Figure 4.3 shows the worldwide distribution of human skin color measured by the percentage of light reflected off the skin at a given wavelength of light. This study is based on data from 102 male samples from indigenous populations (populations whose ancestors have been in the same region for 50,000 years or longer) in the Old World (Relethford, 2005). Skin color is darkest at the equator and lightens with increasing distance north or south from the equator. The reason for this is that ultraviolet radiation is strongest at the equator and weakest away from the equator. Many anthropologists and human biologists agree that the distribution of human skin color in modern humans suggests past evolutionary events relating to natural selection (Blum, 1961; Damon, 1977; Holick, MacLaughlin, & Doppelt, 1981; Jablonski & Chaplin, 2000; Loomis, 1967; Molnar, 2002; Relethford, 2005; Robins, 1991).

Conventional wisdom in biological anthropology suggests that dark skin evolved among our early ancestors in Africa. Later, as some human populations began moving out of Africa and away from the equator, light skin color began to evolve. So what was the selective advantage of dark skin near the equator and light skin away from the equator?

According to the first hypothesis, melanin in the skin prevents the penetration of ultraviolet radiation, which causes skin cancer. Therefore, dark skin has an inherent advantage in environments where the intensity of solar radiation is greatest. Because natural selection is all about survival and reproduction, the former hypothesis is weak because skin cancer usually affects individuals who are long past their reproductive years (Jablonski & Chaplin, 2000). In another popular hypothesis, Loomis (1967) suggested that dark skin protects from overproduction of

FIGURE **4.3.** Worldwide distribution of human skin color measured by the percentage of light reflected off the skin at a given wavelength of light.

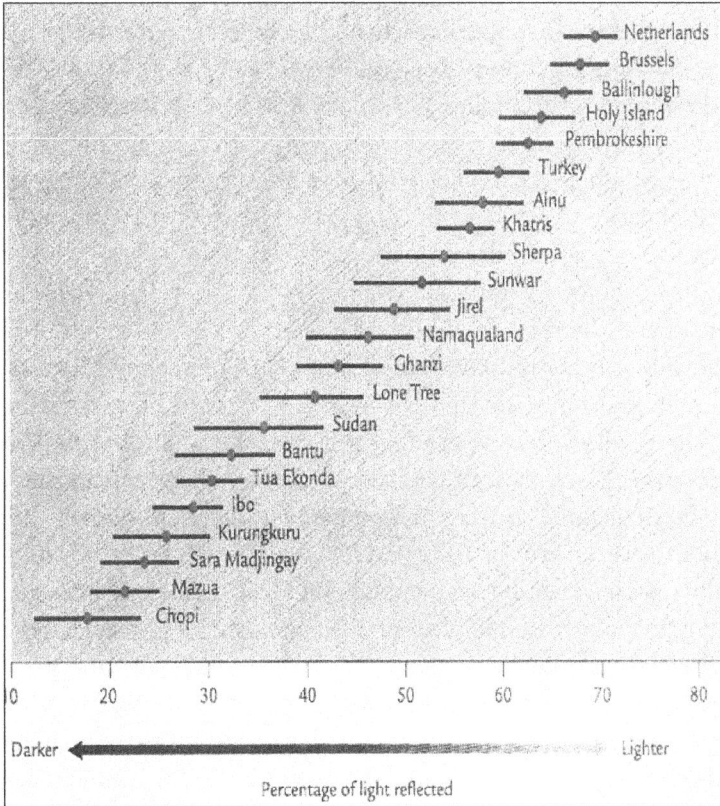

Source. Relethford (©2005 McGraw-Hill. Reprinted with the permission of McGraw-Hill Companies).
Note. This table has been reproduced as best as possible from the original scan.

vitamin D. The major source of vitamin D for humans has always been the sun: sun (sunlight + skin = vitamin D), and vitamin D mediates the absorption of calcium necessary for bone growth (Brace, 1996; Robins, 1991). Too much vitamin D, Loomis argued, would produce toxicity, such as raised blood levels of calcium as well as calcium deposition in the kidneys, causing kidney failure and death. Consequently, darker individuals would be at less risk for vitamin D toxicity. However, Holick et al. (1981) have shown that during continued exposure to ultraviolet radiation, vitamin D synthesis plateaus at a high but not a toxic level.

In a more plausible hypothesis, Jablonski and Chaplin (2000) argued that ultraviolet radiation destroys folate, leading to several serious consequences. Folic acid, a necessary nutrient, is converted to folate in the body. Folate deficiency has been linked to disorders in developing fetuses and reproductive capabilities in adult males. Because survival and reproduction are critical elements of natural selection, evolution would favor a trait that promotes reproduction and survival. This trait, according to Jablonski and Chaplin, would be dark skin, because melanin filters out the harmful effects of ultraviolet radiation, thus protecting folate.

As mentioned earlier, sunlight + skin = vitamin D, and vitamin D mediates the absorption of calcium necessary for bone growth. Vitamin D deficiency causes malformation of the skeleton in growth and development. Consequently, if one assumed that early modern humans migrating out of Africa were dark-skinned (Haviland et al., 2005; Wills, 1994), then low solar radiation in combination with their dark skin and the clothing they likely started wearing to keep warm would have prevented the natural synthesis of vitamin D. Rickets would become prevalent among children and especially serious in females: a malformed pelvis would be dangerous in childbirth. The high mortality rate among infants and children could lead to population reduction and/or extinction. Over time, natural selection would have favored a trait that promoted survival and reproduction; that trait could have been light skin.

Temperature has also been suggested as a factor in the evolution of light skin. Temperatures are high at or near the equator, whereas temperatures drop as the distance from the equator increases. This correlation seems to suggest a link between skin color and cold adaptation. The popular press and the scientific literature (surprisingly) are replete with reasons why the majority of black athletes are not found in winter sports such as ice hockey or skiing. Post, Daniels, and Binford (1975) noted that in cold climates, dark-skinned individuals are at a greater risk for frostbite than light-skinned individuals. World War II and Korean War data seem to support this. During the Korean War, for instance, black American soldiers were more than four times as likely to get frostbite as white American soldiers (Relethford, 2005). There may be a simpler reason for this difference: the rampant racial discrimination in 1950s American society, of which the American military establishment was a subset (in this social environment, it is probable that black soldiers did not receive the proper cold-weather gear). But the cold-injury hypothesis persists and is supported by laboratory experiments on piebald guinea pigs (some of which are dark skinned and some light skinned). It seems that cold injury could be induced more frequently and more severely in the darker patches of the skin (Relethford, 2005). However, Beall and Steegmann (2000) questioned the cold-injury hypothesis. They argue that the higher rates of frostbite among African American soldiers reflect differences in vascular responses to cold and not skin color.[40] They noted that the piebald guinea pig experiment was not really valid because the temperatures used in the laboratory experiments were not typical of those experienced by Paleolithic man.

Face Form

To understand the modern human facial form, we must first look at biological and cultural adaptations in prehistory. In human evolution, the genus *Australopithecus* possessed large, prognathic (projecting) face and teeth.[41] The craniofacial structure of the "robust" species included a ridge of bone in the center of the skull (a sagittal crest) for attachment of large chewing muscles, big brow ridges, a wide face (cheekbones), and huge jaws and teeth. With the advent of tool use, hunting, fire, cooking, and pottery in the genus *Homo*, selection for large jaws and teeth diminished because meat was softer than harsh vegetation and could be made even softer by cooking. Also, food in a pot could be broken down to a drinkable consistency—large facial structures were no longer needed for survival. When traits are no longer needed for survival, their frequencies are reduced and removed by natural selection. With the reduction in these elements in the late Upper Paleolithic time, our fossil ancestors began to look like us. Not all early modern populations underwent the same pattern of change, however, nor were their faces altered at the same rate. Culture is implicated in this process because cooking technology and pottery techniques diffused late to some populations of the world, such as sub-Saharan Africans and, particularly, Australian Aborigines, who not only still have large prognathic faces and teeth but also large brow ridges. Some populations, like the Inuit (Eskimo), retained their large facial features because they continued heavy dental use well into the 20th century.

One distinctive trait used in forensic anthropology to determine race from the skull is facial prognathism, the degree to which the upper and lower jaw project outward. There is a high frequency of prognathism in individuals of African ancestry, but it can also be found in individuals of Asian ancestry. Consequently, non-racialists would argue it is an ambiguous racial trait. Nonetheless, this trait was considered a "primitive" trait in previous centuries and subsequently used to separate and label populations. For instance, a Dutch anatomist, Pieter Camper (1722–1789), compared the angles of the facial profiles of monkeys, apes, and humans (see figure 4.4). His famous "facial angle" is produced by drawing a line touching the forehead and the upper lip and measuring the angle created by that line and a line that runs through the ear opening and between the upper lip and lower border of the nose (Brace, 2005). When he compared Europeans, Africans, and Asians with a monkey and an orangutan, he noted the "marked analogy between the head of the Negro and that of the ape" (as cited in Greene, 1959, p. 190). Camper calculated that the human facial angle fell somewhere between 70 and 80 degrees, starting from a vertical profile. He proclaimed without reservation that:

> everything above eighty degrees belonged to the realm of art, everything below seventy degrees to the animal kingdom...when I inclined that line backwards, I produced a Negro physiognomy, and definitely the profile of an ape, of a Chinese, of an idiot in proportion as I inclined this same line more or less to the rear. (pp. 190–191)

Examples of this type of scientific racism have been discussed in previous chapters. Moreover, many modern populations have prognathic

FIGURE **4.4.** Camper's sketches showing the differences in his famous "facial angle."

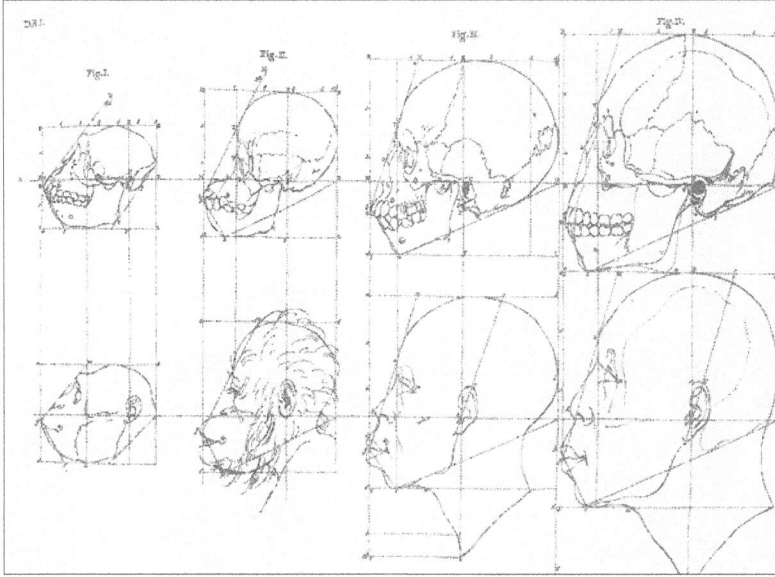

Source. Brace (©2005 Oxford University Press. Reprinted with the permission of Oxford University Press).
Note. Camper's figure I is of an Old World monkey; his figure II is of a juvenile orangutan; his figure III is a "young negro"; his figure IV is a "Kalmouk" from central Asia.

profiles, yet this does not indicate a closer affinity with the animal kingdom or prehistoric fossils. It is simply the result of the presence of large teeth in the maxillary and mandibular dental arches.

People have also used teeth morphology as a racial label. Specifically, shovel-shaped incisors, which describes an incisor tooth that has thickened margins on the lingual surface (tongue side of tooth), have a high frequency in individuals of Asian ancestry (which includes the descendant group Native Americans). In forensic anthropology, it is often used as an additional trait in race assessment using the skull. But as was the case with facial prognathism, shovel-shaped incisors are not uniquely Asian; they can also be found in individuals of European and African ancestries (Bass, 2005; Molnar, 2002). Shovel-shaped incisors are found in various populations because of the way they use their teeth. For instance, the raised surfaces of the tooth provide structural reinforcement that prevents or reduces the possibility of breakage. This may be a simpler explanation than using race; nonetheless, in most cases where shovel-shaped incisors are found in the jaw, the skull is identified correctly as belonging to someone of Asian or Native American ancestry.

Eye Color and Eyelid Shape

The genetics of eye color has not been worked out, but it is likely to be polygenetic (i.e., the result of several loci), which would account for the range of eye colors within and between populations and within some families (Molnar, 2002). But eye color is related to the degree of skin melanin, so blue eyes occur when there is little melanin scattered throughout the iris structure. In short, most instances of blue eyes occur in individuals with fair skin, and most darker eyes do not. Generally, blue-eyed individuals have fair skin, but not all fair-skinned individuals have blue eyes. Likewise, all dark-skinned individuals have dark, brown, or hazel eyes, but all individuals with brown or hazel eyes are not dark skinned. In *Homo sapiens*, eye color becomes extremely complex and more work needs to be done on the connection between eye color and race.

There is variation in eyelid shape within and between populations. But the greatest variation in this trait—compared to most other populations—is found in Asian populations, some Native Americans, and the Khoisan (Bushmen and Hottentot) people of southern Africa. These populations have the epicanthic fold, a fold of skin on the upper eyelid (Campbell, Loy, & Cruz-Uribe, 2006). There is no environmentally adaptive significance to this trait because Asians and sub-Saharan Africans live in different climatic conditions. In short, eyelid shape would make a poor racial trait.

Nose Form

Nasal form and size vary over a wide range. There are people with broad noses and narrow noses and anything in between. In some populations, a certain nose shape does appear more frequently and can be used as a racial trait. Linear measurements of the nose can be taken on the living or from the nasal bones on a skull. A good example of this method is nasal index. This statistic is calculated by dividing the width of nasal opening of the skull with the height of the nose (which includes the nasal bones plus opening) and multiplying the result by 100 (Byers, 2002). For instance, a nasal index of 85% or higher describes a nose that is wide; such high indices are found among most sub-Saharan Africans, Melanesians (New Guinea), and Aborigines of central Australia (Molnar, 2002). Narrower noses, represented by low indices (85% and below), are found among Europeans, North Africans, Native Americans, and the Inuit (Eskimos).

As part of the upper respiratory tract, the nose performs the vital functions of filtering, warming, and moistening the inspired air. The nose is lined with mucosal membranes that cover a dense bed of fatty tissues through which a rich supply of blood flows, and these membranes can secrete large amounts of water (up to 1 liter per day) to moisten inhaled air (Molnar, 2002). Indigenous populations of arid regions of the world could therefore be expected to have a nasal shape that provides the greatest surface-to-volume ratio. And indeed, among desert (hot, dry climate) and mountain populations, including populations in cold climates, the narrow nose is the predominant form. A narrow nasal aperture (opening) provides a much more efficient mechanism for warming and moistening inhaled air than does a short, broad one. Nonetheless, this adaptive significance of size and shape has been challenged by proponents of race because the adaptation hypothesis is not well established in the literature, and in craniofacial forensic analysis, midfacial measurements (i.e., nasal bone length and width, nasal opening, interorbital breadth, midfacial height and width, etc.) are excellent estimators of ancestry (Brace et al., 2006; Brace et al., 1993; Howells, 1973 and 1989).

Hair Form
Like eye color, the genetics (or adaptive significance) of hair form is unknown. Yet, like most of these polygenetic traits, hair on the head varies in length and form from straight to wavy, curly, or spiral shaped. Asians

have straight hair that is thicker than the wavy or curly hair of many Europeans. Frizzy or woolly and spiral-shaped hair are the forms of most sub-Saharan Africans. Some have argued that this woolly or spiral form allows for an air space between the scalp and the outer edges that protect the head from the intensity of the sun's heat in the tropics of sub-Saharan Africa and Melanesia (Molnar, 2002; Stern, 1973). But this is highly speculative.

Head Size and Shape
Head size and shape have been used in the past to define racial groups. As discussed in chapter 2, William Ripley (1899) used head size and shape to group Europeans into three racial entities using Anders Retzius' cephalic index as the objective measure. As a reminder, this index is the ratio of the breadth to the length of the skull; it provides an approximation of shape without regard to size. Human skulls vary from long and narrow to short and broad, which translates to a cephalic index from 70 to about 90 (Molnar, 2002). Most populations are within this range, with the narrowest skull shapes (and similar indices) being found in native South Americans of the Andes, central Europeans, Norwegians, Africans, and Australian Aborigines. Lapps of Scandinavia are at the high end of the spectrum (i.e., have the broadest skull shapes).

These populations all live in different climatic conditions; consequently, environmental adaptation as a direct factor in skull size and shape would seem to be a weak hypothesis. However, Kenneth Beals, Smith, and Dodd (1984) made a comparative study of 20,000 skulls from populations around the world and found a close correlation between environmental temperature and head shape. Populations in colder climates had, on average, rounder heads than populations in the tropics. This correlates to the Bergmann-Allen Rule, which states that as a structure approaches a spherical shape, the surface-area-to-volume ratio will be lower.[42] In contrast, as a structure approaches an elongated shape, the surface-area-to-volume ratio will be higher (Molnar, 2002).

So what can we say about similar cephalic indices found in disparate population groups and environments and the use of skull size and shape in race classification? Richard H. Osborne and Frances V. DeGeorge (1959) showed that head shape had a high genetic component and thus might be used to distinguish populations. They compared monozygotic (identical twins) and dizygotic (nonidentical twins) twins and showed a closer similarity between monozygotic than between dizygotic twins. However, much of the evidence indicates that head size and shape are controlled by many genes that are part of the overall growth and developmental pattern and that are influenced by the environment (e.g., taller individuals have longer heads).

Body Form
In 1988 sports commentator Jimmy "the Greek" Snyder stated his opinion on why blacks were the best athletes by proffering his "theory" based on breeding practices of slave owners—artificial selection—and the resulting body form of the slave offspring. He was subsequently fired by CBS. As the debate on body form and physiological differences between racial groups intensified, in a speech before the British Association for the Advancement of Science in 1995 Roger Bannister, a respected physician, stated,

> As a scientist rather than a sociologist, I am prepared to risk political incorrectness by drawing attention to the seemingly obvious but understressed fact that black sprinters and black athletes in general all seem to have certain natural anatomical advantages. Perhaps there are anatomical advantages in the length of the Achilles' tendon, the longest tendon in the body.

The anecdotes just presented attest to the provocative nature of statements using body form in racial classification. But how is body form actually determined? The measure is known as cormic index, or the ratio between two measurements (standing height divided by sitting height multiplied by 100). This index describes the contribution of the head and trunk length to the total body height. For instance, a cormic index of less than 50 is found in populations—such as Australian Aborigines and Africans—with relatively short torsos and long legs (Molnar, 2002). In contrast, a cormic index of greater than 50 would indicate populations—such as Chinese, Native Americans, and Pygmies—with long trunks and short legs. Although many populations show a tendency toward a particular body form, some researchers argue that body form cannot be used on its own as a racial trait because of the confounding factors of the Bergmann-Allen Rule, as mentioned earlier, and nutritional patterns (Abbie, 1975; Katzmarzyk & Leonard, 1998; Molnar, 2002; Roberts, 1978; Shea & Gomez, 1988).

Skin color, face form, eye color and eyelid shape, nose form, hair form, head size and shape, and body form have been and are currently being used in human society to classify races. The evidence shows these traits are complex and none of them are exclusive to one population or another. In other words, different populations in different geographical regions may share the same traits. We should continue to study the complexity behind these traits and take care how we use the results. But we cannot ignore the fact that populations in the same geographical region generally share more traits than they do with populations in more distant geographical regions. Consequently, the person on the street can clearly tell the difference between an Asian and a sub-Saharan African or between a European and an Australian Aborigine. These visible differences have persisted for thousands of years despite population migrations to new environments and admixture. In summary, one is tempted to state that there may be an evolutionary explanation to race and human classification in that we tend to seek out individuals who resemble us and who share the same language and culture because it gives us some *identity* or *roots* and makes us feel safe. In essence, human classification may be a result of a form of natural selection called *group* selection. I will develop this idea in greater detail in the final chapter.

PART II

RACE IN CONTEMPORARY SOCIETY

CHAPTER 5

RACE, FORENSIC ANTHROPOLOGY, AND HUMAN CLASSIFICATION

A SHORT HISTORY OF FORENSIC ANTHROPOLOGY

In the social realm, is it important for us to physically distinguish an individual of African ancestry from one of Asian or European ancestry? This is a very controversial question, which will be addressed in the last chapter. Nonetheless, in the United States, a country composed of populations from different parts of the globe (and whose ancestors can be traced to those regions), methods were created to categorize and classify these populations into races for practical purposes. Science in general, and biological anthropology in particular, aided in this classification.

Forensic anthropology is defined as the application of physical anthropology to legal investigations. Debra A. Komar and Jane E. Buikstra (2008) published a more thorough definition in their textbook:

> Forensic anthropology is the application of the science of physical anthropology to the legal process. The identification of skeletal, badly

decomposed, or otherwise unidentified human remains is important for both legal and humanitarian reasons. Forensic anthropologists apply standard scientific techniques developed in physical anthropology to identify human remains, and to assist in the detection of crime. Forensic anthropologists frequently work in conjunction with forensic pathologists, odontologists, and homicide investigators to identify a decedent, discover evidence of foul play, and/or the postmortem interval. In addition to assisting in locating and recovering suspicious remains, forensic anthropologists work to suggest the age, sex, ancestry, stature, and unique features of a decedent from the skeleton. (p. 11)

The term *forensic anthropology* was unheard of prior to the 1970s, although many anthropologists were assisting with medico-legal investigations beginning in the latter part of the 19th century (Nafte, 2000; Stewart, 1979). Others have argued that the origin of the science can be traced to the Parkman murder in 1849, where professors of anatomy Oliver Wendell Holmes Sr. (1809–1894) and Jeffries Wyman (1814–1874) were able to reassemble the body of a prominent murder victim, determining that it was a 5-ft, 10½-in. white male who was between 50 and 60 years old at the time of death (Maples & Browning, 1994). But Thomas Dwight is designated the "father of forensic anthropology in the United States" (despite the fact that in his time the American School of Biological Anthropology had died with Morton—see first section of chapter 2) because he was the first American to make major contributions to the field as a "forensic" anthropologist (Byers, 2008; Stewart, 1979; Ubelaker, 1999).

Thomas Dwight (1843–1911) spent nearly 40 years as an investigator and teacher of anatomy. During the last 28 years of his career, he held the Parkman Professorship of Anatomy at Harvard, after having succeeded Holmes (Stewart, 1979; Warren, 1911). He was the first to write articles and give lectures on different aspects of human skeletal identification (the words *forensic* and *anthropology* were considered separate entities at the time). For instance, he experimented with many different skeletal elements—the breast bone (sternum); long bones of arm and legs; suture closure of the skull; and long bones' ends (epiphyses)—in order to determine sex, age, and stature (height) (Byers, 2008).

Even though the evolution of forensic anthropology was slow at the time, Dwight did influence such other scientists as George A. Dorsey (1869–1931), Harris H. Wilder (1864–1928), and Paul Stevenson (1890–1971), who today are considered early pioneers of the field. Dorsey, in particular, became notable because he was the first anthropologist to testify as an expert witness in a criminal case (Byers, 2008; Stewart, 1979). Dorsey was aware of Dwight's work because Dorsey was an anthropology student at Harvard, and he also attended Dwight's Shattuck Lecture in 1894 on long bone articular surfaces and their use in sex determination. From this lecture, Dorsey discovered that the head of the humerus (upper arm bone) is a better indicator of sex than the head of the femur (thigh bone). In the highly publicized Luetgert murder trial of 1897, the prosecution called Dorsey to give his expert opinion on four bone fragments. They were so small that they could fit on a quarter (Byers, 2008; Maples & Browning, 1994), yet Dorsey was able to "identify" the four fragments as human and originating from the hand, foot, and rib. Based on this testimony, coupled with the material evidence, Adolph Luetgert was convicted of killing his wife. I would not attempt to identify bone fragments the size of quarters, and neither would most forensic anthropologists. Opposing anatomists during the trial also pointed to the futility of attempting to identify unidentifiable fragments. As a result, Dorsey was severely criticized and never again consulted on criminal cases.

Certainly, this public criticism was a hindrance to the growth of forensic anthropology. But Harris Wilder (1864–1928) was interested in the more high-profile aspects of skeletal identification, such as facial reconstruction on skulls and dermatoglyphics (configuration of fingerprints). This work led to a book, coauthored with Bert Wenworth and published in 1918, on personal identification. Similarly, Paul Stevenson contributed to the growing literature on human skeletal identification by writing an article on determining age from the epiphyseal union (growth plate) of the long bones and another on the stature of Chinese based on long bone measurements (Byers, 2008; Stewart, 1979). Although not generally associated with forensic anthropology, Earnest Hooton (see second section of chapter 2) worked on a number of cases involving human skeletal identification but did not think this aspect of physical anthropology was important (Stewart, 1979). This is surprising given the numerous materials written about Hooton and his assessment of race.

Interestingly, Wilder's and Stevenson's careers overlapped with those of two prominent physical anthropologists that would usher in a new period of forensic anthropology. The first of these prominent anthropologists is Aleš Hrdlička (see chapter 2). Hrdlička, if you remember, is credited with founding the *American Journal of Physical Anthropology* (1918) and being one of the founding members of the American Association of Physical Anthropologists (1930). But like Earnest Hooton, Hrdlička is not usually thought of as a forensic scientist or an early pioneer of forensic anthropology. As noted in the second section of chapter 2, part of Hrdlička's studies, which included medico-legal training in Paris in 1896, led him to Alphonse Bertillon's criminology laboratory in Paris, where Bertillon utilized anthropometric measurements (measuring the head and face of a criminal at predetermined points with a caliper) and observations for human identification in forensic science (Molnar, 2002; Spencer, 1979). Bertillon recorded the measurements and filed them for future comparison and identification; positive identification would be possible if the same person reoffended. But measurement error resulted in innocent individuals who possessed similar characteristics as known criminals being falsely accused and convicted (Ferllini, 2002). Bertillon also introduced another method, which involved compiling a series of transparencies, each showing a different facial characteristic of criminals. These could be superimposed on each other to create a composite portrait based upon an eyewitness account. He also profited from the influence of Cesare Lombroso (1836–1909), who published a long list of "abnormalities" that were synonymous with the "born criminal," such as receding forehead, large ears, square and projecting chin, broad cheekbones, left-handedness, and addiction to decorating the body (tattoos) (Molnar, 2002). It is not hard to imagine the effect this exposure had on Hrdlička. As a matter of fact, Douglas H. Ubelaker (1999) noted that Hrdlička had a single-minded interest in interpreting evidence of abnormality. Ubelaker also details Hrdlička's direct involvement in both consultation and testimony on medico-legal matters.

From 1896 to 1932 Hrdlička presented court testimony on epilepsy and insanity issues in a jury trial; acted as expert witness for defendants in litigation regarding the "blood status" of Native American allottees of the Chippewa White Earth Reservation in Minnesota; identified human skeletal materials in Argentina and Peru; and determined race, sex, age, and manner of death from a skull recovered in Arizona. Furthermore, beginning in 1936 until his death in late 1943, he gave his expert opinion and conducted skeletal identification for the FBI. On several occasions, exchanges of correspondence took place between Hrdlička and J. Edgar Hoover, the FBI director during that period. Consequently, it is perplexing that the name Aleš Hrdlička is not synonymous with forensic anthropology or noted for beginning the modern period (1939 to 1971) in the history of forensic anthropology. I believe his work in the founding of the AAPA, coupled with the popular questions of human origins and Neanderthals and his bias for the field of medical physiology, all conspired to eclipse his work in the fledgling field of skeletal identification.

The other prominent anthropologist who gets credit for beginning the new period of forensic anthropology is Wilton M. Krogman (1903– 1987). Krogman burst onto the scene with the then-landmark *Guide to the Identification of Human Skeletal Material* (1939). This publication was noteworthy because it had relatively new information on growth and development in the human skeleton, which Krogman studied at Western Reserve University (today called Case Western Reserve University after the merger with Case Institute of Technology in the late 1960s) under the direction of T. Wingate Todd (1885–1938) (Byers, 2008; Rhine, 1998; Stewart, 1979; Ubelaker, 1999; Wolpoff & Caspari, 1997). Data from Todd's new and respected research permeated Krogman's *Guide*, rendering it a publication without competition. It was widely used by anthropologists identifying skeletal remains for the FBI (Stewart, 1979). The same year, Hrdlička published *Practical Anthropometry*, which included information on using skeletal evidence in the identification of deceased individuals and anthropometry in the identification of criminals, but it was not included with Krogman's *Guide* as a reference forensic text for law enforcement personnel in the field. It seems Hrdlička's publication was a general text on criminalistics, the old term for forensic science, and not geared specifically to law enforcement (Ubelaker, 1999).

Krogman's *Guide* would become indispensable in the U.S. Army's program of identifying the skeletal remains of U.S. service members killed in World War II (U.S. involvement 1941–1945), the Korean War (1950–1953), and the Vietnam War (1965–1973). During World War II, because of the fighting, the bodies of soldiers killed in battle could not be recovered from the battlefield until much later. In the meantime, decomposition occurred and the remains became impossible to identify. Because the knowledge on human skeletal identification had grown from the days of Thomas Dwight, culminating with Krogman's *Guide*, the U.S. Army called upon anthropologists to identify the skeletal remains of soldiers overseas for repatriation. In 1947 the U.S. Army Office of the Quartermaster established the Central Identification Laboratory at Hickam Air Force Base in Hawaii, primarily to deal with the Pacific U.S. war dead (Byers, 2008; Stewart, 1979). Charles E. Snow (1910–1967) was the laboratory's first director, followed by Mildred Trotter (1899–1991) in 1948. Although Trotter was hired solely to identify war dead (research on war death was frowned upon by the army), she was eventually able to conduct research on improving ways of determining stature from the lengths of long bones using the skeletons of killed servicemen. The possibility of comparing calculated results based on the long bones to army records of actual heights during life added to the accuracy of the data.

Five years later, with the signing of the armistice on July 27, 1953, ending the Korean War, American physical anthropologists were again engaged in identifying the skeletal remains of U.S. servicemen (Byers, 2008; Stewart, 1979). The U.S. Army established an identification laboratory in Japan, with Thomas Dale Stewart (1901–1997) as its director this time. There was no resistance to research on war dead by the military. In fact, the U.S. Army now encouraged it in order to improve accuracy in the identification of war dead and bring closure for families. Stewart directed research on age estimation from the skeletons of deceased soldiers. Again, comparisons to army records were critical to accuracy. This tradition of large-scale human identification continued during the Vietnam War, where an identification laboratory was established in Saigon (now known as Ho Chi Minh City). Today the identification laboratory is located at its birthplace on Hickam Air Force Base, and it has recently been renamed the Joint POW-MIA Accounting Command (JPAC) Central Identification Laboratory. Most of its search and recovery is concentrated in Southeast Asia.

Because a good number of physical anthropologists were applying their skills to medico-legal investigations, physical anthropologists Ellis R. Kerley (1924–1998) and Clyde C. Snow (b. 1928) believed there should be a separate Section of Physical Anthropology in the American Academy of Forensic Sciences (AAFS). Kerley joined the academy's Section of Pathology-Biology in 1968 and immediately began to encourage other physical anthropologists to apply for membership so that by 1972 there were enough physical anthropologists in the AAFS to create a new section (Byers, 2008; Stewart, 1979). This development is seen as the beginning of the modern period of forensic anthropology. The American Board of Forensic Anthropology (ABFA) was established in 1977 with the purpose of ensuring the competence of physical anthropologists who practice forensic anthropology in North America (Byers, 2008; Nafte, 2000).

In Krogman's 1939 *Guide*, the primary focus was identification of the skeleton. Today forensic anthropologists also assist in identifying the types of trauma that can be inflicted on the skeleton, as well as the types of weapon used to do it. In addition, they assist in identifying weapons used in dismemberments and determine time since death from partially decomposed and skeletonized remains. Finally, they investigate human-rights violations (i.e., in Argentina, Bosnia, Rwanda, Kosovo, Iraq, etc.) by searching and excavating suspected mass graves. Despite all of this varied work, race classification remains most controversial. Therefore, let me discuss and analyze the race concept first from the point of view of proponents of the race concept and then from that of the opponents. For simplicity, I will continue to use the terms *racialist* and *non-racialist*.

EXISTENCE OR NON-EXISTENCE OF RACE

The Racialist Perspective: Forensic Anthropologists and Human Biologists

Human bodies, soft tissue or skeleton, found in suspicious circumstances must be accounted for. In other words, law enforcement must know the identity of the victim. In the case of skeletal remains, forensic anthropologists create a "biological profile" by obtaining metric and nonmetric data. According to Krogman and İşcan (1986), the accuracy of race estimation based on the skeleton, using traditional anthropological methods, is quite high: "On the basis of the usual morphological and morphometric studies, race can be determined from the skull in 85 to 90 percent of the cases" (p. 296). Though their position finds broad support (Bass, 1995; Brues, 1993; Byers, 2002), some forensic anthropologists are more cautious by noting specific population group percentages. For instance, Ousley and Hefner (2005) yield classification accuracy rates of between 84 and 87% for American whites and blacks, using concordance analysis and canonical analysis of the principal coordinates. Asian Americans, Native Americans, and Hispanic Americans attain lower success rates (these groups will be dealt with in more detail in chapters 6 and 7). Nonetheless, the average overall classification rate of 86% is critical to the forensic anthropologists' argument that race must exist because they are so good at finding it. Some of the evidence is discussed in the following sections.

Nonmetric Traits: Skull

The midface is an excellent region to assess race because it is variable from one population to the next (Brace, 1995; Brues, 1977 and 1990; Gill & Gilbert, 1990; Rhine, 1993). For example, in figure 5.1, the area between the eye orbits is narrow in Caucasoids, intermediate in Mongoloids, and wide in Negroids. The nasal openings of these individuals follow similar trends. In figure 5.2, the nasal bones have a high angle in Caucasoids, an intermediate angle in Mongoloids, and a low angle in Negroids. In addition, whereas the region below the nasal opening

FIGURE **5.1.** Front views of midface in Caucasoid, Mongoloid, and Negroid.

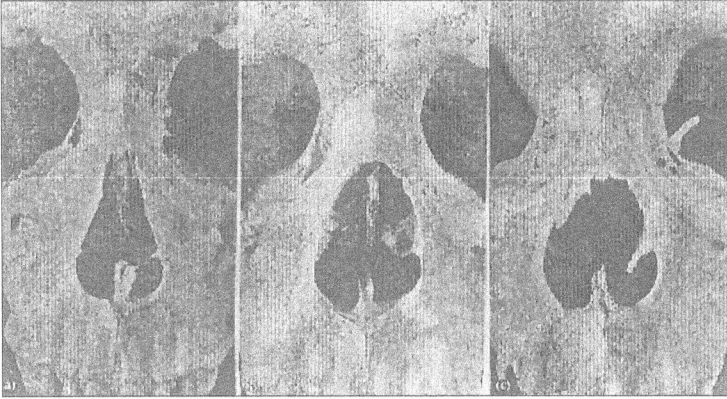

Source. Byers (©2008 Prentice Hall. Reprinted with the permission of the Maxwell Museum of Anthropology and Julie R. Angel).

FIGURE **5.2.** Side views of faces in Caucasoid, Mongoloid, and Negroid showing the degree of nasal and jaw projection.

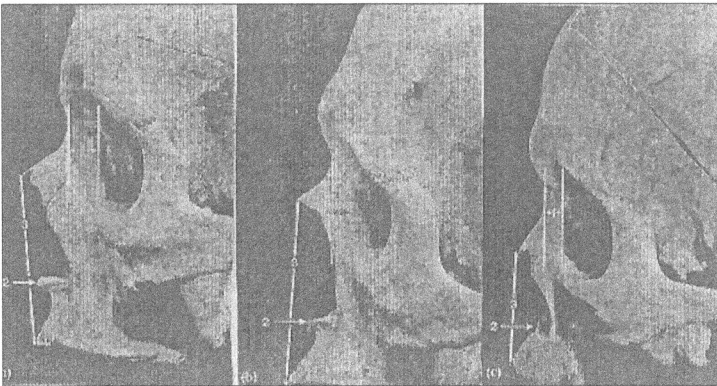

Source. Byers (©2008 Prentice Hall. Reprinted with the permission of the Maxwell Museum of Anthropology and Julie R. Angel).

(alveolar region) in Negroids and Mongoloids is projecting, the maxillary area (midfacial region) of Caucasoids is projecting. These traits, although they cross population lines, are significant when they are found in high frequencies in one population or another. According to Brues (1990), for a trait to be labeled racial, it must have a high genetic component (population history) or a high frequency in one geographical region.

Metric Traits: *Skull*
Figure 5.2 shows side views of the midface of these individuals. Distance 1 shows the length from where the nasal bones meet the anterior plane of the eye orbit. In Caucasoids, this distance is wider than in Mongoloids and Negroids. Arrow 2 points to the nasal spine. It is very large in Caucasoids, intermediate in Mongoloids, and very small in Negroids. Finally, distance 3 shows the length from the tips of the nasal bones to the most forward projection of the alveolar region. This distance is shorter in Negroids than in Caucasoids and Mongoloids.

These midfacial traits and cranial traits can be measured and the numbers plugged into a multivariate statistical package to generate a scatter plot. This technique is called a discriminant function analysis (Giles & Elliot, 1962). The aim is to get the maximum discrimination between populations based on the measurements. Despite the fact that only two populations can be compared at one time, for example, Caucasoids and Negroids or Caucasoids and Mongoloids, this particular discriminant analysis provides a very good separation between populations. Racialists argue that metric and nonmetric techniques enable them to frequently find race. The developers of the latest version of a more sophisticated statistical program called Fordisc 3.0, which is a database of cranial measurements for hundreds of sample groups, boast that their program generates even better results in discriminant analysis of population groups (Jantz & Ousley, 2005). Fordisc 3.0 classifies an unknown skull to the closest documented sample group in the database based on the measurements and angles. I will discuss Fordisc, as it relates to my research, in greater detail in the next chapter.

Phenotypical Traits and Physiological Mechanisms

Racialists take issue with the statement "there is no such thing as race." And a large percentage of society would probably agree with them. In terms of skin color, one forensic anthropologist has stated (with some humor) that if proponents of this statement were dropped by parachute into downtown Nairobi, they would be unable to tell by looking around whether they were in Nairobi or Stockholm (Brues, 1993). In contemporary American society, President Barack Obama or golfer Tiger Woods, though multiracial, are *viewed* by the greater public as black Americans; they would not be mistaken for any other race. And most westerners would identify individuals with a certain characteristic eyelid shape (epicanthic fold) as East Asians. So despite the overwhelming data on the adaptive nature of complex traits discussed earlier in this chapter, skin color, eyelid shape, and nose and hair form are used every day to identify and classify people. All racialists agree that, though not exclusive, particular forms of these traits have a higher frequency in one geographic region or another, rendering the major ancestral groups of human populations—that is, sub-Saharan Africans, East Asians, and Europeans—as well as their descendants, easier to identify.

A minority of biologists believe racial variation is significant. Vincent Sarich and Frank Miele received the following question after sending out a few e-mails on their objection to the "no such thing as race" philosophy:

> One thing that intrigues me about this subject is the tendency of the "no race" people to avoid defining what it is that they claim doesn't exist. *In other words, what characteristics would human races have if they did exist?* Would anyone care to try to address that one? Or provide a reference to a recent effort that does? (2004, p. 162; italics added)

In the first section of chapter 4, I noted the famous assessment made by Richard Lewontin, dating back to 1972, that there was more variation within populations than between populations. Lewontin looked at the data from 17 genetic loci in the major geographical populations to answer the question of how much variability in these genetic markers was responsible for the differences between these populations. He found only 15% for the variance (6% variance between races but 9% variance within races). In other words, 85% of the genetic variability was among individuals within populations. Sarich and Miele (2004) agree that these percentages remain true for a much larger body of data that has accumulated since 1972, but they argue that Lewontin's assessment is simply an average across the genetic loci on hand that says nothing about the variation at the individual loci. They note that any two sub-Saharan West African individuals have dark skin, frizzy hair, and an absence of Duffy blood groups Fy^a and Fy^b. In other words, sub-Saharan Africans are more similar to one another than to Europeans or Asians or Native Americans.

In a related study, Noah Rosenberg et al. (2002) studied human population structure using genotypes at 377 autosomal microsatellite[43] loci in 1,056 individuals from 52 populations (usually defined by culture or geography, not necessarily as a reflection of underlying genetic relationships). They confirmed Lewontin's 1972 findings, obtaining a within-population genetic variation of 93 to 95% and a between-group variation of 3 to 5%. Nonetheless, without using prior information about the origins of individuals, they identified—applying a model-based clustering algorithm that identifies subgroups that have distinctive allele frequencies—five main genetic clusters: Africa, Europe, Asia, America, and Oceania. In addition, there were subclusters that corresponded to within-individual populations. Furthermore, they found that genetic clusters often corresponded closely to predefined regional or population groups or to collections of geographically and linguistically similar populations. Rosenberg and colleagues concluded that the structure of human population (in other words, racial differences) is relevant in various epidemiological contexts, such as variation in genetic and nongenetic risk factors, disease rates, and response to pharmaceuticals.

In another study, where the general aim was to understand racial genetic variation underlying disease susceptibility for the purpose of providing personalized health care, Michael Bamshad et al. (2003) assayed 100 *Alu* insertion polymorphisms[44] in a heterogeneous collection of 565 individuals (from sub-Saharan Africa, East Asia, southern Asia, and Europe), 200 of whom were also typed for 60 microsatellites. After they removed all information about race (continent of origin) and ethnic affiliation, they used a model-based clustering method to estimate the number of clusters into which the sample data fit with posterior probability. Correct assignment to the continent of origin, with a mean accuracy of at least 90%, required a minimum of 60 *Alu* markers or microsatellites—and reached 99 to 100% when 100 or more loci were used. For the *Alu* data, they found that the mean prediction rates ranged from 40 to 50% for one locus to an impressive 95 to 99% for 100 loci (depending on true population origin). As additional loci were added, the rate of correct allocation increased more quickly for sub-Saharan Africans than for East Asians or Europeans. When only 20 markers were used, Bamshad et al. found that 88% of sub-Saharan Africans were assigned correctly, whereas the rates of correct assignment for East Asians (76%) and Europeans (71%) were lower. Interestingly, sub-Saharan Africans were rarely allocated to Asia or Europe, and East Asians and Europeans were rarely allocated to Africa (as popularized by mtDNA and the "Out of Africa" model for modern human origins—see chapter 3 for a complete discussion). Moreover, it was easier for Bamshad and colleagues to distinguish Africans from non-Africans than to distinguish other groups from each other.

When 60 *Alu* markers were used, 98% of the sub-Saharan African samples were correctly allocated to Africa, versus 96% using microsatellites. For the researchers, combining the *Alu* and microsatellite data increased the power to correctly predict the continent of origin for the East Asian and European samples. For instance, using 20 loci generated a mean correct prediction rate of 91% for the sub-Saharan African samples, followed by 82% for East Asians and 79% for Europeans. In summary, Bamshad et al. found significant genetic variation among these widely separated populations of Africa, Asia, and Europe, and they believed this situation is likely to be similar at many loci influencing disease susceptibility or drug response. But in their analysis, they found that detection of population structure and assignment of samples from geographically intermediate regions (e.g., Middle East, central Asia) was less accurate, possibly because these are admixed populations. This last result may be positive news for non-racialists because it seems to undermine traditional concepts of race.

In a more provocative study, Sarich and Miele (2004) found that racial morphological (cranial/facial) distances between human populations are much greater than those seen among gorillas or chimpanzees (and, on average, even greater than between the sexes). They collected 28 craniofacial measurements from 29 human populations (2,500 individuals), 17 from the two species of chimpanzee (347 individuals), and 25 measurements on the two species of gorilla (590 individuals). Within one of the species of chimpanzee (*Pan troglodytes*) and gorilla (*Gorilla gorilla*), there are several subspecies or races. Generally, the aim was to obtain the amount of morphological differences within (male-male and male-female paired comparisons) and between populations. The numbers given are the percent increases in distance going from within-group to between-group comparisons of individuals. For instance, the distance among the three chimpanzee subspecies or races is approximately 6%. The distance between the two chimpanzee species (*Pan troglodytes* and *Pan paniscus*) is 14.6%. Furthermore, the distances within the gorilla species are variable. But the distance between the two species of gorilla (*Gorilla gorilla graueri* and *Gorilla beringei beringei*) is 24.7%.

When the data on human populations are compared, Sarich and Miele (2004) showed that the Dogon of Mali (West Africa) or the Teita (Kenyan Bantu speakers) have a distance of 14.9% to the Khoisan (!Kung San "Bushmen"), similar to the 14.6% separating the two chimpanzee species. They also found that the distance separating Norse (northern Europeans) and South Australian sample groups is 26%, slightly greater than the largest distance between gorilla species. Even more provocative are the findings that the largest differences are found when comparing African with either Asian or Amerindian sample groups, such as Teita to Tierra del Fuegans (32.4%); Zulu to Tierra del Fuegans (36%); Zulu to Santa Cruz Island (California) (36%); and Teita to Buriat (Mongolia) (46%).

In addition, racialists present evidence in physiology and medicine: they argue that health journals continuously publish scientific studies that show clear differences among races in susceptibility to disease, different reactions to pharmaceuticals, and other aspects of medicine and physiology. They list several general examples: black men are 40% more likely to suffer from lung cancer than are white men; in regard to breast cancer, black women tend to develop tumors that are more malignant than those found in white women; black infants are almost two-and-a-half times more likely to die within the first 11 months of life than white infants; and American Indians are far more likely than blacks or whites to carry an enzyme that makes it harder for them to metabolize alcohol, leading to a high frequency of alcoholism. The other reports we hear are the racial differences in rates of cardiovascular disease, diabetes, kidney disease, Tay-Sachs, cystic fibrosis, sickle-cell trait, life expectancy, and many other pathologies (Tay-Sachs, cystic fibrosis, and sickle-cell were discussed in detail in the first section of chapter 4). But the most controversial disease (in recent history) that has been linked to race is hypertension (or high blood pressure) and its high frequencies in blacks. I say controversial because it has also been linked to pernicious socioeconomic ills such as the aftereffects of American slavery and discrimination, that is, the effect those ills have on African Americans' nutrition, health care, and life expectancy. Racialists argue that since the 1980s, medical literature has shown that U.S. blacks are almost twice as likely as whites to suffer from hypertension, which could lead to cardiovascular diseases. Furthermore, they report that black men are reported to have a 27% higher death rate from cardiovascular disease than white men, with the rate in black women being 55% higher than in white women. It has been hypothesized for the past 30 years that West Africans (ancestors of black Americans) have a genetic adaptation to low-sodium diets because western central Africa is a region with a low salt supply, which makes their descendants (African Americans) sensitive to even moderate intakes of sodium (Molnar, 2002; Shreeve, 1994; T. W. Wilson, 1986).

In a recent study of hypertension in black Americans, Randall Tackett (of the University of Georgia) et al. (1995) showed that a physiological mechanism was a more likely cause than socioeconomic circumstances for the higher incidence of hypertension. They exposed veins to chemicals that stressed the tissues and caused them to constrict. They found that veins taken from blacks were slower to return to normal size than those taken from whites. Because constricted veins cause the heart to work harder (having to pump blood through a narrow space), the result is a hypertensive environment. Tackett et al. concluded, "This is the first direct demonstration that there are racial differences at the level of the vasculature" (p. 876).

Furthermore, Sarich and Miele (2004) reported on the differences in the effectiveness of two types of hypertension medication between black and white patients. Black patients, on average, did not benefit from one class of ACE (angiotensin-converting enzyme) inhibitors as much as white patients did (this drug is considered the standard treatment for heart failure resulting from hypertension). The cause for this difference is nitric-oxide insufficiency in blacks. Nitric oxide is a gas that is normally produced by the cells that line the blood vessels. It functions to relax blood vessels and thereby reduce blood pressure. Sarich and Miele note that ACE inhibitors probably interact with nitric oxide, lowering blood pressure. Consequently, individuals with less of the gas will not respond as well. Interestingly, a drug called BiDil, patented by Jay N. Colin, a professor of medicine at the University of Minnesota School of Medicine, may replenish nitric oxide (Sarich & Miele, 2004). BiDil is a diuretic and a vasodilator, and it has preliminary support from the Food and Drug Administration. Most racialists have labeled non-racialists illogical for not accepting this particular racial difference—by acknowledging it, they could improve medical care and treatment. It seems the Association of Black Cardiologists and the Congressional Black Caucus have acknowledged this racial difference, indirectly, by supporting testing for BiDil (Sarich & Miele, 2004).

In summary, racialists believe that in the human soft tissue and skeleton "there is something there." They emphasize that when we are on the street in New York City, London, or Paris, we have no problem identifying races; this is the social or important reality. And based on the genetic and physiological evidence presented here, they would argue that it is therefore silly to say, "There is no such thing as race."

The Non-Racialist Perspective: Conventional Wisdom
(The Majority of Human Biologists)
Metric and Nonmetric Traits: Skull and Skin Color

Proponents of the statement "there is no such thing as race" do not intend it to be humorous. This prestigious camp, which includes human biologists and most anthropologists, counters with some compelling arguments. First, the biological anthropologists state that no trait is entirely genetic or racial because there may be a strong environmental factor asserting its influence (Armelagos, 1994; R. Boyd & Silk, 2006; Brace, 1964, 1995, and 2005; Goodman & Armelagos, 1996; Gould, 1994; Huxley & Haddon, 1936; F. Livingstone, 1962; Molnar, 2002; Montagu, 1964; Relethford, 2005; Shreeve, 1994). They are actually referring to midfacial traits, particularly nasal form (opening), which is a favorite trait among forensic anthropologists in race assessments using the skull.

In soft tissue, nasal form is combined with hair form and skin color to classify individuals. For example, most Americans associate wide noses with African Americans. But according to most non-racialists, this is wrong—non-racialists firmly believe that nose form might be an adaptive trait (Brace, 1996; Brace et al., 1993; Molnar, 2002; Relethford, 2005). I discuss this adaptive aspect of nose form in detail in the last section of chapter 4. But to briefly review this topic, in regions where the air is dry and hot or dry and cold, the expectation is a geometric nasal shape that provides the greatest internal surface-to-volume ratio (not only to moisten air but also to warm cold air). Therefore, the nasal form of populations who have a long history in hot or cold dry geographical regions is high-bridged and elongate. In contrast, populations who have a long history in tropical regions, where humidity is high, do not require a large internal nasal surface. Consequently, the nasal shape in these populations is low-bridged and broad.

Non-racialists assert that this environmental-adaptation perspective on nasal form delivers a powerful blow to racialists who use nose form as a racial trait. This begs the question, how many skulls have been labeled European or Caucasoid due to similar nasal form (opening) when they were actually North African (from a dry and hot region)? Or can we call Melanesians or Australian Aborigines sub-Saharan Africans?

Non-racialists relish these types of questions because they weaken the arguments of racialists.

Non-racialists also get support from evolutionary biology because most researchers in this field reject the notion that there are special racial traits (Bowcock et al., 1991; Lewontin, 1972; Templeton, 1999). For instance, consider the Melanesians and sub-Saharan Africans in the evolutionary tree of human populations as estimated from genetic-distance data in figure 5.3 (Bowcock et al., 1991; Templeton, 1999). These two human populations form two separate branches (genetic divergence) within this evolutionary tree of humanity with respect to genetic markers. Nonetheless, Melanesians and sub-Saharan Africans share dark skin, hair form, and craniofacial traits typically used to classify people into races. From this gross disparity between racially defining traits and molecular genetic data, non-racialists have additional proof indicating that classifications based on these racial traits have no real validity. They state that it is as ridiculous as grouping East Asians and the Khoisan into a single race based on eyelid shape (as both populations have epicanthic folds).

Phenotypical Traits and Physiological Mechanisms
Non-racialists reject the proposition that populations can be classified by head size and shape as in Ripley's tripartite races of Europe (discussed in detail in the second section of chapter 2). They note Howells' (1989) published results on worldwide skull size and shape, which showed that skull shape varies within and between populations. Non-racialists also note Boas' provocative study of changes in body form in second-generation immigrants (American-born descendants) (see the second section of chapter 2 for discussion). As a reminder, Boas rebutted Ripley's work by showing that in the first American-born generation of immigrants the general shape of the skull changed significantly because of environmental and cultural factors, for example, nutritional changes and ending the European practice of dressing infants and children in skull caps in order to "bind the ears closer to the head" (Boas, 1911). Additionally, non-racialists add climate (discussed in the second section of the previous chapter) as another problem in using skull size and shape to classify populations.

FIGURE 5.3. Evolutionary tree showing genetic distances between human populations.

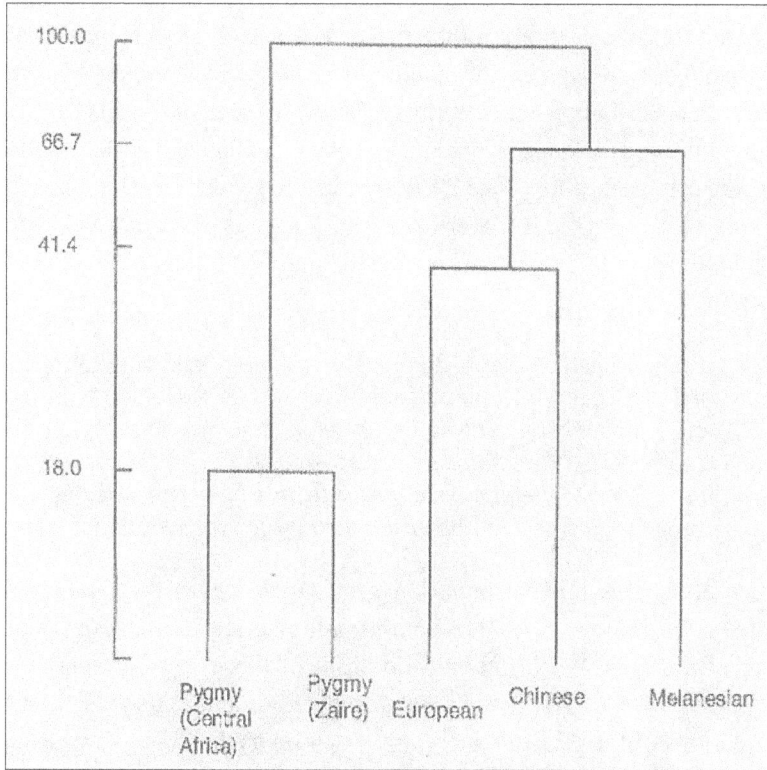

Source. Bowcock et al. (©1991 Nature Publishing Group. Reprinted with the permission of Nature Publishing Group).

Early-20th-century biological anthropologists labeled some living populations as "primitive" based on skull size and shape, essentially placing racial differences far back in time (see chapter 3 for a complete treatment of this topic). And even in the 1990s a prehistoric human fossil was classified as "Caucasoid." Non-racialists use this incident as an example of the chaos the race concept creates. In 1996 human skeletal remains were discovered in a pooled area of the Columbia River in Kennewick,

Washington. It was radiocarbon-dated at approximately 8,000 to 8,500 years BP (Taylor, Kirner, Southon, & Chatters, 1998). A preliminary examination was performed on the skeleton, and it was said to have "Caucasoid-like" traits (Chatters, 2000). Although the "Caucasoid" label for Kennewick Man has been frequently attributed to Dr. James Chatters, Dr. Chatters rejects this attribution and accuses various writers of misquoting him despite his explanation to the contrary (Chatters, 2000 and 2002; Chatters, personal communication, June 29, 2009). In a paper published in *American Antiquity* entitled "The Recovery and First Analysis of an Early Holocene Human Skeleton from Kennewick, Washington," Chatters (2000) noted the following:

> Cranial characteristics, femoral morphology and stature together led me, in the forensic venue, to suggest an affiliation with modern Euroamericans. *Once the skeleton's age was known, however, I referred to the remains as "Caucasoid-like".... I did not state, nor did I intend to imply, once the skeleton's age became known, that he was a member of some European group.* (p. 306; italics added)

Nonetheless, this misinterpretation sent shock waves throughout biological anthropology, with those anthropologists specializing in the peopling of the New World feeling the brunt of those waves: *Caucasians in the New World 8,000 years ago?* More importantly, it shook the very foundations of the Native Americans' position as the "First Americans." Later, however, a detailed multivariate analysis was done on a battery of measurements taken on the skull, indicating that, morphologically, Kennewick Man was "nearest" to Polynesians and East Asians (J. Powell & Rose, 2004). Non-racialists insist that the concept of race cannot be applied to 8,000- or 9,000-year-old fossils because race, as defined by categories such as Asian American or African American or by skin color and so forth, is a phenomenon created in recent times.

Skin color is the trait traditionally used to classify human populations. Non-racialists believe it is not racial but an adaptive trait coded by many genes (polygenic) and affected by the environment. Specifically, they argue that skin color follows the intensity of solar radiation in a *clinal* (a gradient in a measurable trait) distribution (Brace, 1964 and 2005; Brace et al., 1993; F. Livingstone, 1962; Molnar, 2002; Relethford, 2005). They also note that the distribution of skin color in the world today suggests past evolutionary events relating to natural selection, such as dark skin prevents skin cancer or protects folate levels from the damaging effects of ultraviolet radiation (see discussion in the second section of the previous chapter). Non-racialists report on a study done by John Relethford (1997) on skin color, suggesting that—despite using skin color—human populations cannot be classified into discrete categories.

John Relethford (b. 1953) measured skin color at specific wavelengths using a reflectance spectrophotometer. Specifically, the more light reflected off the skin, the lighter the individual, and the less light reflected off the skin, the darker the individual. Initially, three populations were studied. Figure 5.4 shows the three populations. The dots represent the mean skin reflectance measured at a wavelength of 685 nanometers, and the lines represent one standard deviation about the mean. Relethford suggested that three populations along the horizontal axis indicated three categories, giving us a false sense of the true nature of human variation. But when he added more populations—a representative approximation of the world's populations—he got a totally different picture (see figure 4.3). There is tremendous overlap among all populations—we do not see any categories anymore. According to Relethford, it is very difficult to tell where one population starts and another ends. This result is what non-racialists emphasize most because it shows a clear overlap in the sample populations. They herald this result as significant (and ironic) because skin color is the very trait used in human classification for the past 600 years or more.

Racialists study the literature in physiology and medicine and report that there are racial differences in rates of cardiovascular disease, diabetes, kidney ailments, life expectancy of newborns and adults, alcoholism, hypertension, and other physiological pathologies. Non-racialists argue that the disparities in health status reflect the impact of past and present social inequality, of which the root cause is racial discrimination (Duster, 2005; Flint, 1995; Krieger, 1987; Krieger, Rowley, Herman, Avery, & Phillips, 1993; Leon & Walt, 2001; D. R. Williams, 1999). In essence,

FIGURE **5.4.** Distribution of human skin color for three populations measured by the percentage of light reflected off the skin at a given wavelength of light.

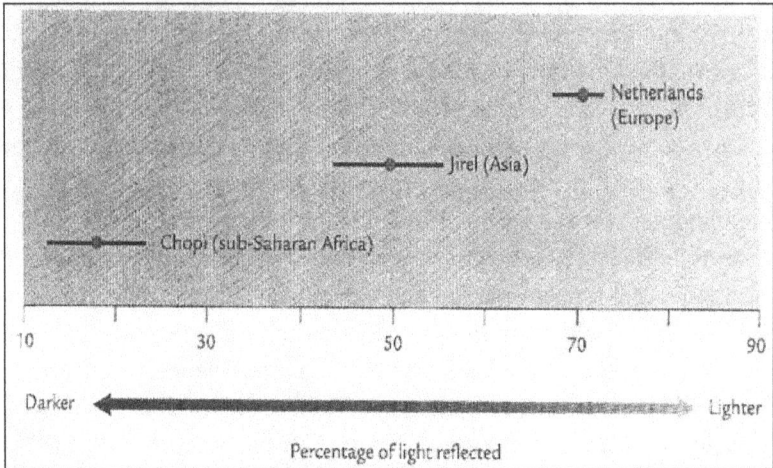

Source. Relethford (©2005 McGraw-Hill. Reprinted with the permission of McGraw-Hill Companies).
Note. This table has been reproduced as best as possible from the original scan.

they are urging scientists not to classify by race. For instance, on the controversial subject of hypertension (discussed earlier in this chapter), Tackett et al. (1995) found that when the veins from blacks and whites were exposed to chemicals that stressed the tissues, veins from blacks were slower to return to normal size than those taken from whites. Some non-racialists note that Tackett's sample of African Americans was limited to 22 individuals from southern Georgia (Duster, 2005; Shreeve, 1994). Others add that the simplest explanation for hypertension in some minority groups may be the frustration and tensions encountered in their daily lives that can lead to anxiety and increased blood pressure (Boaz & Almquist, 2002; Krieger, 1987; Little & Baker, 1988; Molnar, 2002). Whereas racialists note that African Americans with darker skin frequently had higher blood pressure, non-racialists counter by showing that it was not the skin color that produced a direct causal outcome in hypertension, but that darker skin color in the United States was associated with less access to needed resources (Duster, 2005; Klag, Wheldon, Coresh, Grim, & Kuller, 1991; Molnar, 2002). What if we compare the American population with populations from around the world? Non-racialists note results from Richard Cooper et al.'s (2005) study that compared racial differences in hypertension by sampling whites from eight surveys completed in Europe, the United States, and Canada and contrasted these results with those of a sample of three surveys among blacks from Africa, the Caribbean, and the United States. Hypertension rates were measured in 85,000 subjects. The study found that the data from Brazil, Trinidad, and Cuba indicated a significantly smaller racial disparity in blood pressure than what was found in North America.

Non-racialists attribute Cooper's results to the stresses of North American high-tech industrial society rather than racial differences. They assert that populations living in isolated rural communities frequently show lower average blood pressures than their relatives living in urban areas (Little & Baker, 1988; Molnar, 2002; Shreeve, 1994). They also add that when aboriginal populations move to cities and adopt Western lifestyles, one of their earliest physiological responses is increased blood pressure, and this physiological response is found in populations as genetically or physically diverse as the Inuit, New Guinea highlanders, Solomon Islanders, and Australian Aborigines. Non-racialists would view the 22 blacks from southern Georgia used in Tackett's study as experiencing socioeconomic stress based on the history of racial discrimination in the region.

Prominent human biologist Jared Diamond is biased toward the environmental arguments for population differences in hypertension. He believes that using skin color, nose form, hair form, head shape, and body form to classify human populations is as ridiculous as using any other, random trait (Diamond, 1994). If we use the sickle-cell gene, according to Diamond, then African blacks would be grouped with Greeks, South Asians, New Guineans, Italians, and North Africans. He notes that these groupings are not based on skin color, obviously, but on the prevalence of malaria (see discussion in the first section in chapter 4). In contrast, Swedes would be grouped with the Khoisan because of the absence of the sickle-cell gene. Furthermore, the lactase enzyme enables us to digest the milk sugar lactose. As infants, we have lactase because we need milk, but we stop producing it after weaning. However, many populations retain their lactase into adulthood because their cultures have a long history of mammal domestication. Adult lactase is found in low frequency in southern Europeans, East Asians, Australian Aborigines, Native Americans, and sub-Saharan Africans. According to Diamond, if the lactase enzyme is used to classify populations, then Swedes belong with Fulani (lactase-positive), whereas other African blacks, Japanese, and Native Americans belong together in a separate group (lactase-negative).

Finally, fingerprint patterns are identified by arches, loops, and whorls. Europeans and sub-Saharan Africans' fingerprints tend to have many loops, whereas Australian Aborigines' fingerprints tend to have many whorls. If we use fingerprints to classify populations, according to Diamond, Europeans and sub-Saharan Africans would sort together in one race, Jews and some Indonesians in another, and Australian Aborigines in a third.

Non-racialists present solid scientific evidence that challenges the validity of human races. Additionally, in the past 400 years or more, there has been population admixture in the United States—more so in the last 50 years because of immigration. This fact has made America much more complicated in terms of race. Non-racialists note the genetic analysis on populations such as Ethiopian or Afro-Caribbean, where the associations between race and genes were dismantled because these were admixed populations (Romualdi et al., 2002; Wilson et al., 2001). They also note Bamshad et al. (2003), maintaining that populations from geographically intermediate regions (e.g., Middle East, central Asia) could not be genetically allocated to their respective regions. In other words, they emphasize that our ability to accurately classify individuals according to different geographical regions is not equivalent to allocating races. Additionally, geneticists and forensic anthropologists using skulls have found it difficult to classify Hispanics (Long et al., 1991; Parra et al., 2001). But does admixture vindicate non-racialists in their claim that race is an illusion? We will address this important question in chapters 6 and 7.

CHAPTER 6

RACE AND
POPULATION ADMIXTURE

A BRIEF HISTORY OF U.S. IMMIGRATION

Before the important date of 1492, North America was already populated with people who claim (and rightly so) the title of "First Americans." Genetic dating based on mutation rates of mtDNA and Y-chromosomes indicates that their ancestors (North Asians) migrated from Asia to North America via the Bering Land Bridge (or Beringia) sometime between 20,000 and 15,000 years ago (Larsen, 2008; Relethford, 2005).Their descendants—or Native Americans—populated the Atlantic Seaboard from present-day southern Maine to North Carolina, where the Algonquian-speaking peoples combined intensive horticulture with small- and big-game hunting and fishing (Morison et al., 1980; University of Calgary, 2001). Also, other nations in the Great Lakes region and the St. Lawrence River area harvested wild rice, hunted big game, and traveled by canoes, interacting with other groups through warfare and peaceful trading.

Within this social interaction, there was more than likely interbreeding (population admixture or gene flow) through alliances and warfare (taking females by force).

Societies in the South and Midwest and on the Pacific coast were also densely populated with nations interacting through alliances and warfare (Morison et al., 1980; University of Calgary, 2001). The Mississippian and Hopewell societies in the south were complex, hierarchical social organizations. To the west, on the Great Plains, lived the big-game hunters. On the Pacific coast, from southern Alaska to the Acoma Pueblo towns of Southern California, mobile trading nations traveled along the coast and inland along the Columbia River to trade iron, pelts, copper, dried fish, fish oil, and human slaves with other coastal nations. Again, we see another form of violent population admixture—slavery.

European migration to North America began in the 17th century along the Atlantic coast. This migration would continue in greater numbers into the 20th century, and the immigrants and their descendants would be joined by migrants from Africa, Asia, Latin America, and the Caribbean, resulting in the present biologically (and culturally) complex United States.

There were several push and pull factors that forced Europeans to immigrate to North America: general overpopulation caused by high birth rates leading to unemployment in urban centers; political persecution in the form of repressive legislation and unlawful imprisonment; and religious persecution under the rule of Charles I (reign: 1629–1640), who valued the Catholic ceremonial elements in the Church of England and allowed management of the church to rest with Archbishop Laud, who was anti-Protestant (Hartmann, 1979; Morison et al., 1980). Later, under Oliver Cromwell (1640s and 1650s), England persecuted dissenting Protestant groups, Anglicans, and Catholics. At the end of Cromwell's rule, the English Parliament reinstated a Catholic king, Charles II (reign: 1649–1651 in Scotland; 1660–1685 in England and Scotland), despite the generally Protestant population. In France, the Jesuit-favoring monarch Louis XIV (reign: 1643–1715) was intolerant of both dissenting Catholic groups and Protestant Huguenots. These groups were imprisoned, executed, or exiled.

During this time, Africans were forced from their homeland and taken across the Atlantic to the Americas for hard labor in the sugarcane fields and cotton and tobacco plantations. As the plantation system expanded because of these successful crops, they needed more slaves. For example, tobacco in Virginia and the opening of large cotton plantations in Alabama, Mississippi, and Louisiana after the Louisiana Purchase and the War of 1812 led to a large concentration of slaves in the Deep South (Hartmann, 1979; Morison et al., 1980).

There was a division of labor among slaves; the young men did the manual labor as planters, boiler men, blacksmiths, masons, or carpenters, to name a few, whereas women worked as cooks, domestics (washing clothing, washing floors, baking, milking cows), and nannies. Although working in the house of the plantation owner provided some protection from the hardships of life in the field, there were drawbacks. Frequently, slave women had to suffer the degradation of being raped or becoming a concubine to a plantation owner or other white master. As with the Native Americans discussed earlier, population admixture is occurring, but it is not through the taking of women in warfare; in this case, interbreeding is occurring violently between white men and black women (and in a few cases, black men and white women).

The racial makeup of the United States (including Florida, Louisiana, and the Spanish Southwest) at that time (based on the 1790 Census) was Black (856,770) and White (3,226,944) (American Council of Learned Societies, 1932). Of course, Native Americans were omnipresent, but they were not considered part of the American population. In addition, terms such as *mixed-race*[45] and *multiracial* were not coined yet (although dictionaries chart 16th-century usage of the word *mulatow*[46]), and this hybrid population would not be given official consideration until the 1870 Census. In the last section of chapter 1 and the second section of chapter 2, I discuss in detail Bachman and Morton's insistence that blacks were a different species despite the ubiquitous evidence of multiracial individuals or "mulattoes." To review, a child born of one black and one white parent was referred to as a mulatto, and the child of a mulatto and a white was called a quadroon. Furthermore, a child born of one black or white parent and one American Indian was con-sidered mixed-blood. In essence, early America had three large, distinct populations outside their ancestral geographical regions in considerable conflict with each other. Yet there was considerable cultural and genic (consensual and forced interbreeding) exchanges between Europeans, Africans, and Native Americans.

In the late 1840s a new wave of European migration to America was motivated by revolutions, political crackdowns occurring throughout Europe, and letters from friends already in America noting that it was "the land of opportunity" and "the home of the free." The discovery of gold in California (1849–1850) also influenced migrations to America (particu-larly the West Coast). Moreover, Chinese, Germans, Czechs, Hungarians, British, and especially the Irish—85,000 émigrés to North America in a single year because of the Great Famine in Ireland (1845–1849)—left the Old World for a better life (Hartmann, 1979). Included in this migration to the West Coast were populations (Chileans and Mexicans) south of the U.S. border. The racial makeup of the U.S. population based on the 1870 Census was *White*, *Black*, *Mulatto*, *Chinese*, and *Indian* (see figure 6.1). This reflected an increased diversity of the U.S. population compared to 1790.

Between 1860 and 1890 approximately 10 million Europeans came to the United States, of which 80% were from northwestern European countries (Hartmann, 1979). By 1914 immigrants from eastern and southern Europe and the Middle East were added to the growing wave of immigrants. But those Americans who could trace their ancestry back to the American Revolution gradually started to develop anti-immigrant hostility—there was a fear of "the other" similar to the fear of Afri-cans and Native Americans. A good many of the newcomers, although white—the idea of what *white* is will be addressed later in this chapter—spoke different languages, wore different clothing, cooked different types of food, and, extremely provocative, were Roman Catholic, East-ern Orthodox, or Jewish in their religious faith. All of these cultural dif-ferences, despite the fact that all Europeans had white skin, were cultural reproductive-isolating mechanisms or cultural barriers to interbreeding.

FIGURE 6.1. Racial makeup of the United States by states and territories, 1790–1870.

WHITE, COLORED, FREE COLORED, SLAVE, CHINESE, AND INDIAN, AT EACH CENSUS.

POPULATION BY STATES AND TERRITORIES—1790–1870.

TABLE I.—THE UNITED STATES.

Source. U.S. Census Bureau (1870).

Note. This table has been reproduced as best as possible from the original scan.

Even today, radical movements to tighten our immigration laws and fortify our southern border using the military are rooted in fear of immigrants, especially illegal immigrants, competing for jobs. It was no different in the late 19th and early 20th centuries. But another form of xenophobia reared its head, and many educated people supported it. This xenophobia was coupled with race.

In the first section of chapter 2, I discussed in great detail Samuel George Morton and the founding of the American School of Biological Anthropology, which provided "scientific" justification for slavery. If you recall, after Morton's death, his memory was kept alive by Josiah Clark Nott and Louis Agassiz, both prominent in the eyes of European scientists and scholars. Nathaniel Southgate Shaler became Agassiz's successor as professor of paleontology at Harvard. Shaler is being reiterated in this chapter because he taught more than 6,000 Harvard students, who were from upper-middle-class or rich native-born American families. These students were groomed for positions in the federal government (immigration or foreign office), politics, law, and business, equipped with Shaler's legacy—America was suitable only for "Teutons" (Nordic type or Anglo-Saxon)—of racial and religious bigotry. Soon his views became incorporated into official American immigration policy. In 1882 Congress passed the famous Chinese Exclusion Act, which practically suspended Chinese immigration, initially for 10 years and, starting in 1902, for an indefinite time (Hartmann, 1979).

Up to 1890 the majority of Americans were of Anglo-Saxon or German stock because most of the immigrants who had arrived before that year had come from northwestern Europe. But by 1914 millions of immigrants had come from southern and eastern Europe and the Middle East. And most of them did not fit the "ideal" type of tall, blond, and blue-eyed advocated by William Ripley (see the second section of chapter 2 for a full discussion) (Ripley, 1899). So would a racially inferior stock finally replace the original, superior American stock? (Even today, extremist groups frequently pose this type of question.)

The "powers that be" were worried about the future of America; consequently, the Immigration Restriction League organized in 1894 to begin the process of closing America to "inferior" immigrant groups (Morison et al., 1980).

In 1903 a special commission called the Dillingham Commission was set up to study the whole "problem" of immigration (Hartmann, 1979; Morison et al., 1980). For 8 years, the commission accumulated data, and in 1911 it delivered its final conclusion. To the dismay of immigration-restriction advocates, the commission did not favor restriction based on race. Looking toward the future in terms of business, economic interests, and all Americans, the commission wanted to adopt a more realistic policy. But radicalism and the fear of Communism during World War I resulted in a restrictive program. One new aspect of this restrictive program was a literacy test for any immigrant who wanted to settle in the United States. One of the people studying the results of the tests was Princeton psychologist Carl C. Brigham (1890–1943). Brigham emphasized the lower scores for foreign-born immigrants from southern and eastern Europe and concluded that they were innately inferior to the "Nordic type." Testing immigrants who had been drafted for the army as a more efficient means to formulate immigration restriction legislation, Brigham and the data he generated from this testing (*A Study of American Intelligence*) would be instrumental in justifying the immigration-restricting Johnson-Lodge Act of 1924 (Brace, 2005; Brigham, 1923). Brigham (1923) declared, "Our data from the army tests indicate clearly the intellectual superiority of the Nordic race group.... The Alpine race, according to our figures...seems to be considerably below the Nordic type intellectually" (p. 197). "Mediterraneans" were one step lower than the Alpine. Concerning the Russians and the Poles, Brigham had "no serious objection, from an anthropological standpoint, to classifying the northern Jew as an Alpine, for he has the head form, stature, and color of his Slavic neighbors. He is an Alpine Slav" (p. 190). Brigham continued, "Our figures, then, would rather disprove the popular belief that the Jew is highly intelligent" (p. 190). The reader will note that Brigham's conclusions are reminiscent of the writings of William Ripley and Madison Grant discussed earlier in this chapter and in greater detail in chapter 2.

In the period up to and following World War II, immigration legislation continued to favor Europeans over non-Europeans. But in 1962 the introduction of a points system for immigration regulation dramatically increased the rate of immigration of other racial population and ethnic categories (Hartmann, 1979). Although the largest numbers of immigrants continued to come from Britain and Italy, Asian immigration started to steadily increase. Between 1820 and 1965 Asians emigrated mainly from the Philippines, China, Taiwan, Hong Kong, Korea, and India (Morison et al., 1980). Even within this period, the census categories reflected a different social understanding: Black, White, and *Other* (see figure 6.2). By the 1970s and 1980s a significant number of Asian immigrants (fleeing civil unrest and war, the "boat people") came from Thailand, Cambodia, Laos, and Vietnam, increasing the complexity of race in America.

Like Asian immigration, Central and South American immigration was deeply affected by U.S. policies toward individual nations in the region. For instance, it served the United States' international interests to accept migrants from Cuba because of the Communist regime of Fidel Castro. Consequently, thousands of Cuban refugees (some of whom could be more accurately described as economic migrants) sailed to Miami. In contrast, the United States denied asylum to Haitians fleeing persecution and brutality under the governments of the Duvalier regimes in the 1970s because they were viewed as economic migrants, even though Haiti was seen as an important ally in combating communism in the Caribbean.

Migration from Africa to North America in the period following World War II has been caused, as in the case of so many of the countries mentioned before, by economic imbalance, civil unrest, war, and so forth. Interestingly, high levels of poverty within Africa have prevented many of the poorest from leaving, but those who can accumulate sufficient funds to migrate will often do so in search of a better life. Despite the fact that the African continent contains the highest number of refugees in the world, under American laws, Africa has the lowest refugee ceiling of any continent. For example, African refugees entering the United States were limited to 7,000 per annum in the early 1990s, though there were

FIGURE 6.2. The 1950 Census of the U.S. population.

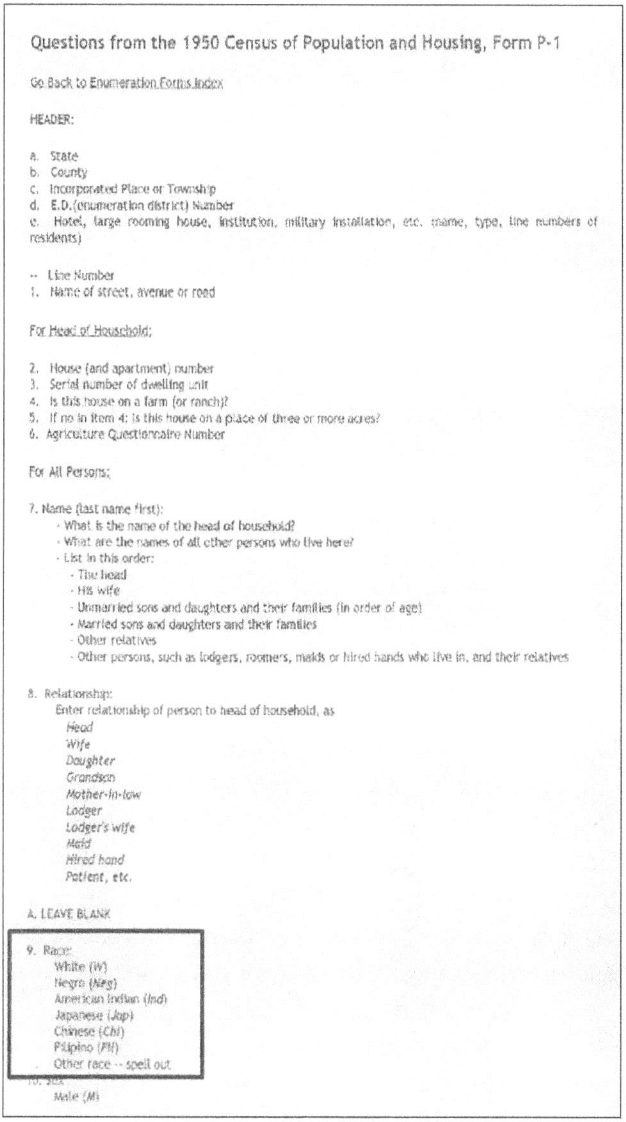

Questions from the 1950 Census of Population and Housing, Form P-1

Go Back to Enumeration Forms Index

HEADER:

a. State
b. County
c. Incorporated Place or Township
d. E.D.(enumeration district) Number
e. Hotel, large rooming house, institution, military installation, etc. (name, type, line numbers of residents)

-- Line Number
1. Name of street, avenue or road

For Head of Household:

2. House (and apartment) number
3. Serial number of dwelling unit
4. Is this house on a farm (or ranch)?
5. If no in item 4: is this house on a place of three or more acres?
6. Agriculture Questionnaire Number

For All Persons:

7. Name (last name first):
   - What is the name of the head of household?
   - What are the names of all other persons who live here?
   - List in this order:
     - The head
     - His wife
     - Unmarried sons and daughters and their families (in order of age)
     - Married sons and daughters and their families
     - Other relatives
     - Other persons, such as lodgers, roomers, maids or hired hands who live in, and their relatives

8. Relationship:
   Enter relationship of person to head of household, as
   Head
   Wife
   Daughter
   Grandson
   Mother-in-law
   Lodger
   Lodger's wife
   Maid
   Hired hand
   Patient, etc.

A. LEAVE BLANK

9. Race:
   White (W)
   Negro (Neg)
   American Indian (Ind)
   Japanese (Jap)
   Chinese (Chi)
   Filipino (FN)
   Other race -- spell out

10. Sex:
   Male (M)

Source. U.S. Census Bureau (1950).
Note. This table has been reproduced as best as possible from the original scan.

an estimated 5.8 million refugees in Africa in 1993 (Hartmann, 1979; Morison et al., 1980; University of Calgary, 2001).

But American immigration policies have not stopped illegal immigration from many of the countries mentioned previously. Notably, the close proximity of Central and South America and the Caribbean has vastly increased the number of immigrants from countries such as Mexico, Chile, Puerto Rico, El Salvador, Guatemala, Nicaragua, Costa Rica, Haiti, Jamaica, and the Bahamas, among others (illegal immigrants are, more than likely, not figured in the census racial population numbers, see table 2) (U.S. Census Bureau, 2000).

In essence, whether legal or illegal, these migrations have—no doubt— made America more complex in terms of race. And they have led to further subdivision of the racial categories by the U.S. Census Bureau (compared to the 1950 Census) to reflect the growing racial (i.e., black, white, etc.) and multiracial populations. They have also been instrumental in forging an alliance between non-racialists and multiracial (mixed-race or multiethnic) individuals in their fight to eliminate the race concept.

The U.S. Census and Recent Racial Classification Changes

In 1977 the U.S. Office of Management and Budget (OMB) issued Statistical Policy Directive No. 15: *Race and Ethnic Standards and Administrative Reporting*, which established four racial and two ethnicity (sociocultural identity) categories (U.S. Census Bureau, 2000; U.S. Office of Management and Budget, 2000). The racial categories were white, black, American Indian or Alaskan Native, and Asian/Pacific Islander. The ethnicity categories were Hispanic origin and not of Hispanic origin. The U.S. government uses racial information to track minority employment, school enrollments, and the granting of government contracts and to ensure voting rights and compliance with redistricting requirements, affirmative action, law enforcement, and much more.

Due to population admixture because of immigration and interracial marriages and births up to 1977, a growing number of people objected

TABLE 2. Population by race and Hispanic origin for the United States (2000).

Race and Hispanic or Latino	Number	Percent of total population
RACE		
Total population	284,421,906	100.0
One race	274,595,678	97.6
White	211,460,626	75.1
Black or African American	34,658,190	12.3
American Indian and Alaskan Native	2,475,956	0.9
Asian	10,242,998	3.6
Native Hawaiian and Other Pacific Islander	398,835	0.1
Some other race	15,359,073	5.5
Two or more races	6,826,228	2.4
HISPANIC OR LATINO		
Total population	281,421,906	100.0
Hispanic or Latino	35,305,818	12.5
Not Hispanic or Latino	246,116,088	87.5

Source. U.S. Census Bureau (2000).

to categories based on race. In response to this growing opposition, the OMB initiated a review of Racial and Ethnic Standards and convened public hearings. The bureau found that Arab Americans (a group that includes persons from the Middle East, Turkey, and North Africa) were unhappy with their official designation as "White, non-European." Many indigenous Hawaiians wanted to be recategorized from Pacific Islander to Native American, a shift that would provide them with greater minority benefits.

Furthermore, some Hispanics wanted the Census Bureau to identify them as a race and not as an ethnic origin. To many researchers, "Hispanic" refers to a wide variety of Spanish speakers, from Mexicans to Bolivians (Boaz & Almquist, 2002; R. Boyd & Silk, 2006; Cartmill,

1999; Hinkes, 1993; Gordon & Bell, 1993; Komar & Buikstra, 2008; Molnar, 2002; Relethford, 2005; F. L. E. Williams, Belcher, & Armelagos, 2005). Some Hispanics also prefer the term "Latino" because "Hispanic" originates from the colonization of Latin America by Spain and Portugal (ironically, the adjective "Latin" is also associated with Europe). Other Hispanics prefer to be identified by their families' country of origin, such as Puerto Rican, Colombian, or Cuban American, the way European Americans tend to identify themselves as, for example, Irish, German, or Polish American.

Some African Americans wanted the Census Bureau to retire the term *Black*—and immigrants from the Caribbean, like some Hispanics, prefer to be labeled by their families' country of origin, such as Jamaican, Haitian, or Bahamian American.

In 1997 champion golfer Tiger Woods classified himself as "Cablinasian," defined as "CAucasian, BLack, American INdian, and Asian" (in other words, part European, part African, part Native American, part Thai, and part Chinese). At approximately the same time, the OMB announced the revised standards for federal data on race and ethnicity. Nick Gillespie (1997), writer for *Reason Magazine*, has implied that this was not a coincidence, suggesting that high-profile public pressure stimulated the OMB to act. The minimum categories for race are now American Indian or Alaskan Native, Asian, Black or African American, Native Hawaiian or other Pacific Islander, and White (U.S. Census, 2000). Instead of allowing a multiracial category as was suggested in public hearings and in congressional hearings, the OMB adopted the recommendation based on the review of Racial and Ethnic Standards: respondents would be allowed to select one or more races when they self-identified.

In essence, the most significant change to the question on race for Census 2000 was the addition of a sixth racial category: Some Other Race(s) (see figure 6.3). Furthermore, there are 15 check-box response categories and three write-in areas on the Census 2000 questionnaire, compared with 16 check-box response categories and two write-in areas in 1990. The three separate identifiers for the American Indian and Alaska Native populations (American Indian, Eskimo, or Aleut)

FIGURE 6.3. The 2000 Census of the U.S. population.

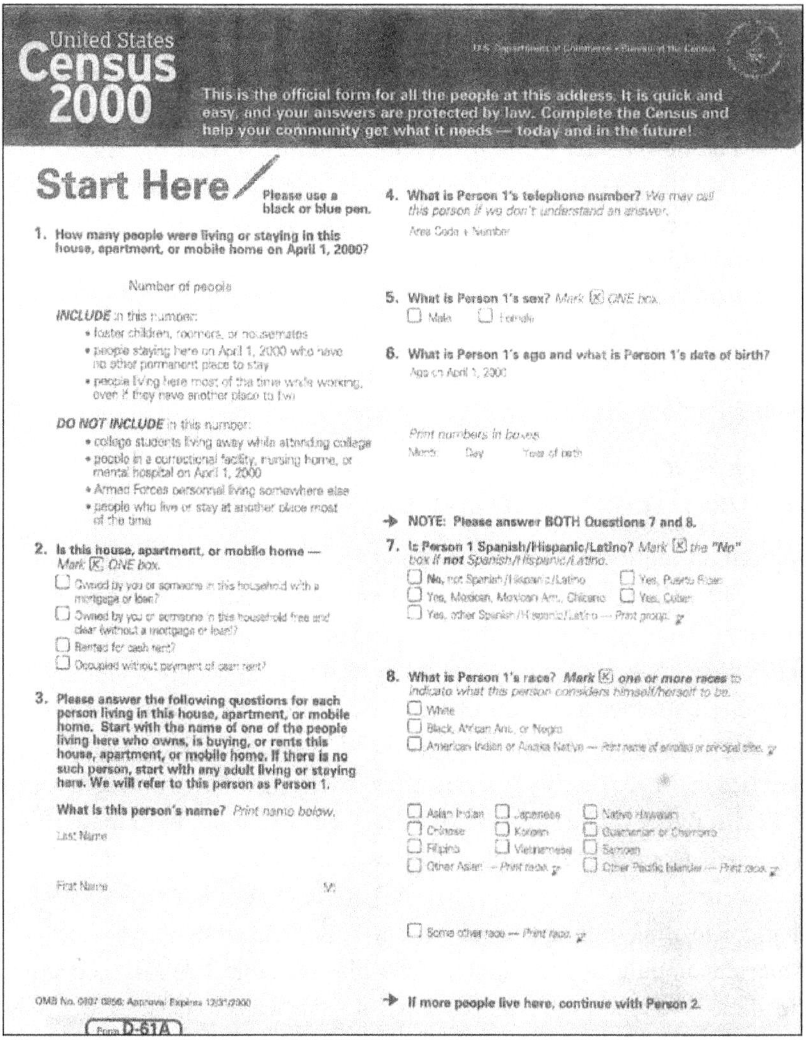

United States
Census
2000

This is the official form for all the people at this address. It is quick and easy, and your answers are protected by law. Complete the Census and help your community get what it needs — today and in the future!

Start Here Please use a black or blue pen.

1. **How many people were living or staying in this house, apartment, or mobile home on April 1, 2000?**

   Number of people

   INCLUDE in this number:
   - foster children, roomers, or housemates
   - people staying here on April 1, 2000 who have no other permanent place to stay
   - people living here most of the time while working, even if they have another place to live

   DO NOT INCLUDE in this number:
   - college students living away while attending college
   - people in a correctional facility, nursing home, or mental hospital on April 1, 2000
   - Armed Forces personnel living somewhere else
   - people who live or stay at another place most of the time

2. **Is this house, apartment, or mobile home —** *Mark ☒ ONE box.*
   - ☐ Owned by you or someone in this household with a mortgage or loan?
   - ☐ Owned by you or someone in this household free and clear (without a mortgage or loan)?
   - ☐ Rented for cash rent?
   - ☐ Occupied without payment of cash rent?

3. **Please answer the following questions for each person living in this house, apartment, or mobile home. Start with the name of one of the people living here who owns, is buying, or rents this house, apartment, or mobile home. If there is no such person, start with any adult living or staying here. We will refer to this person as Person 1.**

   What is this person's name? *Print name below.*

   Last Name

   First Name MI

4. **What is Person 1's telephone number?** *We may call this person if we don't understand an answer.*

   Area Code + Number

5. **What is Person 1's sex?** *Mark ☒ ONE box.*

   ☐ Male ☐ Female

6. **What is Person 1's age and what is Person 1's date of birth?**

   Age on April 1, 2000

   Print numbers in boxes.

   Month Day Year of birth

→ **NOTE: Please answer BOTH Questions 7 and 8.**

7. **Is Person 1 Spanish/Hispanic/Latino?** *Mark ☒ the "No" box if **not** Spanish/Hispanic/Latino.*
   - ☐ **No,** not Spanish/Hispanic/Latino
   - ☐ Yes, Puerto Rican
   - ☐ Yes, Mexican, Mexican Am., Chicano
   - ☐ Yes, Cuban
   - ☐ Yes, other Spanish/Hispanic/Latino — *Print group.*

8. **What is Person 1's race?** ***Mark ☒ one or more races*** *to indicate what this person considers himself/herself to be.*
   - ☐ White
   - ☐ Black, African Am., or Negro
   - ☐ American Indian or Alaska Native — *Print name of enrolled or principal tribe.*
   - ☐ Asian Indian ☐ Japanese ☐ Native Hawaiian
   - ☐ Chinese ☐ Korean ☐ Guamanian or Chamorro
   - ☐ Filipino ☐ Vietnamese ☐ Samoan
   - ☐ Other Asian — *Print race.* ☐ Other Pacific Islander — *Print race.*
   - ☐ Some other race — *Print race.*

→ **If more people live here, continue with Person 2.**

OMB No. 0607-0856: Approval Expires 12/31/2000

Form D-61A

Source. U.S. Census Bureau (2000).
Note. This table has been reproduced as best as possible from the original scan.

used earlier have been combined into one category (American Indian or Alaska Native) and a space to write tribal affiliation. The Asian and Pacific Islander category has been split into two categories: Asian and Native Hawaiian and Other Pacific Islander. Specifically, there are six Asian and three Pacific Islander categories, as well as Other Asian and Other Pacific Islander, both of which have write-in areas for respondents to provide the race not listed in the Asian and Pacific Island categories. Finally, the category Some Other Race also has a write-in area to capture responses such as "Cablinasian."

The unusual racial category "Other" means something real and important to those who refuse to use the traditional racial categories as self-identifiers. They feel that the current categories inadequately account for the tremendous diversity in contemporary America.

MULTIRACIAL VERSUS RACIAL IDENTIFICATION

Population admixture has been going on ever since the establishment of the 13 colonies in North America and has steadily increased despite such key biological and cultural reproductive isolating mechanisms as skin color, nose form, eye color, body form, socioeconomic status, and religion. This fact has been obvious since the 1870 Census, when the phenotypic category "mulatto" was listed. It was also documented using genetics in a 1963 study (10 years after Watson and Crick's revolutionary 1953 discovery of the structure of DNA). For example, Workman, Blumberg, and Cooper (1963) showed how admixture of Europeans' genes had occurred in the Claxton African American population, indicated by changes in allele frequencies of African American compared to European American populations in Claxton, Georgia (see table 3). We would expect the allele frequencies of Claxton African Americans to be similar to West Coast Africans because of the descendant-ancestor relationship. But in this table, the allele frequencies of the Claxton African Americans lie between West Coast African and Claxton European American frequencies. If we study this table more carefully, European gene flow (note that the Duffy alleles Fy^a and Fy^b are not present in the ancestral West Coast

TABLE **3.** Allele frequencies of African American and European American populations in Claxton, Georgia: Evidence of admixture.

Locus	Allele	West Coast Africans	Claxton African Americans	Claxton European Americans
Rhesus	*d*	0.211	0.230	0.358
ABO	*A*	0.148	0.158	0.246
ABO	*B*	0.151	0.129	0.050
MN	*M*	0.476	0.485	0.508
Duffy	FY^e	0.000	0.046	0.422
P	*p*	0.780	0.757	0.526
Hemoglobin	*S*	0.110	0.043	0.000

Source. Workman et al. (©1963 Elsevier. Reprinted with the permission of Elsevier).

African population, but the Fy[a] allele is at nearly a 5% frequency in African Americans) has caused the Claxton African American allele frequencies to move farther away from the West Coast African frequencies.

In a more recent study, Jeffrey Long et al. (1991) studied admixture in Mexican Americans in the states of Arizona, Texas, and California. They typed 730 Mexican Americans for the HLA-A, HLA-B, ABO, Rh, MNSs, Duffy, Kidd, and Kell loci and used them to estimate ancestral contributions. They tested a dihybrid model with Amerindians and Spaniards (of European ancestry), and a trihybrid model with Amerindians, Spaniards, and Africans as proposed ancestors. Long et al. used a modified weighted least squares method that allows for linkage disequilibrium to estimate ancestral contributions for each model.[47] They found significant admixture of Spaniards and Amerindians in these Mexican Americans (see table 4). More surprising was a small amount of African ancestry, supported by the presence of the Duffy Fy[4] marker, which indicates African descent.

In another recent study, Esteban Parra et al. (2001) analyzed admixture in samples of six different African American populations from South

TABLE 4. Using HLA-A, HLA-B, ABO, Rh, MNSs, Duffy, Kidd, and Kell loci to estimate ancestral contributions (trihybrid model: Amerindians, Spaniards, and Africans) in Mexican Americans.

System Arizona	Spanish	African	Indian
HLA-A	0.698	0.125	0.178
HLA-B	0.736	0.081	0.184
Rhesus	0.524	0.050	0.426
MNS	0.576	−0.070	0.494
ABO	0.460	0.146	0.394
Duffy	0.492	0.061	0.447
San Antonio system			
ABO	0.596	NA	0.404
Los Angeles system			
HLA	0.834	NA	0.166

Source. Adapted from Long et al. (1991).
Note. Kidd and Kell loci data not available for this single-locus trihybrid analysis.

Carolina: Gullah-speaking Sea Islanders in coastal South Carolina; residents of Berkeley, Charleston, Colleton, and Dorchester Counties in the "Lowcountry"; and residents living in the city of Columbia. Using a battery of autosomal, mtDNA, and Y-chromosome markers, the researchers found a high level of European admixture in Charleston and Dorchester Counties and the city of Columbia (see table 5).

In chapter 5, I detailed a study by Bamshad et al. (2003) on microsatellite DNA and *Alu* insertions that showed a high degree of genetic variation (or good classification by geographical region) between samples from Africa, Asia, and Europe. Bamshad also admitted less accurate genetic clustering for samples (possibly admixed populations) from geographically intermediate regions. It is interesting that my results after the metric comparison of nine skulls tagged "China" (bought for educational purposes) to a database of worldwide cranial samples showed an overall classification by geographical region, that is, Pacific Islander and

TABLE 5. European admixture in American blacks from South Carolina.

Group	European Admixture
Gullah Sea Islands	3.5 +/– 0.9%
Charleston Co.	9.9 +/– 1.8%
Dorchester Co.	14.0 +/– 1.9%
Columbia	17.7 +/– 3.1%

Source. Adapted from Parra et al. (2001).

East Asia (with tremendous admixture), and not always by nationality or ethnicity.

Specifically, in my study, the accuracy of a racial label (or the social question of race) was tested against the biological or skeletal reality using Fordisc 3.0, the latest version of a computer program used to metrically determine race and sex.[48] Fordisc 3.0 is designed to standardize the way in which forensic anthropologists assess population affinity. It helps investigators ascribe a social race to unknown individuals. The concept of *social race* structures mating and preserves preexisting differences; therefore, it is the most practical means for identifying unknown individuals (Jantz & Ousley, 2005).

I tested the null hypothesis that nine skulls bought from a private company originated in China or that they were from Chinese individuals. The alternate hypothesis was that the skulls originated from the broad regions of East Asia and the Pacific Islands and could not be tagged with the social label "Chinese." The null hypothesis was tested nonmetrically using traditional nonmetric traits and also metrically, where each skull was subjected to William W. Howells' series (1989) because his sample groups are worldwide. Because facial flatness is a feature associated predominantly, but not exclusively, with East Asian populations (Hanihara, 2000; Ishida, 1992; Woo & Morant, 1934; Yamaguchi, 1973), five measurements that emphasized facial size and shape were used in order to assess this feature. Initially, each skull was assessed against East Asian,

Pacific Islander, Guatemalan, Native American, and sub-Saharan African sample groups. East Asians and Pacific Islanders are closer geographically than Europeans or New World populations; it follows that the closer populations are geographically, the more gene flow occurs between them and the smaller the genetic distance (Bamshad et al., 2003; Relethford, 2005; Rosenberg et al., 2002). This becomes important in assessing cranial variation because populations in the geographical extremes or at the "edges" of the species range could be accurately sorted as a result of less within-population variation compared to populations at the geographical center (F. L. E. Williams et al., 2005; Wolpoff & Caspari, 1997). Subsequently, a full battery of measurements was applied in the Howells series. Next, each skull was subjected to the FDB series. If the null hypothesis was correct, then all the skulls would be ascribed to the Chinese sample group with high probabilities. Probabilities should be very low for blacks, whites, Guatemalans, Native Americans, or Hispanics.

My findings showed that the "Chinese" tags placed on the nine skulls were inaccurate. Several runs were ambiguous in that most of the skulls could not be classified into a specific sample group consistently or confidently. Nonetheless, the general pattern was overwhelmingly East Asian and Pacific Islander (see figure 6.4). Consequently, I rejected the null hypothesis and accepted the alternative hypothesis, namely that the skulls originated from the broad regions of East Asia and the Pacific Islands and should not be tagged with the national label "China."

Curiously, there is a small American Indian and Hispanic component, which may result from ancestry and admixture. Native American ancestry can be traced to East Asia, and Hispanics may be trihybrid, with the proposed ancestors being Africans, Spaniards, and Amerindians (Long et al., 1991). Nonetheless, one major question emerges from this study (and is pertinent to the Bamshad et al. [2003] study): Is region equivalent to geographical race?

The answer of non-racialists (Boaz & Almquist, 2002; Brace, 1964, 1995, and 2005; Cartmill, 1999; Larsen, 2008; F. Livingstone, 1962; Molnar, 2002; Relethford, 2005; Sauer, 1992) would be an emphatic "no." As forensic anthropologist Norman Sauer (1992) noted, "The ability to

FIGURE 6.4. The nine purchased skulls tagged with the label "China."

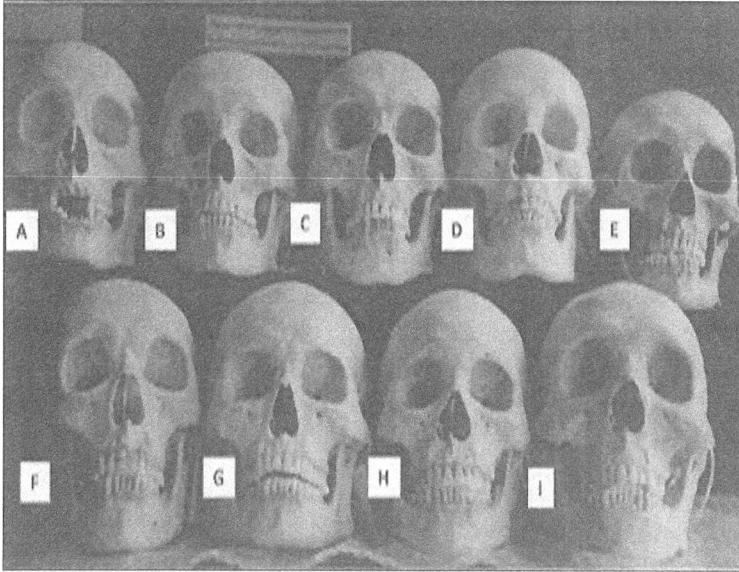

Note. These nine skulls were classified (using Howells' data) into the following races: A (North Japanese males); B (Guatemalan males); C (North Japanese males); D (Pacific Islander males); E (Pacific Islander males); F (Guatemalan males); G (South Japanese males); H (Hainan [China] females); I (Anyang [China] males). The grand average typicality probability for classification in the China samples is 0.169.

identify a person having ancestors from say, Northern Europe, does not identify a biological race of Northern Europeans" (p. 110). Using Bamshad et al.'s research as an example, non-racialists ask how we can classify Middle Eastern, Mediterranean, Ethiopian, central Asian, and other admixed populations. These issues and others, such as not having a multiracial category on the census race classification section, are key factors in the rejection of race by multiracial individuals.

Social concepts are usually not original; they are inherited from the past, repackaged, and presented as something new. It is the same for the "new" multiracialism. As noted in the first section of this chapter (and in the first section of chapter 2, where Morton and his statements on hybridity in 1850 and 1851 are discussed in detail), multiracial or mixed-race individuals were major problems in the strict 19th and early 20th centuries' social environments. Consequently, these populations had to be monitored for economic purposes, and if their numbers increased, existing laws were enhanced to prevent mixing of the races. In the 1870 U.S. Census, racial categories were *White*, *Mulatto* (which included quadroons, octoroons, and all persons having any perceptible trace of African blood), *Chinese*, and *Indian*. Later, *Quadroon* and *Octoroon* designations were added to the census (Morning, 2003). In the 1890s the definitions of black/white ancestry became even more detailed, "drawing on notions of blood proportions, or quanta, that had already been widely applied to American Indian mixed bloods" (Morning, 2003, p. 45). In the 1890s the U.S. Census' definition of black/white ancestry was as follows:

> The word "black" should be used to describe those persons who have three-fourths or more black blood; "mulatto," those persons who have from three-eighths to five-eighths black blood; "quadroon," those persons who have one-fourth black blood; and "octoroons," those persons who have one-eighth or any trace of black blood. (Morning, 2003, p. 45)

It is interesting that this 19th-century obsession with the question "What color is black?" is still prevalent today. One third of African Americans said blacks should not be considered a single race (Klein, 1995).

The term *mixed-race* (mixed-blood), also commonly listed as "half-breeds," was also defined and elaborated by the early census. In 1870 "half-breeds" were simply defined as "persons with any perceptible trace of Indian blood, whether mixed with white or with Negro stock" (U.S. Census Office, 1872, p. xiii). In this definition, they added cultural and behavioral factors:

> Where persons reported as "half-breeds" are found residing with whites, adopting their habits of life and methods of industry, such persons are to be treated as belonging to the white population. Where, on the other hand, they are found in communities composed wholly or mainly of Indians, the opposite construction is taken. In a word, in

> the equilibrium produced by the equal division of blood, the habits, tastes, and associations of the half-breed are allowed to determine his gravitation to the one class or the other. (p. xiii)

A cross with mulattoes (or trihybrid cross) was also discussed. Although the early 1900s saw an elaboration of the quanta of blood and fractions of Indian blood that were recorded ("full-blood," "half to full," "quarter to half," and "less than ¼"), by 1930 a simple full-blood/ mixed-blood dichotomy was used so that black/white ancestry was designated as Negro. Black/Indian ancestry was also designated as Negro; and white/Indian ancestry was designated as Indian (Morning, 2003). In short, in all instances of multiracialism—black/white, black/Indian, or white/Indian—the real concern was the nature of whiteness or "mongrelization" of the white race (Morning, 2003).

Like the reemergence of the "what is black" question today, a similar intraracial questioning ("What is white?") has occurred in whites. The question was first raised in the late 19th and early 20th centuries because of the great influx of new eastern and southern European immigrants, who were deemed the racially "inferior" stock (compared to the northern "Nordic" Europeans). Gradually America became enlightened about multiracial unions, and today the boundaries of whiteness have expanded and the high pedestal on which whiteness once stood has eroded. Some argue that recognizing multiracialism or, on the other side of the coin, calling for the elimination of the race concept by the "powers that be" might be motivated more by the fact that whites are predicted to lose their numerical majority in the 21st century in the United States than by any ideas about the complexity of human variation or the "unity of man" (Morning, 2003; Patterson, 2001; Warren & Twine, 1997). In addition, other criticisms are linked to social and economical factors that directly affect all Americans.

MULTIRACIALISM AND THE GROWING NUMBER OF RACIAL CATEGORIES: CLARITY OR CONFUSION?

According to the 2000 Census, the total population of the United States was 281,421,906, with 6,826,228, or 2.4%, self-identifying as being of two or more races (see table 6) (DeBose, 2003). The number of multi-racial people, whose biological parents are from different racial groups, is steadily increasing the negative attitudes about the race concept. This, in turn, has relaxed the stigma against interracial relationships. There were 149,000 interracial marriages in 1960, compared with 964,000 in 1990 and 1,264,000 in 1997 (U.S. Census Bureau, 2001). The exact number of multiracial children from these unions is not certain, but the

TABLE 6. Multiracial composition of the United States according to the 2000 Census.

Two or More Races	Number	% of Total Population
White and Black	784,764	0.28
White and American Indian	1,082,683	0.38
White and Asian	868,395	0.31
White and Native American	112,964	0.04
White and some other race	2,206,251	0.78
Black and American Indian	182,494	0.06
Black and Asian	106,782	0.04
Black and Native American	29,786	0.01
Black and some other race	417,249	0.15
American Indian and Asian	52,429	0.02
American Indian and Native Hawaiian	7,328	0.00
American Indian and some other race	93,842	0.03
Asian and Native Hawaiian	138,802	0.05
Asian and some other race	249,108	0.09
Native Hawaiian and some other race	35,108	0.01
Three or More Races	458,153	0.16
Total	6,826,228	2.4

Source. U.S. Census Bureau (2001).

census recorded less than 500,000 such children in 1960, compared with 1,937,496 in 1990 (U.S. Census, 2001; DeBose, 2003). Incidentally, the multiracial identification on the 2000 Census was skewed toward the individuals in this group who were 18 years old or younger. For instance, nearly 4% of these individuals (compared with 1.9% of adults 18 years or older) self-identified as two or more races (Morning, 2003). In short, people younger than 18 years contributed 42% of all multirace responses even though they constitute only 26% of the U.S. population. So, as I have stated in the introduction, America is getting complicated—a fact scholars on both sides of the argument agree with. But racialists view the multiracial category as hypocrisy. They ask how non-racialists and multiracialists can call for an end to categorical thinking and simultaneously ask for another category (Murdock, 2001; Powell, 2004; Wright & Hartman, 1994). Put another way, racialists are concerned that allowing people to choose one or more racial categories will cause tremendous confusion and affect, in a negative way, the distribution of goods and services. Another point that is confusing to racialists is the fact that non-racialists and multiracialists emphasize that it is important for physicians to know the entire background of a patient to make a well-informed diagnosis yet at the same time argue against biological determinism and accuse racialists of using biology and racial background when discussing medicine and treatment.

Mary Texeira (2003), a sociologist at California State University–San Bernardino, argues that a multiracial category is similar to the mulatto, quadroon, and octoroon of the mid-19th and early 20th centuries. For instance, during a series of conferences and public meetings on adding a multiracial category in 2000, the U.S. Census Bureau made a concession to several interest groups (Multiracial Americans of Southern California, Association of Multiethnic Americans, and Project RACE[49]) that it would allow persons to designate more than one race. But for civil rights/data collection purposes, the individual would be counted in the "minority" group (Texeira, 2003). This, some have responded, is reminiscent of the "one drop rule" (Murdock, 2001; Wright & Hartman,

1994). Deroy Murdock, a columnist for National Review Online, goes even further:

> By cynically and artificially assigning citizens of mixed-race back-grounds solely to minority categories, OMB magically can inflate the apparent number of minorities in a given locale. This will sup-ply federal, state and local officials with abundant raw materials for mischief, ranging from redistricting to set-asides to college admis-sions. (p. 2)

Despite this concern, the black lobby supports the concession by the U.S. Census Bureau. The members of Project RACE feel it is most important for every individual to be able to classify themselves according to how *they* identify themselves, not as others might see them (DaCosta, 2003). But a National Center for Health Statistics study (1993) found that 6% of people who called themselves black were seen as white by a census interviewer. Nearly a third of people self-identifying as Asian and 70% of those self-identifying as American Indian were classified as white or black by independent observers. Racialists have argued that this kind of free-for-all will lead to chaos and the impact on social programs will be catastrophic.

George Washington University professor Amitai Etzioni (2000) states that new multiracial categories could water down civil rights efforts. And the NAACP (National Association for the Advancement of Colored People), National Urban League, National Council of La Raza, Lawyers' Committee for Civil Rights Under Law, and National Congress of Indian Americans all agree that in a democratic country anyone has the right to call themselves what they wish (Texeira, 2003). But they also agree that there is still a need to track injustice based on race (using the exist-ing categories). According to Hilary Shelton, director of the NAACP's Washington bureau:

> The fundamental fear is that you're going to have people who look African-American, who have grown up in communities that are African-American, who are going to experience the discrimination that African-Americans have historically experienced, but not have

even the existing civil rights protections because they're being identified now in this census in a way that's inconsistent with how it's been monitored in the past and how law enforcement is tooled to enforce it now. The numbers aren't important. The enforcement of civil rights are. No matter what you're calling yourself, we want to make sure you don't get lost or left on the periphery of civil rights protection. (as cited in Texeira, 2003, p. 31)

Shelton is probably implying that the entire civil rights regulatory program concerning housing, employment, education would have to be reassessed; school desegregation plans would be put on hold; legislative districts would have to be redrawn; affirmative action programs would be reassessed; jury selection would be reassessed; and much more.

Lawrence Wright and Chester Hartman (1994) posit the following example: "Suppose a court orders a city to hire additional Black police officers to make up for past discrimination, will mixed-race officers count? Will they count wholly or in part?" (p. 2). Law enforcement uses race every day in profiling terrorists, finding criminals, and searching for the missing. I determine race for the Bloomsburg Police Department and Pennsylvania State Police when skeletal remains are found. *Alu* genetic markers and microsatellites are the basis for the establishment of genetic databases of Caucasoid, African American, Asian, and Hispanic individuals used in DNA fingerprinting. In short, law enforcement finds race every day. No matter how negatively non-racialists and multiracial groups view the race concept, if any one of them ever goes missing, law enforcement will use the traditional racial categories (Caucasian or white; African American or black; Asian American; Native American or American Indian; Pacific Islander; and Hispanic or Latino) to find them. Furthermore, the FBI uses skin color, hair form, nose form, eyelid shape, body form, height, and other easily noticed characteristics to identify individuals they are attempting to apprehend. The point here is that law enforcement works in the social realm, interacting with people every day. They see human differences and need to keep it simple—in apprehending a criminal, it is generally more important to arrive at a description that will *readily* suggest the general appearance of the individual.

If police officers had to deal with 57 possible multiple race ancestries (from the six main categories on the 2000 Census) to find a fugitive or a missing person, it would certainly cause confusion for them (and for the public, who are generally a huge help to law enforcement, particularly in missing persons cases).

Most racialists and non-racialists believe that promoting diversity, the unity of humanity, multiculturalism, and multiracialism are all positive goals, and these goals are very popular in the sciences as well as the social sciences. From a cultural anthropological perspective, this is what we should strive for: cultural relativism/self-identity, respecting how cultures and individuals view themselves. But is it or is it not dangerous to make decisions in law enforcement and other social justice programs based on a colorblind system? Non-racialists have provided overwhelming evidence to show that there is tremendous admixture in the American population, which leads them to the conclusion that race is an illusion. But racialists counter with their own evidence showing that we cannot have a colorblind society because there are important differences between the races. So what is the compromise? What is the future of racial identification and classification in America? I will answer these questions in the next and final chapter.

CHAPTER 7

THE FUTURE OF RACIAL IDENTIFICATION AND CLASSIFICATION IN THE UNITED STATES

THE CONVENIENCE OF SOCIAL RACE AND IDENTIFICATION

The election of Barack Obama as the 44th president of the United States was a boon for non-racialists and an added boost (even greater than Tiger Woods) for the multiracialist movement. To a large percentage of Americans, Obama's rise indicates that America has finally transcended race and that the phrase "there is no such thing as race" may become credible. Yet Obama is consistently and universally identified as the first *African American* president, and he also self-identifies as African American. This is a notable fact because it shows the overwhelming importance and persistence of race in social life. The fact of Obama's categorization as the *African American* president is a significant point in the arguments of racial classification. It says that racial classification has practical benefits (even though Obama's campaign consistently deemphasized the race issue). Tiger Woods does not classify himself solely as African American; instead he created a category called *Cablinasian* for himself. (Regardless, Tiger Woods is perceived by the public as the first great *African American* golfer.) This example is instructive; it shows that human beings will always create a category or group that fits their perception of themselves when one is not available. In essence, we *need* our identity and we *need* to make sure that we can be identified (as part of a group).

We all agree that racism is bad, but I believe human beings are willing to suffer the negative elements of racialism for the putative biological (largely visible) and cultural unity and comfort (or comfort zone) that racial unity brings. Skin color, nose form, and hair form are the result of long-term environment adaptation during human evolution. And these traits are important to millions of people worldwide because they suggest kinship. Obama is the American people's president, but he is classified (visibly and culturally) and self-identifies (through kinship) as an African American. Of course, this behavior of self-identification and perception is not confined to Obama or Woods—it is ubiquitous in the United States (and the world).

We might blame our obsession with family "trees" and "roots." In the mid-1970s African American author Alex Haley (1921–1992) wrote his autobiography, titled *Roots*, where he, supposedly, traced his origins all the way back to the 18th-century slave trade. It was a story of the tragedy and resilience of a black family, and it spoke to all African American families, unifying them in a common experience and kinship. The subsequent television series was even more provocative. *Roots*, whether fact or fiction, was successful in motivating people—whites and blacks—to find their "roots." People want to know where they came from; because we are a social species, we want to be identified with a category or group, whether it be racial, ethnic, or even multiracial. This is found in every country on this planet, whether it be the Tutsi versus the Hutu, the Irish versus the British, the Muslims versus the Jews, the

Serbs versus the Bosniaks, the Bantu peoples versus the Afrikaners, and so forth. In identifying ourselves in the United States, specifically, we put the name of our ancestral country, ethnicity, or religion first and then the word *American*. We are *African* American, *Irish* American, *Italian* American, *German* American, *Mexican* American, *Japanese* American, *Cuban* American, and *Jewish* American, to name a few. This emphasis on identity is likely here to stay because "roots" anchor individuals to their group and all of the advantages and disadvantages that come with being a member of that group.

THE PERSISTENCE OF HUMAN CLASSIFICATION: AN EVOLUTIONARY PERSPECTIVE

In animal taxonomy, humans are in the order Primates. The nonhuman primates are prosimians, monkeys, and apes. These nonhuman primates make the best living models for the earliest human behavior.[50] Consequently, to understand why humans are prone to classifying each other or identifying ourselves with a specific group, we must discuss nonhuman primates whose behaviors give us insights into modern human origins. From this point on, I will refer to nonhuman primates simply as primates.

First, why do primates live in groups? Pia Nystrom and Pamela Ashmore (2008) believe that primate sociality had important advantages during natural selection, specifically in regards to the ecology of predator protection (more eyes and ears available to look out for predators), resource defense (the greater number of individuals that band together, the better they will be at defending access to scarce resources such as food, water, and sleeping sites), assistance in infant rearing (if a mother dies, relatives and female friends will help raise the infant), and access to mates. In essence, primates have evolved to live in groups.

Second, and more critical, why do primates designate even members of their own respective species as "us" versus "them"? The well-debated mechanism of kin selection has been used to answer this question. Kin selection is a form of natural selection, in which an individual's fitness (survival and reproduction, i.e., the ability to pass one's genes to the next generation) is influenced by the fitness of its relatives, who share a proportion of its genes (R. Boyd & Silk, 2006; Nystrom & Ashmore, 2008; Strier, 2007). For instance, a primate giving an alarm call to warn others in the group about an approaching predator runs the risk of being killed—an act that has real or potential costs to the primate's fitness. If this primate is killed, the cost (to the primate) may be offset by the benefits to the members of its group, assuming they are relatives (kin) and manage to survive. According to William D. Hamilton (1964), this type of altruistic behavior can only evolve if the benefits are sufficiently greater than the costs.

Hamilton (1964) developed an equation for predicting when an altruistic act by an individual monkey might be beneficial to the group. In Hamilton's equation, three variables must be estimated: 1) the cost (c) of the alarm call to the monkey's individual fitness; 2) the benefits (b) of the alarm call to the recipient monkeys' individual fitness; and 3) the degree of relatedness (r), or the proportion of genes shared between the altruistic monkey and the recipient monkeys through common descent. Essentially, a monkey will help a relative whenever $c < b \times r$. Multiplying r by b means that b (the fitness benefits of the recipient monkey) multiplied by r (the relatedness factor) must be larger than c (the fitness cost to the monkey making the alarm call).

Certainly, more research needs to be done on how primates recognize relatives. But it seems plausible that living together in a group from infancy to adulthood leads to familiarity and learned relationships among individuals. Additionally, there is a good reason why monkeys, apes, and humans have forward-facing eyes and color vision, as opposed to eyes on the side of the head and a snout (as in dogs, for example). In primate evolution, these traits are an adaptation to life in a mosaic, arboreal environment. Specifically, we have evolved binocular-stereoscopic color vision, which is overlapping fields of vision that produce depth and distance—traits uniquely suited to life in the colorful environment of the trees (Nystrom & Ashmore, 2008; Strier, 2007). It would seem our eyes and visual system evolved to see things that mattered most to our ancestors, like food, danger, and other ancestors (Berreby, 2005). The faces of apes are variable just like those of humans; we identify our relatives by using physical characteristics, such as face and skin color. Recognizing relatives is an important requisite for kin selection.

Altruistic behavior, such as food sharing, grooming, and coalition formation, occurs more frequently among related individuals. For instance, among chimpanzees at Gombe Stream National Park in Tanzania, researchers (McGrew, 2001) found that 86% of food sharing involved maternal kin, who constituted 5% of the individuals in the group. Food sharing also occurs in two species of tiny monkeys called marmosets and tamarins. Food items are spontaneously offered to infants and juveniles by older group members. Because infants are closely related to most of the group members, this food sharing might be a product of kin selection (R. Boyd & Silk, 2006).

Social grooming is critical in primate groups because, in addition to bits of dead skin, debris, and parasites being removed from the fur, it reduces tension after conflict and reinforces social bonds. Grooming is more common among kin, particularly mothers and their offspring, than nonkin. This was illustrated by Carol Berman and Ellen Kapsalis (1999) of the University of Buffalo, who documented the effect of maternal relatedness among rhesus macaques on Cayo Santiago. In that population, females groom close kin at higher rates than nonkin.

Many studies have shown that primates form coalitions with close kin. Female pigtail macaques defend their offspring and close kin more often than distant relatives or nonkin (R. Boyd & Silk, 2006). Among vervet monkeys, females respond more quickly when the distress call comes from close kin (in conflicts) than from nonkin. Comparable forms of assistance and affiliation occur among males in the patrilineal societies of chimpanzees, where males join forces to attack unrelated groups of males (Strier, 2007).

The aforementioned examples indicate that the tendency to help one's own ("us") as opposed to strangers ("them") is rooted in primate origins.

In humans, at a basic level, family members will help other family members rather than strangers. At a general level, individuals who are phenotypically similar will tend to promote their own group (race) rather than another group. Of course, there are many examples where individuals support others regardless of race. Nonetheless, our deep-seated tendencies to classify people into *groups* and to distinguish between "us" and "them" may be rooted in a primate's daily struggle for survival. In other words, our brain evaluates the ongoing conflict in human societies and guides us through the path of least resistance, that is, associating with groups that share our phenotype. Because societal conflicts vary in type and degree, the brain simply modifies the template from the "them" who are phenotypically different from "us" to the "them" who are only different in language and culture. An example of this shift in group classification is found in David Berreby's award-winning book *Us and Them: The Science of Identity* (2005), which notes the work of former University of Oklahoma psychologist Muzafer Sherif (1906–1988). Sherif published *The Robbers Cave Experiment: Intergroup Conflict and Cooperation* (Sherif et al., 1961).

In the late 1950s 22 white, Protestant, middle-class children were bused to a summer camp in the Sans Bois Mountains, Oklahoma, in two groups of 11. The first bus arrived hours before the second one, and the 11 boys began to divide themselves into groups, such as "us Southsiders" versus "them" (p. 168). Almost immediately, the tendency to classify began. But the camp "leaders" (Sherif and colleagues) had decided in advance that they would all live together in one bunkhouse. When the 11 boys in the other bus finally arrived, they were deliberately separated from the first group. In fact, the two groups would not see each other until much later in the experiment.

The first group of boys spent the week playing games and swimming, and they automatically created "our" ways of doing things (p. 168). They also decided that they should have a name for their tribe—they called themselves "Rattlers" (the second group chose the name "Eagles") and created a symbol (p. 168). A few days into the experiment, the Rattlers heard the other boys (the Eagles) playing in the distance. Their immediate reaction was to "run them off" (p. 168). The Eagles, in turn, heard the Rattlers, and one Eagle boy wanted to know who "those nigger campers" were that he could hear but not see (p. 169). When it turned out that all the boys were white, this boy (and others) shifted to other derogative names for the other group (communists, sissies, cheats, etc.) to explain his feelings. It is also important to note that the boys in both groups constantly tried to emphasize their similarities (simultaneously distancing themselves from the other group) even though they were all white.

In 1950s Oklahoma, a white boy's code for "not our kind" included communists, criminals, homosexuals, and racial minorities (Berreby, 2005). Today we continue to use this same mental code to label individuals (derogatorily or otherwise) for the convenience of identification. For instance, law enforcement uses skin color, hair form, nose shape, and so forth (the phenotypic [race] code) in order to find missing people or fugitives.

The unchanging theme here is that our brains are programmed to classify humans in myriad groups based on the changing conditions of our social environment. Although the American population today is more enlightened in terms of the "other," categories such as *race* (and *homosexuality*) are still hard-wired into our mental map, and we are enculturated into our group and keep track of our cultural norms because

> interacting with people who do not share our norms creates significant fitness costs because the game of reciprocity is more difficult to play when the players have different expectations and rules. Humans have evolved to be sensitive to these costs. (Gil-White, 2001, p. 519)

In the same way, we feel a sense of comfort when we cluster with our own "kind."

Cultural anthropologist Francisco Gil-White (2001) of the University of Pennsylvania notes that "cognitive studies with children and ethnobiological work increasingly support the hypothesis that there may be a universal cognitive adaptation for processing living kinds as categories endowed with 'essences'" (pp. 517–518). In other words, humans come equipped with the mental machinery for processing ethnic and racial groups as biological realities, even though there is valid research

(see chapter 4) that challenges this assumption. In the 1990s Lawrence Hirschfeld, professor of psychology at the New School for Social
Research, conducted an experiment that looked for the mental roots of
race (Hirschfeld, 1996). He showed three sets of color-wash line drawings to 109 children in the Ann Arbor, Michigan, area. Each set included
drawings of an adult and three children of the same sex. The adults and
children in the picture varied with respect to three kinds of obvious outward cues: body build (thin versus stocky), occupation (wearing tools or
a police uniform), and color (dark versus light). When asked which pic-
tured kid was the adult's child, the children generally matched by color
(racial types). They also matched images by occupation and body build
(albeit to a lesser extent).

David Berreby (2005) argues that when the children matched kids
and adults by color, they were treating the visible facts as mental codes:
"Their minds saw the visible cues as representations of a fact they could
not see. It told them to ignore similarities in build and clothing and treat
color as the deciding trait for grouping people together" (pp. 134–135).
In human evolution, race may have been an easier trait to learn/identify
than ethnic or religious affiliation.

Human history is replete with the classification of people into groups
because of physical differences. But what do we say about the classification of people by others who are phenotypically similar (i.e., American "Nativists" classified eastern and southern Europeans and European
Jews; Hutus classified Tutsis as "cockroaches" during Rwanda's civil
war; Serbs used a policy of ethnic cleansing of the Bosniaks, etc.)? Again,
our mental machinery is designed to locate physical differences and classify. But even when there are no physical differences, we tend to *racialize*
nonetheless. Gil-White (2001) details an example:

> The Weimar Jews were quite assimilated to German society in
> speech, custom, and dress, had fought as Germans in World War
> I, and, without relinquishing a Jewish identity, often considered
> themselves genuine Germans. But in the ensuing anti-Semitic
> rampage not merely those who preserved Jewish ascriptions and
> traditions for themselves but even those with a small fraction of

Jewish ancestry (sometimes as little as one-eighth) were slated for persecution. Nazi anti-Semitism openly essentialized its victims, attributing to them a corrupt nature. Not all were convinced by this ideology to the point of justifying the persecution of Jews, but the question remains: Why was it so plausible to Nazi converts that even a little bit of Jewish "blood"—unknown perhaps even to their bearers and against all the powers of German enculturation—would pass on this supposedly corrupt nature? Perhaps because we intuitively process ethnic groups as if they were "species," reasoning implicitly that the corresponding nature is passed down reproductively and hence, in the "blood." (p. 518)

The culture of most Weimar Jews was no different from the non-Jewish Germans. But the Germans nevertheless racialized the Weimar Jews.

Berreby (2005) attempted to answer the critical question of what it is about the human mind that makes us believe in categories such as race, ethnicity, nationalism, and religion. I believe his argument supports my conclusion (which I will detail later in the chapter) about the future of racial classification. In the preface of his book, Berreby argued:

[G]rouping people is an inborn, automatic, involuntary activity of the mind. It's like learning to walk, or talk, or recognize faces. It can't be shut off. It's not evil. It's not good. It is just there, a mental faculty *we can't help using*, with rules different from the ones used by other parts. (p. xiii; italics added)

He lamented that the advances in biological knowledge and in computing power have led to more measurement of differences between populations. In chapters 4 and 5, I discuss in great detail research highlighting the genetic differences between the races. One controversial and high-profile topic I discuss is hypertension and its high frequency in black Americans. I also discuss the new drug BiDil (a diuretic and vasodilator) created for hypertensive patients. The fact that BiDil is now on the U.S. market as the first drug created for a specific racial group—African Americans—is a strong example of our inborn tendency to find differences and to classify. Another prominent example that has not yet been discussed is the Human Genome Diversity Project—the 15-year, $3-billion, coordinated effort by scientists on every continent to record the dwindling regional genetic diversity of *Homo sapiens* by taking DNA samples from several hundred distinct human populations and storing those samples in gene banks (Gutin, 1994). One might argue that storing DNA samples of *distinct human populations* is akin to maintaining the race concept. Moreover, the good intensions of celebrating diversity and difference have the unintentional effect of emphasizing categories and reifying the race concept. Researchers are studying DNA for clues to the *evolutionary histories of populations and to their resistance or susceptibility to particular diseases*. This statement supports Berreby's (2005) conclusion that we believe in dividing human populations into African Americans, Irish Americans, Jewish Americans, and so forth and that because we believe in these categories we gather the data. I would go further and state that, ironically, human biological differences are being racialized.

In an interesting study geared to find out if there is an inborn human tendency to categorize by race, anthropologist Robert Kurzban (Kurzban, Tooby, & Cosmides, 2001) of the University of California at Santa Barbara devised an experiment where he asked undergraduate student volunteers to look at eight photographs of black and white male and female students (according to the racial categories used in the United States) wearing the same gray sweater. To introduce the idea that the eight people in the photographs were in conflict, Kurzban instructed the volunteers to read a sentence on a computer screen. The sentences were all about group conflict: "They were the ones who started the fight!" The inborn tendency in humans to categorize did not fail. The volunteers, in their answers, tended to pair blacks with blacks and whites with whites, even though the two sides in the fictional fight were blacks against whites. In the next phase of their experiment, Kurzban et al. made a simple change by using Photoshop to modify the color of the sweaters in the photos from gray to yellow and green. The volunteers now had two color schemes to think about: black or white skin; yellow or green sweaters. Kurzban et al. were pleased to learn that in this *alternate social world*, the volunteers reasoned that the sentences they heard actually implied a conflict between the Yellows and the Greens, not between the blacks and the whites. I italicized "alternate social world" because in the United States we live in a social world with deep-rooted racial categories. I can think of only one situation where the human tendency to racially classify would be suppressed, and this would be in contact with extraterrestrials. In the short-lived late-1980s TV series *Alien Nation* (which was loosely based on a movie of the same name), a slave ship from outer space carrying 250,000 aliens crash-landed in the Mojave Desert, California. These aliens were initially quarantined and eventually released into the city of Los Angeles. Phenotypically, these aliens—or Tenctonese, the fictitious name of this extraterrestrial species— were similar to humans in every way except for a slightly different shaped, hairless skull permeated with spots. It was not long before *Homo sapiens* as a species (i.e., American blacks, whites, Asians, and Indians—histor- ical racial enemies) were in solidarity in their hatred for the "slags," the derogatory label applied to the aliens. The human intrapopulation racial hatred was suppressed or, more correctly, transferred to another species— the tendency to classify never ended. Despite the fact that this is a fictional example, it is quite instructive. The inborn human tendency to classify "can't be shut off" (Berreby, 2005, p. xiii).

In the 19th century, linguists and anthropologists transformed the Sanskrit word *noble* into "Aryan" (Berreby, 2005). In fact, the word *Aryan* had originally been used by Sir William Jones (1746–1794), a British colonial administrator in India, in the late 18th century to desig- nate the language—Indo-European—that was the common ancestor of the languages spoken today in northern India, Greece, Italy, Germany, and other parts of western Europe (Brace, 2005). If you recall (see chap- ter 2), Gobineau believed that the Nordic race, or his putative Aryans, had a Germanic or "Teutonic" origin. He went even further by assigning them innate biological and behavioral characteristics, in effect creating an "Aryan race" (Brace, 2005). German scholar Friedrich Max Müller (1823–1900) believed that the discovery of common Indian and Euro- pean ancestry was a powerful argument against racism, arguing:

> an ethnologist who speaks of Aryan race, Aryan blood, Aryan eyes and hair, is as great a sinner as a linguist who speaks of a dolichocephalic dictionary or a brachycephalic grammar…and

> that the blackest Hindus represent an earlier stage of Aryan speech
> and thought than the fairest Scandinavians. (Müller, [1888] 2004,
> p. 120)

In the noise of European nationalism, Müller's non-racialist protest was drowned out—as detailed in most of the examples in this section of the chapter, the deep-rooted human tendency to group and label took over. The term *aryan* took on tribal trappings (see Gobineau earlier) that continued into the 20th century, with disastrous results.

Southern and eastern European immigrants and the Irish (see chapter 6) were not considered white by most native-born 19th- and early-20th-century Americans, but their descendants are—they have been reclassified. Again, the human "programming" that says "When in doubt, classify," never ends; the classification simply takes new forms.

Berreby (2005) provided an example from the 18th century of how perceptions of race could change:

> The experience of Charles Johnston is a good example. He grew
> up in North Carolina as a white man with ordinary eighteenth-
> century American attitudes towards nonwhites. Then, in 1790, he
> was seized by a band of Shawnee Indians. Their only other cap-
> tive was a black slave. In his memoirs the white man recalled:
> "The poor Negro, whom I should have kept at a distance under
> other circumstances, now became my companion and friend, and
> I felt quite at home." Those circumstances had placed Johnston
> in a situation where the human kinds "white" and "black" were
> not useful; where, in fact, another way of dividing human beings
> (Shawnee versus English speaker) was a better fit. And so circum-
> stance was enough to make Johnson set his lifelong race divide
> aside. (pp. 69–70)

Johnston's unusual situation did change his mental map from black/white to Shawnee/English speaker. But his general category thinking did not change: us versus them. In addition, the Shawnee probably classified their captives as white and black men. More importantly, although the kinship formed between Johnston and black fellow captive made him "set his lifelong race divide aside," this feeling did not carry over into the greater society. There are many isolated circumstances where individuals with racial and ethnic differences accept each other—and this gives us some hope. But these isolated circumstances remain just that—isolated—and the reality of difference—for better or worse—reemerges. Berreby (2005) made this very clear:

> A white person and a black person in today's New York City can agree over coffee that race is "all in your mind." But when they leave Starbucks and raise their hands to hail a taxi, the white person is more likely to get a cab. In that moment, race is as real as gravity. (p. 322)

This is a critical statement. As long as our mental map perceives human kinds as analogous to a "salad bowl" and not a "melting pot," group classification will always be the norm.

A Compromise: Having Our Cake and Eating It Too

The discussion in the previous section shows very clearly that human classification is persistent. For thousands of years, *Homo sapiens* has adapted to ever-changing physical and social environments. Our big brains have helped us cope with these complex situations by imposing a "reality" we can understand. It does not matter that this reality might be suspect; to people living in the social environment it is real. Berreby (2001) articulated it very well: "We live in a virtual world, where belief matters more than fact, and perception shapes reality. This is not a new aspect of life in the media-soaked 21st century, but an *eternal aspect of human nature*" (p. xix; italics added). Therefore, the clash of three large physically and culturally different population groups in the foundation of early America and the institutionalized racial segregation and discrimination that continued all the way through the first half of the 20th century sustain racial classification, and the specter of economic, political, and racial discrimination still plagues black inner cities. In this stressful environment, our mental machinery helps us cope by finding the path of least resistance toward a comfort zone of allies. In other words, the "us" versus "them" mentality as a coping mechanism kicks in.

We cannot change our evolutionary inheritance, nor can we change the social history of the United States that we have inherited. Therefore, we really don't have a choice but to accept race. If we stand on the main street of any big city in America, we have no problem picking out different races of people. This means that our mental machinery is working and that difference is real. And we have to compromise for more practical and substantive reasons, too. Racial classification impacts civil rights compliance and educational accountability for students, distribution of federal aid to minorities, minority districting in congressional elections, and law enforcement because the FBI, state, and local police use the familiar categories of Caucasoid or white, African American or black, Asian, Hispanic (Mexican or Cuban), and Native American or Indian to find missing people and apprehend criminals. Law enforcement has been accused of profiling or stereotyping. For instance, local and federal law enforcement agencies concentrated on one specific phenotype after the September 11 attacks on the United States: Middle Eastern (Sephardic) males. Why? Up to that infamous date, the majority of suicide bombings occurred in the Middle East performed by Middle Eastern (Sephardic) men. We know that most Middle Eastern (Sephardic) males are not terrorists. But what other strategy could law enforcement use to find these respective terrorists if not race? Could they have used the lactase enzyme, sickle cell gene, or blood type (as Diamond [1994] has skillfully shown don't work)? Probably not. Similarly, when dealing with the recent drug violence on the U.S.-Mexican border, law enforcement has no choice but to use race as a tool in apprehending the culprits. This means that they profile Latinos (Mexican immigrants and Chicanos— Mexican Americans who arrived in the United States decades earlier), all the while knowing full well that most Latinos are not drug dealers.

In chapters 4 and 5, I discussed in detail the arguments regarding genetic variation, physiology, and racial differences in response to pharmaceuticals. Recall the blood-pressure drug BiDil mentioned earlier (see chapter 5 for a complete discussion). BiDil is currently on the U.S. market and supported by the Association of Black Cardiologists and the Congressional Black Caucus. The fact that this drug has support from both the black medical and political establishment (and to some extent from whites) suggests there is some acknowledgment that racial physiological differences exist and that it is important or practical to explore these differences. Along the same lines, the evolutionary histories of the populations and their resistance or susceptibility to particular diseases are being studied as a result of the Human Genome Diversity Project. The initial funding of $3 billion by the National Institutes of Health, the Department of Energy, and the National Science Foundation indicates that learning about racial differences is practical for medicine and physiology.

Race is analogous to standardized tests such as the SAT, ACT, or GRE. The historical social function of these tests was to measure intelligence. The function of race is to explain human biological variation, such as skin color, nose shape, hair form, and body shape to name a few. But like body shape, for example, intelligence is a complex trait that cannot be easily measured. More than likely, a standardized test measures the quality of the taker's education instead. And race is a convenient way to explain phenotypic ancestral traits. Nonetheless, standardized tests are a necessary tool in American education. Without them, there is no way to tell whether students are acquiring basic literacy and numeracy (Lemann, 1999). Likewise, eliminating the concept of race altogether would impact civil rights compliance and educational accountability for students by race and ethnicity; distribution of federal aid to minorities; and minority districting in congressional elections. It might also erode black or Hispanic solidarity and confuse law enforcement because the FBI, state, and local police depend on race for much of their day-to-day work.

As we continue to use race for practical purposes, non-racialist academics can find new strategies in teaching the public about the complexities of racial variation. Instead of the blanket statement "there is no such thing as race," non-racialists can note that individuals from different parts of the world can share many traits and have many of the same characteristics: for instance, sub-Saharan Africans and Melanesians have dark skin and curly hair, and the Khoisan (!Kung San of South Africa) and East Asians share a characteristic eyelid shape. In addition, non-racialists can emphasize the fact that in animal taxonomy, race is defined as a sub-species, and a subspecies, in turn, is defined as a population in the midst of becoming a new species—whereas human populations are not in the midst of becoming different species. We can hope that educated members of the public, while continuing to see racial differences, might then recall the non-racialist information about the complexities behind race and behavior and continue to educate themselves on our differences. This strategy may not overcome our deep-rooted tendency to classify human beings, but it may, in time, steadily erode our primal fear of the "other."

Racialists and non-racialists are both right and both wrong. The complexities of human origins are the root cause of this disagreement. Because survival meant being able to distinguish "us" from "them," phenotypical—or racial—differences and our ability to classify them are evolutionary adaptive. These traits may not be desirable in terms of human relationships, but natural selection is selfish: it is all about the good of the individual or group. Consequently, we must err on the side of race but continue to educate the public on the complexities of human variation.

THE FUTURE OF RACIAL CLASSIFICATION IN THE UNITED STATES

It is a safe assumption that racial classification in the United States will continue indefinitely. And multiracialism will not change this assessment. Recall my earlier discussion of the significant changes in the 2000 U.S. Census and the rise of multiracialism. Hundreds of thousands of multiracial Americans are demanding visibility, acceptance, and, in many cases, an identity that goes beyond "black" or "white." The fact that multiracial Americans want a "separate identity" is another example of racial classification. More than other racial groups, multiracial Americans see themselves as a unique category—and, as such, display the same human tendency to classify themselves.

In the American political and economic landscape, race has always been an important factor in how resources (money, education, services, etc.) are distributed—and it will continue to be a factor, albeit maybe to a lesser extent. Jon Meacham et al. (2000), writing for *Newsweek* magazine, provided some information as to why racial classification will "continue to" be in the minds of most people:

> *By 2010, Latinos will outpace blacks as the nation's largest minority population.* By 2020 the number of people of Asian descent will double, from 10 million to 20 million. *By 2050 whites will make up a slim majority—53 percent.* Last week the Bureau of Labor Statistics announced that the number of foreign-born workers has hit 15.7 million, the highest level in decades. Nashville is desperate for Spanish speakers to respond to 911 calls, and teachers in Rogers, Ark., are dispatched to Mexico in the summers to better absorb the culture from which so many of their pupils come. A lawyer in Birmingham recently built a new swimming pool. The languages spoken by the workers: Polish, Italian, Spanish and Arabic. (p. 40; italics added)

This quote suggests that national elections and immigration will conspire to emphasize racial classification. And the election of Obama or Deval Patrick (the first *black* governor of Massachusetts) will not make people "colorblind."

Certainly, there are many people who adhere to the notion that at the genetic level it is very difficult to classify populations. There is much evidence to support this (see chapters 4 and 5). But the average person on the street cannot see genes; therefore, genes do not seem real to him. Though he can interact with and touch the physical expression of genes—that is, skin, bone, blood, in essence the human being—he cannot interact with genes. The common phrase "seeing is believing" very much applies here. The public puts a high premium on what it can see or perceive in the social world, which makes racial classification a perpetual behavior. Several key events in the 1980s and 1990s that received national attention emphasize the persistence of race: In 1984 Bernhard Goetz, a self-employed electrical engineer living in Manhattan, shot four black males who allegedly were attempting to rob him (Fletcher, 1990; Lesly, 1988). He was dubbed the "Subway Vigilante." Did Goetz's mental machinery associate blacks with violence and crime? Public opinion tended to fall into three camps: Those in the first camp believed Goetz's version of the incident, namely that he feared for his life. Those in the second camp believed the version told by the four black men, who said they were simply panhandling. A third group believed Goetz was threatened but overreacted (associating blacks with violent crime). In the criminal trial, Goetz was tried before a mainly white Manhattan jury (six of whom had been victims of street crime), and he was acquitted of the attempted murder and first-degree assault charges (Lesly, 1988). A lawsuit was filed by one of the alleged robbers, and in the civil trial 11 years later, a jury that included four blacks and two Hispanics found that Goetz acted recklessly and deliberately, particularly in firing twice at the plaintiff. In both the criminal and civil cases, one can speculate that race and behavior was prominently on the jurors' minds.

In another incident that sparked outrage across the country, Rodney King, a black resident of Los Angeles, refused to pull over after signaled to do so by the L.A. Police Department. He believed a DUI would violate his parole for a previous robbery (Mydans, 1992). Eventually, King pulled over but resisted arrest. He was repeatedly beaten by the police, and the beating was caught on tape. The Los Angeles district attorney charged the officers with the use of excessive force. In the criminal trial, a jury consisting of Ventura County residents—10 whites, 1 Latino, and 1 Asian—acquitted three of the officers (Mydans, 1992). The acquittal triggered the Los Angeles riots of 1992. This event prompted the Department of Justice to investigate and charge the officers with violation of federal civil rights.

During the L.A. riots, a largely African American mob in South Central Los Angeles was in the streets, shouting "Black justice!" In this racial fervor, Reginald Denny, a white construction truck driver, was pulled from his truck and brutally beaten by four black men. In the criminal case, a jury of five whites, three blacks, three Latinos, and one Asian was chosen. Although the prosecution argued that the four men had knowingly tried to kill Denny, the defense challenged the video evidence and portrayed the four as victims of poverty and racism (Mydans, 1992). After a few jury changes, a hung jury nullified all charges except for a felony count of mayhem against one defendant and misdemeanor charges against the others. In this case, the jury was chosen based on race (an attempt at choosing a wide cross-section of individuals), and the acquittals in the Rodney King case may also have influenced the outcome in the Reginald Denny beating.

Three years later, in what was dubbed the "Trial of the Century," O. J. Simpson, former African American football star and actor, was brought to trial for the 1994 murder of his ex-wife Nicole Brown Simpson and her friend Ronald Goldman. In the criminal trial, a jury consisting of nine blacks, one Hispanic, and two whites returned a verdict of not guilty. The prosecution's case was supported by tremendous DNA evidence (Meier, 1994). Whether the jury understood the genetic evidence is unknown, but it is certain that race relations (the phenotype) overshadowed the DNA evidence (the genotype).

In conclusion, these high-profile cases speak to the persistence of race. The numerous similar cases that occur regularly in American society (albeit with different actors), the terrorist attacks on U.S. soil (which resulted in the profiling of Middle Eastern males), and the legal and illegal immigration of (largely) racial and ethnic minorities from developing nations will compel the U.S. government to continue classifying populations for economic, political, and national security reasons. Though the disagreement on the existence or non-existence of race will not be resolved in academia, for the general public race has always existed. This fact was clear in the Bernhard Goetz, Rodney King, Reginald Denny, and O. J. Simpson cases and many other incidents where people of different cultures and skin colors have interacted in the social environment. Berreby's (2005) example brings the point home. I reiterate it here:

> A white person and a black person in today's New York City can agree over coffee that race is "all in your mind." But when they leave Starbucks and raise their hands to hail a taxi, the white person is more likely to get a cab. In that moment, race is as real as gravity. (p. 322)

Grouping people according to skin color, hair form, nose shape, body type, eye color, and so forth is rooted in our evolutionary history. It is involuntary and automatic. "It's like learning to walk, talk, or recognize faces. It can't be shut off. It's not evil. It's not good. It is just a mental faculty we can't help using" (Berreby, 2005, p. xiii). Based on this statement and many other examples in this chapter, racial classification, as it has in the past and does in the present, will continue into the distant future.

NOTES

1. The theoretical stance racialism is not meant to hurt, but the data can be misinterpreted and used in a negative way. Consequently, non-racialists believe the race concept used in any aspect of human biology (i.e., genetics, physiology, skeletal identification, etc.) is not valid (Goodman & Armelagos, 1996; Muir, 1993).
2. Racialists are individuals who believe that genetics, physiology, and even the skeleton indicate racial differences.
3. The post-Renaissance world of the 18th century is known as the Enlightenment, or the "Age of Reason," to give it the name designated in the title of Thomas Paine's book in 1796. As with most other periods, it has no precise dates of demarcation. "Still, there is utility in recognizing the Age of Reason, and it plays a very important, if somewhat curious, role in the development of the concept of 'race'" (Brace, 1995, p. 22).
4. In Aristotelian hierarchy, all life was linked in a "great chain" commonly known as the Great Chain of Being or Aristotle's *scalae naturae*. This model went as far as proposing a hierarchy of life roughly similar to the one listed here: God: angels: humans: animals: inanimate objects. This hierarchy was fixed, with everything set nicely in its own place. Within the human realm, Aristotle placed Europeans, particularly Greeks, on top (Brace & Montagu, 1977; Jurmain & Nelson, 1994).
5. The Scottish Enlightenment's "Philosophy of Common Sense" is a mid-18th-century school of thought advocating that the common sense with which everyone is endowed can counter the extremes of skepticism. In essence, every human being was considered to have the common sense to determine the true and false and the good and bad. This was the impetus for the growth of science, and according to one, its fall in the late 18th century paved the way for the proliferation of the race concept (Brace, 2005).
6. According to skeletal and genetic evidence, Asians and Native Americans show remarkable similarities. The highest frequencies of shovel-shaped incisors are found in Asians and Native Americans. This evidence indicates an evolutionary relationship between these two populations. More compelling evidence for a peopling of the Americas is the fact that Native Americans share haplogroups (A, B, C, D—genes on chromosomes that do not recombine and are inherited as a unit) with northeast Asians. These haplogroups were present in Asians who migrated to the Americas.

The presence of all four groups throughout the Americas and the strong similarity of the nucleotide sequences suggest they share a common ancestry in a single founding population that arrived in the Americas from Asia (Larsen, 2008).

7. The Neolithic and Bronze Age worlds were very large in the sense that traveling great distances took months as opposed to hours today because traveling in these archaic periods was done on foot, horseback, or small sailboats. One can assume most people could not afford a horse or boat; consequently, they had no choice but to travel on foot or not at all. This limited their knowledge of the world, as one could not travel very far on foot—approximately 25 miles a day from the natal farm in a lifetime (45–50 years). One author calls this personal ignorance of the world "the Peasant Perspective." For more discussion on this, see Brace (2005, pp. 18–21).

8. There were other populations, such as Asians, but their numbers were small. The 1850 Census lists only three categories: Negroes, Whites, and Blacks.

9. The Rosetta Stone was found by Napoleon's forces in the Nile Delta in 1799 and finally deciphered by Jean Francois Champollion.

10. The theory of "deep time" states that the earth is billions of years old and thus has a long history of development and change. The geologist John McPhee coined the term to distinguish geological time from the scale of time that governs our everyday lives. McPhee meant the term to refer to the immense intervals, measured in millions of years, discussed as if they were days or weeks in the conversation of geologists; yet in reality, the intervals of geological time are too long to be readily comprehensible to minds used to thinking in terms of days, weeks, and years (Gee, 1999). For more discussion on this, see John McPhee, *Basin and Range* (1982).

11. The term *Romanticism* frequently evokes an image of sexual and mindless sentimentality. In some sense this is true, but the whole movement is much more complex. Romanticism permeated 19th-century America, giving birth to polygenism, or separate creations for whites, blacks, and Native Americans, which led to the "scientific" support for separate species designations for blacks and Native Americans when there were viable mixed-race children and adults in plain view. This was "feeling over reason."

12. George R. Gliddon (1809–1857) and Josiah Clark Nott (1804–1873) were considered, by European scholars of the mid-19th century, as members of the American School of Biological Anthropology. Whereas Morton kept above the muck of slavery, Gliddon and Nott reveled in it. After Morton's death, they would link the American School of Biological Anthropology

directly to the South and slavery and attach Morton's name to give added prestige. Gliddon was well liked by most of his educated friends, but most thought he was a "traveling showman" as he undertook his lecture tour of the eastern United States in 1840. Nott earned his doctor of medicine degree at the University of Pennsylvania Medical School in Philadelphia in 1827. While Morton and Louis Agassiz provided the "scholarship," Nott articulated the American School in the language of Southern racism. For more, see Brace, *Race Is a Four-Letter Word* (2005), pp. 110–130.

13. Catastrophism, the doctrine Georges Cuvier (1769–1832) proposed, asserted that global warming melted glaciers, resulting in a "great flood" or "catastrophe" that caused the extinction of past life-forms represented by prehistoric fossils in his collection. After the flood, Cuvier suggested that animals from other regions moved in to "fill-up" the empty landscape. And God speeded things up by creating more animals. Cuvier's work provided the first basic understanding of extinction.

14. The Lowell Institute Lecture Series was initiated on January 3, 1840, by the renowned chemist Benjamin Silliman (1779–1864) of Yale. It was endowed by John Lowell Jr. of Boston with a bequest of $250,000 (Weeks, 1966). The series chose speakers and lecture topics carefully, rejecting anyone and any topic that was controversial.

15. Nathaniel Southgate Shaler posited a "Teutonic" origin for American democracy that could be traced back to the "primitive folk meetings deep in the heart of the old Germanic forest" (D. N. Livingstone, 1987, p. 191). Shaler adopted this view from the readings of Joseph-Arthur Comte de Gobineau, "the father of racism," who believed that civilization was appropriate only for his "Teutons." Subsequently, Shaler argued America was suitable only for "Teutons." This view was instilled into the hearts and minds of Harvard graduates in the late 19th century, and they carried these ideas into the 20th century, incorporating them into U.S. government and social policy.

16. The "white man's burden" was the title of a verse written by England's poet of the empire Rudyard Kipling in 1899 (Kipling, 1907). Kipling believed that the white race or Nordics were natural rulers and it was the duty of the white race to govern "lower" races—hence the support for empire and colonialism. Kipling sent an advance copy of the verse to Pres. Teddy Roosevelt, who accepted it as a logical reason for American colonialism. One might speculate that this view of the manifest superiority of the European race, which could be traced back to the American Shaler and originated with the European Gobineau, drove the intervention in the Panama Canal Zone in 1903 under the banner of Manifest Destiny.

17. The Chinese Exclusion Act was a U.S. federal law passed on May 6, 1882, following revisions made in 1880 to the Burlingame Treaty of 1868 (Gyory, 1998). Those revisions allowed the United States to suspend Chinese immigration. The act excluded Chinese "skilled and unskilled laborers and Chinese employed in mining" from entering the country for 10 years under penalty of imprisonment and deportation. The few Chinese nonlaborers who wished to immigrate had to obtain certification from the Chinese government that they were qualified to immigrate, which tended to be difficult to prove. The act also affected Chinese who were already in the United States. Any Chinese who left the United States had to obtain certifications for reentry, and the act made Chinese immigrants permanent aliens by excluding them from U.S. citizenship. After the act's passage, Chinese men in the United States had little chance of ever reuniting with their wives or of starting families in their new home.

18. Joseph-Arthur Comte de Gobineau (1816–1882) has been referred to as "the father of racism" and declared civilization was appropriate only for his "Teutons" or Germanic people (Biddiss, 1970). Gobineau hated democracy and equality, and this hatred was manifested in his *Essai sur l'Inegalité des Races Humaines*, published in four volumes between 1853 and 1855. High on his list of values were "liberty" and "order," but "his liberty was a privileged state enjoyed by the aristocratic elite in a hierarchical social order" (Brace, 2005, p. 120). He applied the Great Chain of Being to the social world, where the inferior races at the bottom served the superior race on top.

19. Madison Grant (1865–1937) wrote *The Passing of the Great Race, or the Racial Basis of European History* (1916 and three editions by 1921), and Lothrop Stoddard (1883–1950) wrote *The Rising Tide of Color Against White World Supremacy* (1920). These men were proud of the fact that they were descendants of the 17th-century colonial settlers and despised immigrants. They had inherited enough money to live in comfort without having to do anything to earn an income. Because Stoddard was a friend and protégé of Grant and Grant wrote the introduction to Stoddard's book, their ideas about race were identical:

> Democratic ideals among an homogeneous population of Nordic blood, as in England or America, is one thing, but it is quite another for the white man to share his blood with, or intrust his ideals to, brown, yellow, black or red men.... This is suicide pure and simple, and the first victim of this amazing folly will be the white man himself. (Grant, 1920, p. xxxii)

20. Marcellin Boule (1861–1942), an eminent French paleoanthropologist, examined the most complete Neanderthal skeleton found at La Chapelle-aux-Saints. He concluded that the La Chapelle individual must have walked with a bent-kneed gait—as in chimpanzees that walk bipedally—and did not have the ability to speak (Larsen, 2008). Professor Boule's scientific writings influenced future generations of anthropologists in their interpretation of Neanderthal phylogeny, behavior, and place in human evolution.

21. Gregor Mendel (1822–1884), an Augustinian monk living in a monastery in what is now Brno, Czech Republic, using the pea plant showed how traits are inherited and in the course of his work laid the foundations for our understanding of genetics. For instance, Mendel inferred that a *discrete* physical unit (passed from parent to offspring) was responsible for the respective characteristics. Today we know this discrete physical unit is called a gene.

22. Sir Arthur Keith was a British anatomist who, according to Loring Brace (2005), was the original source—imported by Earnest Hooton—of the Harvard outlook on race. Keith believed the races were sorted into superior and inferior as a result of competition. In essence, the lower races lost out in the competition. Using sports as an analogy, Keith (1931) asserted,

> What modern football team could face the goal-posts unless it developed as it took the field a spirit of antagonism towards the players wearing opposite colours? Nature endowed her tribal teams with the spirit of antagonism for her own purposes. It has come down to us and creeps out from our modern life in many shapes, as national rivalries and jealousies and as racial hatreds. The modern name for this spirit of antagonism is race-prejudice. (p. 35)

23. Carleton Putnam (1901–1998) was a former head of Delta Airlines who wrote a book titled *Race and Reason: A Yankee View* (1961) (Tucker, 2002). At the 1962 American Association of Physical Anthropologists meeting, the membership voted 91 to 1 in favor of condemning this book.

24. The Modern Synthesis is a unified theory of evolution that combines Mendelian genetics with Darwinian natural selection.

25. The "new physical anthropology" was a rebellion by some Harvard PhDs (e.g., Sherwood Washburn) against the Harvard school of thought in physical anthropology or a break from the Hooton philosophy of ambivalence and insensitivity to race and social issues. This new physical anthropology built on the foundation of the Boasian tradition, which advocated change in body form as a result of changes in environment and culture. In addition,

the post–World War II Boasian school brought anthropology into the public arena, where public monies were used to fund research (as opposed to pre–World War II anthropology, which was dominated and funded by private men of wealth).

26. Charles Darwin's revolutionary book's impact is still being felt today.

27. Natural selection is the name Charles Darwin (1809–1882) used for his explanation of evolution. According to Darwin, individuals have more offspring than can survive. In this situation, there will be a struggle for existence. However, those individuals with favorable traits will survive and reproduce and those with unfavorable traits will die. Those who survive and reproduce will pass their adaptive traits to their offspring. These adaptive traits will increase in future generations. Darwin got the idea for the name "natural selection" from animal breeders who "artificially select" certain traits in animals.

28. *Anthropoid* comes from the word *Anthropoidea*, which is the suborder of Primates in animal (or Linnaean) taxonomy. It includes all monkeys, apes, and humans (and prehistoric bipedal ancestors).

29. Ernst Haeckel's recapitulation theory stated that *ontogeny* (or development of the organism) *recapitulates phylogeny* (evolutionary history of the organism). In other words, the embryos of many animals look very similar, indicating a common ancestry millions of years ago. A classic example is the juvenile chimpanzee who resembles an adult human more than an adult chimpanzee. This is sometimes referred to as neotenic or neoteny.

30. *Pithecanthropus* is the name first proposed by Ernst Haeckel for the oldest hominid. Eugene Dubois (1858–1940), a physician for the Dutch colonial government in Indonesia, found a partial skull and complete femur ("Java Man") on the riverbank near the village of Trinil in 1891 (Larsen, 2008). He used the name *Pithecanthropus* for this discovery (which later became known as *Homo erectus*) because as a teenager he was fascinated by Haeckel's ideas about evolution.

31. *Sinanthropus* was the name Franz Weidenreich assigned to the famous fossil *Homo erectus* remains from the Lower Cave at Zhoukoudian, China.

32. Trinil is where Dubois found the famous "Java Man" skullcap on the island of Java, Indonesia, in 1891. It has the reputation of being the "first *Pithecanthropus*," dated at approximately 1.6 million years.

33. Ngandong is up the other Indonesian or Java *Homo erectus* fossil. Ngandong is dated a little over 500,000 years ago.

34. The Australian paleoanthropologist Alan Thorne (1981) initially proposed the "Center and Edge" hypothesis. He argued that populations at

the "edges" of the species range (Australia, etc.) show a continuity of features through time compared to populations at the "center" (Africa). He compared cranial features of Australian fossils dated at different periods in Australian Paleolithic history and found continuity in features, suggesting a single lineage through time. The assertion here is that populations on the edges of the species range, such as islands, are more homogenous because of limited genes from outside the population. Also, genetic drift increases the difference between populations. In contrast, populations in Africa and Europe are heterogeneous.

35. *Polymorphic* refers to the presence of two or more separate phenotypes for a certain gene in the population. For example, the ABO blood group is polymorphic because there are many different forms, such as A, B, AB, and O.

36. *Clines* refer to adaptive traits that are distributed in a gradation. For example, human skin color is distributed in a gradation. If we use latitude as an example, at the equator, skin color is darkest in order to protect populations from high UV radiation. As one moves up or down to the higher latitudes (less UV radiation), skin color gradually gets lighter.

37. Platonic Essentialism was the worldview of medieval scholars who believed the reality in the world consisted of fixed and separate entities, that is, animals, plants, and inanimate objects, whose perfect representations were to be found only in the mind of God. This view was merged with Aristotle's hierarchy, so when human races were ranked, there was an "ideal type" or racial group that set the standard of perfection.

38. !Kung San occupy southern Africa's Kalahari Desert. They are noted for the "clicks" (noted by the exclamation mark before the letter "K" in Kung) in their speech, which is a feature of the Khoisan languages of Africa.

39. The epicanthic fold is a fold of skin above the inner border of the eye. It is a characteristic eyelid shape of East Asians and the Khoisan/Xhosa of South Africa.

40. Vascular response to cold is a more efficient physiological response to cold stress (than shivering) in that there is a minimization of heat loss through alternate constriction and dilation of blood vessels (Beall & Steegmann, 2000; Relethford, 2005). For instance, vasoconstriction acts to minimize heat loss from the body to the extremities (i.e., the hands and feet) in cold stress. Less blood flow leads to a drop in skin temperature, and cellular necrosis may occur. Should this start to happen, vasodilation begins causing blood and heat to flow from the interior of the body to the extremities. Now the body is losing heat and the cycle begins again. The point here is

that this hypothesis is a better explanation for low or high frequencies of frostbite than skin color (or race).

41. *Australopithecus* is a genus of fossil hominin that lived between 4 million and 1 million years ago and is characterized by bipedal locomotion, small brain size, large face, and large teeth.

42. The Bergmann-Allen Rule states that, generally, populations in cold climates have a large volume and a small surface-area-to-volume ratio and populations in hot climates have a small volume (efficient in maintaining heat) and a large surface-area-to-volume ratio (efficient in releasing heat). As far as body shape is concerned, populations in cold climates are, generally, short and stocky, whereas populations in hot climates are slim and tall (or small).

43. Microsatellites are the numerous noncoding parts of the DNA (or introns) that surround the coding parts of the DNA (exons). They are also short sequences of repeated DNA and highly variable from one individual to the next.

44. *Alu* insertion polymorphism is a sequence of DNA repeated at different locations on different chromosomes. *Alu* markers and microsatellites have comparable power to detect population structure and assign origin (Bamshad et al., 2003).

45. Mixed-race (another term for multiracial or hybrid) denotes people whose genealogical ancestry combined distinct races regardless of whether this mixture stemmed from their parents' generation or farther back (Morning, 2003).

46. *Mulatow* written in this form appears in a list in the 1595 *Drake's Voy*: "By meanes of a Mulatow and an Indian, we had, this night, forty bundles of dried beife" (Sollors, 2000). In the *Oxford English Dictionary*, mulatto is defined as "one who is the offspring of a European and a Black; also used loosely for anyone of mixed race resembling a mulatto" (*Oxford English Dictionary*, 1989).

47. Linkage disequilibrium refers to nonrandom association of alleles (alternate forms of a gene) at two or more loci (position of a gene on a chromosome). Genes on the same chromosomes are said to be linked.

48. Fordisc 3.0 or forensic discrimination is a multivariate statistical software program with a worldwide database of cranial measurements. It classifies unknown skulls into the closest sample group (with probabilities) based on those measurements.

49. Project RACE is a grassroots movement that became a national organization in its activism for recognition of multiracialism. Their main goal is for

a multiracial classification on all school, employment, state, federal, local, census, and medical forms requiring racial data.

50. Inferring the earliest human behavior by studying prehistoric skeletons, tools, or shelters is a very important part of paleoanthropology. But living models have the potential of increasing accuracy. Consequently, living primates—particularly the chimpanzee species—are used as referential models for the earliest human behavior or a window into human evolution.

References

Abbie, A. A. (1975). *Studies in physical anthropology* (Vols. 1–2). Canberra: Australian Institute of Aboriginal Studies, RRS5.

Agassiz, L. (1845). Notice sur la géographie des animaux. Extrait de *La Revue Suisse*. H. Wolfrath.

Agassiz, L. (1850a). The geographical distribution of animals. *Christian Examiner and Religious Miscellany*, *48*, 181–204.

Agassiz, L. (1850b). The diversity and origin of human races. *Christian Examiner and Religious Miscellany*, *49*, 110–145.

Aird, I., Bentall, H. H., & Roberts, J. A. F. (1953). A relationship between cancer of the stomach and the ABO groups. *British Medical Journal*, *1*, 799–801.

American Anthropological Association. (1998, March 23). Statement on "race." Retrieved August 15, 2005, from http://www.aaanet.org/stmts/racepp.htm

American Association of Physical Anthropologists. (1996). Statement on biological aspects of race. *American Journal of Physical Anthropology*, *101*, 569–570.

American Council of Learned Societies. (1932). Report of committee on linguistic and national stocks in the population of the United States. In *American Historical Association annual report for 1931* 1, 120–304. Washington, DC: American Historical Association.

Armelagos, G. J. (1994). Racism and physical anthropology: Brue's review of Barkan's *The retreat of scientific racism*. *American Journal of Physical Anthropology*, *93*, 381–383.

Avise, J. C., Arnold, J., Ball, R. M., Bermingham, E., Lamb, T., Neigel, J. E., Reeb, C. A., & Saunders, N. C. (1987). Intraspecific phylogeography: The mitochondrial DNA bridge between population genetics and systematics. *Annual Review of Ecological Systematics*, *18*, 469–522.

Bachman, J. (1854). An examination of a few the statements of Prof. Agassiz in his "Sketch of the natural provinces of the animal world and their relations to different types of men." *Charleston Medical Journal and Review*, *9*, 790–806.

Bachman, J. (1855). An examination of Prof. Agassiz's sketch of natural provinces of the animal world, and their relation to the different types of man, with a tableau accompanying the sketch. *Charleston Medical Journal and Review*, *10*, 482–534.

Baker, J. (1974). *Race*. New York: Oxford University Press.

Baker, P. T. (1967). The biological race concept as a research tool. *American Journal of Physical Anthropology*, *27*, 21–25.

Bamshad, M. J., Wooding, S., Watkins, W. S., Ostler, C. T., Batzer, M. A., & Jorde, L. B. (2003). Human population genetic structure and inference of group membership. *American Journal of Human Genetics*, *72*, 578–589.

Barkan, E. (1988). Mobilizing scientists against Nazi racism, 1933–1939. In G. Stocking, Jr. (Ed.), *Bones, bodies, behavior. Essays on biological anthropology* (pp. 181–205). Madison: University of Wisconsin Press.

Bass, W. M. (1995). *Human osteology: A laboratory and field manual* (4th ed.). Special Publication No. 2. Columbia: Missouri Archaeological Society.

Bass, W. M. (2005). *Human osteology: A laboratory and field manual* (5th ed.). Special Publication No. 2: Missouri Archaeological Society.

Beall, C. M., & Steegmann, A. T., Jr. (2000). Human adaptation to climate: Temperature, ultraviolet radiation, and altitude. In S. Stinson, B. Bogin, R. Huss-Ashmore, & D. O'Rourke (Eds.), *Human biology: An evolutionary and biocultural perspective* (pp. 163–224). New York: John Wiley.

Beals, K. L., Smith, C. L., & Dodd, S. M. (1984). Brain size, cranial morphology, climate, and time machines. *Current Anthropology*, *25*, 301–330.

Bendyshe, T. (Ed.). (1865). *The anthropological treatises of Johann Frederick Blumenbach.* London: Longman, Green, Longman, Roberts, and Green.

Berreby, D. (2005). *Us and them: The science of identity.* Chicago: University of Chicago Press.

Berman, C. M., & Kapsalis, E. (1999). Development of kin bias among rhesus monkeys: Maternal transmission or individual learning? *Animal Behaviour, 58*, 883–894.

Biddiss, M. D. (1970). *Father of racist ideology: The social and political thought of Count Gobineau.* London: Weidenfeld & Nicolson.

Blum, H. F. (1961). Does the melanin pigment of human skin have adaptive value? An essay in human ecology and the evolution of race. *Quarterly Review of Biology, 36*, 50–63.

Boas, F. (1911). *The mind of primitive man.* New York: Macmillan.

Boas, F. (1912). Changes in bodily form of descendants of immigrants. *American Anthropologist, 14*, 530–562.

Boas, F. (1920). Review of *The rising tide of color: Against white world supremacy* by Lothrop Stoddard. *Nation, 111*, 658.

Boaz, N. T., & Almquist, A. J. (2002). *Biological anthropology: A synthetic approach to human evolution.* Upper Saddle River, NJ: Prentice Hall.

Bowcock, A. M., Herbert, J. M., Mountain, J. L., Kidd, J. R., Rogers, J., Kidd, K. K., & Cavalli-Sforza, L. L. (1991). Study of an additional 58 DNA markers in five human populations from four continents. *Gene Geography, 5*, 151–173.

Bowcock, A. M., Ruiz-Linares, A., Tomfohrde, J., Minch, E., Kidd, J. R., & Cavalli-Sforza, L. L. (1994). High resolution of human evolutionary trees with polymorphic microsatellites. *Nature, 368*, 455–457.

Bowman, J. (1997). The management of hemolytic disease in the fetus newborn. *Seminars in Perinatology, 21*, 39.

Boyd, W. C. (1950). *Genetics and the races of man*. Boston: Little Brown.

Boyd, R., & Silk, J. B. (2006). *How humans evolved* (4th ed.). New York: W. W. Norton.

Brace, C. L. (1964). A non-racial approach towards the understanding of human diversity. In M. F. A. Montagu (Ed.), *Concept of race* (pp. 313–320). New York: Free Press of Glencoe.

Brace, C. L. (1982). The roots of the race concept in American physical anthropology. In F. Spencer (Ed.), *A history of American physical anthropology 1930–1980* (pp. 11–29). New York: Academic Press.

Brace, C. L. (1995). Region does not mean race: Reality versus convention in forensic identification. *Journal Forensic Sciences, 40*, 171–175.

Brace, C. L. (1996). A four letter word called "race." In L. T. Reynolds & L. Lieberman (Eds.), *Race and other misadventures: Essays in honor of Ashley Montagu in his ninetieth year* (pp. 106–141). New York: General Hall Publishers.

Brace, C. L. (1997). Race concept. In F. Spencer (Ed.), *History of physical anthropology: An encyclopedia* (pp. 861–867). New York: Garland Publishing.

Brace, C. L. (2005). *"Race" is a four-letter word: The genesis of the concept*. New York: Oxford University Press.

Brace, C. L., & Montagu, A. (1977). *Human evolution: An introduction to biological anthropology* (2nd ed.). New York: Macmillan.

Brace, C. L., Seguchi, N., Quintyn, C. B., Fox, S. C., Nelson, R. A., Manolis, S. K. …Qifeng, P. (2006). The questionable contribution of the Neolithic and the Bronze Age to European craniofacial form. *Proceedings of National Academy of Sciences, 103*, 242–247.

Brace, C. L., Tracer, D. P., Yaroch, L. A., Robb, J., Brandt, K., & Nelson, R. A. (1993). Clines and clusters versus "race": A test in ancient Egypt and the case of death on the Nile. *Yearbook of Physical Anthropology, 36*, 1–31.

Brigham, C. C. (1923). *A study of American intelligence*. Princeton, NJ: Princeton University Press.

Broca, P. (1860). *Recherches sur l'hybridité animal en general et sur l'hybridité humaine en particulier, considérées dans leurs rapports avec la question de la pluralité des espèces humains*. Paris: J. Claye.

Brues, A. M. (1977). *People and races*. New York: Macmillan.

Brues, A. M. (1990). The once and future diagnosis of race. In G. W. Gill & S. Rhine (Eds.), *Skeletal attribution of race: Methods for forensic anthropology* (pp. 1–8). (Anthropological Papers No. 4). Albuquerque, NM: Maxwell Museum of Anthropology.

Brues, A. M. (1993). Racial concepts: The objective view of race. In C. Gordon (Ed.), *Race, ethnicity, and applied bioanthropology* (pp. 74–78). (Bulletin No. 13). Arlington, VA: American Anthropological Association.

Burdeau, G. (1989). The perceived attractiveness of preterm infants with cranial molding. *Journal of Obstetric, Gynecologic and Neonatal Nursing, 18*, 38–44.

Byers, S. N. (2002). *Introduction to forensic anthropology: A textbook*. Boston: Allyn Bacon.

Byers, S. N. (2008). *Introduction to forensic anthropology: A textbook*. (3rd ed.). Boston: Allyn Bacon.

Campbell, B. G., Loy, J. D., & Cruz-Uribe, K. (2006). *Humankind emerging*. New York: Pearson Education.

Cann, R. L. (1987). In search of Eve. *The Sciences, 27*, 30–37.

Cann, R. L., Stoneking, M., & Wilson, A. C. (1987). Mitochondrial DNA and human evolution. *Nature, 325*, 31–36.

Cartmill, M. (1999). The status of the race concept in physical anthropology. *American Anthropologist, 100*, 651–660.

Cavalli-Sforza, L. L., Menozzi, P., & Piazza, A. (1993). Demic expansions and human evolution. *Science, 259*, 639–646.

Cavalli-Sforza, L. L., Menozzi, P., & Piazza, A. (1994). *The history and geography of human genes*. Princeton, NJ: Princeton University Press.

Chatters, J. C. (2000). The recovery and first analysis of an early Holocene human skeleton from Kennewick, Washington. *American Antiquity*, *65*, 291–316.

Chatters, J. C. (2002). *Ancient encounters: Kennewick man and the first Americans*. New York: Simon & Schuster.

Code Network Media Group. (2006). Map of Africa. Retrieved December 4, 2009, from http://www.map-of-africa.co.uk/

Coon, C. S. (1939). *The races of Europe*. New York: Macmillan.

Coon, C. S. (1962). *The origin of races*. New York: Alfred A. Knopf.

Coon, C. S. (1981). *Adventures and discoveries: The autobiography of Carleton S. Coon*. Englewood Cliffs, NJ: Prentice Hall.

Coon, C. S., Garn, S. M., & Birdsell, J. B. (1950). *Races: A study of the problems of race formation in man*. Springfield, IL: Charles C. Thomas.

Coon, C. S., & Hunt, E. E. (1965). *The living races of man*. New York: Alfred A. Knopf.

Cooper, R. S., Wolf-Maier, K., Luke, A., Adeyemo, A., Banegas, J. R., Forrester, T.,...Thamm, M. (2005). An international comparative study of blood pressure in populations of European vs. African descent. *BMC Medicine*, *3*, 2–8. Retrieved January 26, 2009, from http://www. biomedcentral.com/1741-7015/3/2

DaCosta, K. M. (2003). Multiracial identity: From personal problem to public issue. In L. I. Winters & H. L. DeBose (Eds.), *New faces in a changing America: Multiracial identity in the 21st century* (pp. 68–84). Thousand Oaks, CA: Sage Publications.

Damon, A. (1977). *Human biology and ecology*. New York: W. W. Norton.

Danan, C., Sternberg, D., Van Steirteghem, A., Cazeneuve, C., Duquesnoy, P., Besmond, C.,...Amselem, S. (1999). Evaluation of parental mitochondrial inheritance in neonates born after intracytoplasmic sperm injection. *American Journal of Human Genetics, 65,* 463–473.

DeBose, H. L. (Ed.). (2003). "Introduction." In L. I. Winters and H. L. DeBose (Eds.), *New faces in a changing America: Multiracial identity in the 21st century* (pp. xi–xxi). Thousand Oaks, CA: Sage Publications.

Diamond, J. (1991). Curse and blessing of the ghetto. *Discover, 12,* 60–65.

Diamond, J. (1994). Race without color. *Discover, 15,* 83–89.

Dobson, J. (1994). *Baby beautiful: A handbook of baby head shaping.* Carson City, NV: Heirs Press.

Dobzhansky, T. (1944). On species and races of living and fossil man. *American Journal of Physical Anthropology, 2,* 251–265.

Dobzhansky, T. (1950). Comment on "The problem of the earliest claimed representatives of *Homo sapiens,*" by T. D. Stewart. *Cold Spring Harbor Symposia on Quantitative Biology, 15,* 106–107.

Dobzhansky, T. (1962). *Mankind evolving: The evolution of the human species.* New Haven, CT: Yale University Press.

Dobzhansky, T. (1963). The possibility that *Homo sapiens* evolved independently 5 times is vanishingly small. *Scientific American 208,* 169–172.

Durant, W., & Durant, A. (1967). *Rousseau and revolution: The story of civilization* (Part X). New York: Simon & Schuster.

Duster, T. (2005). Race and reification in science. *Science, 307,* 1050–1051.

El-Najjar, M., & McWilliams, K. R. (1978). Forensic anthropology: The structure, morphology, and variation of human bone and dentition. Springfield, IL: Charles C. Thomas.

Elman, R. (1976). *The living world of Audubon mammals*. New York: Grosset and Dunlap.

Erickson, P. A. (1977). Phrenology and physical anthropology: The George Combe connection. *Current Anthropology, 18*, 92–93.

Etzioni, A. (2000, May 31). *A new American race*. Retrieved February 12, 2008, from http://www.multiracial.com/readers/etzioni.html

Ferllini, R. (2002). *Silent witness: How forensic anthropology is used to solve the world's toughest crimes*. Willowdale, ON: Firefly Books, Ltd.

Fischer, A., Pollack, J., Thalmann, B. N., & Pääbo, S. (2006). Demographic history and genetic differentiation in apes. *Current Biology, 16*, 1133–1138.

FitzSimmons, E., Prost, J. H., & Peniston, S. (1998). Infant head molding: A cultural practice. *Archives of Family Medicine, 7*, 88–90.

Fletcher, G. P. (1990). *A crime of self-defense: Bernhard Goetz and the law on trial*. Chicago: Chicago University Press.

Flint, A. (1995, March 5). Don't classify by race, urge scientists. *The Boston Globe*, p. B1.

Gabriel, S. E., Brigman, K. N., Koller, B. H., Boucher, R. C., & Smuts, M. J. (1994). Cystic fibrosis heterozygote resistance to cholera toxin in the cystic fibrosis mouse model. *Science, 266*, 107–109.

Garn, S. M. (1960). *Readings on race*. Springfield, IL: Charles C. Thomas.

Gee, H. (1999). *In search of deep time: Beyond the fossil record to a new history of life*. New York: The Free Press.

Giles, E., & Elliot, O. (1962). Race identification from cranial measurements. *Journal of Forensic Sciences, 7*, 147–156.

Gill, G. W. (1998). Craniofacial criteria in the skeletal attribution of race. In K. J. Reichs (Ed.), *Forensic osteology: Advances in the identification of human remains* (2nd ed.) (pp. 293–317). Springfield, IL: Charles C. Thomas.

Gill, G. W., & Gilbert, B. M. (1990). Race identification from midfacial skeleton: American blacks and whites. In G. W. Gill & S. Rhine (Eds.), *Skeletal Attribution of Race* (pp. 47–57). (Anthropological Papers No. 4). Albuquerque, NM: Maxwell Museum of Anthropology.

Gillespie, N. (1997, July 1). Blurred vision: Seeing beyond government racial categories. Retrieved October 24, 2007, from http://reason.com/archives/1997/07/01/blurred-vision

Gil-White, F. J. (2001). Are ethnic groups biological "species" to the human brain? Essentialism in our cognition of some social categories. *Current Anthropology, 42*, 515–554.

Gobineau, J. A., Comte de. (1853–1855). *Essai sur l'inegalité des races humaines* (Vols. 1–4). Paris: Didot Frères.

Goodman, A. H., & Armelagos, G. J. (1996). The resurrection of race: The concept of race in physical anthropology in the 1990s. In L. T. Reynolds & L. Lieberman (Eds.), *Race and other misadventures*: *Essays in honor of Ashley Montagu in his ninetieth year* (pp. 174–186). New York: General Hall Publishers.

Gordon, C. C. (1993). Why classify race? In C. Gordon (Ed.), *Race, ethnicity, and applied bioanthropology* (pp. 1–6). (Bulletin No. 13). Arlington, VA: American Anthropological Association.

Gordon, C. C., & Bell, N. (1993). Problems of racial and ethnic self-identification and classification. In C. Gordon (Ed.), *Race, ethnicity, and applied bioanthropology* (pp. 34–47). (Bulletin No. 13). Arlington, VA: American Anthropological Association.

Gould, S. J. (1981). *The mismeasure of man*. New York: W. W. Norton & Company.

Gould, S. J. (1987). Bushes all the way down. *Natural History, 96*, 12–19.

Gould, S. J. (1988). Honorable men and women. *Natural History, 97*, 16–21.

Gould, S. J. (1994). The geometer of race. *Discover, 15,* 65–69.

Gould, S. J. (1996). *The mismeasure of man* (Rev. ed.). New York: W. W. Norton & Company.

Grant, M. (1916). *The passing of the great race.* New York: Charles Scribner's Sons.

Grant, M. (1918). *The passing of the great race: Or the racial basis of European history* (Rev. ed.). New York: Charles Scribner's Sons.

Grant, M. (1920). "Introduction." In *The rising tide of color: Against white world supremacy* (pp. xi–xxxii). New York: Charles Scribner's Sons.

Grant, M. (1921). *The passing of the great race: Or the racial basis of European history* (4th Rev. ed. with preface by Henry Fairfield Osborn). New York: Charles Scribner's Sons.

Grant, M. (1933). *The conquest of a continent, or the expansion of races in America.* New York: Charles Scribner's Sons.

Greene, J. C. (1959). *The death of Adam: Evolution and its impact on western thought.* Ames: Iowa State University Press.

Guillén, A. K., Barrett, G. M., & Takenaka, O. (2005). Genetic diversity among African great apes based on mitochondrial DNA sequences. *Biodiversity and Conservation, 14,* 2221–2233.

Gutin, J. (1994). End of the rainbow. *Discover, 15,* 71–75.

Gyory, A. (1998). *Closing the gate: Race, politics, and the Chinese Exclusion Act.* Chapel Hill: University of North Carolina Press.

Hamilton, W. D. (1964). The genetical evolution of social behavior, I and II. *Journal of Theoretical Biology, 7,* 1–52.

Hanihara, T. (2000). Frontal and facial flatness of major human populations. *American Journal of Physical Anthropology, 111,* 105–134.

Harrison, G. (1978). *Mosquitoes, malaria and man: A history of the hostilities since 1880.* New York: E. P. Dutton.

Hartmann, E. G. (1979). *American immigration*. Minneapolis, MN: Lerner Publications.

Harvey, O. J., White, B. J., Hood, W. R., & Sherif, M. (1961). *The Robbers Cave experiment: Intergroup conflict and cooperation*. Middletown, CT: Wesleyan University Press.

Haviland, W. A., Prins, H. L., Walrath, D., & McBride, B. (2005). *Anthropology: The human challenge* (11th ed.). Belmont, CA: Thomson Learning, Inc.

Hinkes, M. J. (1993). Realities of racial determination in a forensic setting. In C. Gordon (Ed.), *Race, ethnicity, and applied bioanthropology* (pp. 48–53). (Bulletin No. 13). Arlington, VA: American Anthropological Association.

Hirschfeld, L. A. (1996). *Race in the making: Cognition, culture and the child's construction of human kinds*. Cambridge, MA: MIT Press.

Holick, M. F., MacLaughlin, J. A., & Doppelt, S. H. (1981). Regulation of cutaneous previtamin D_3 photosynthesis in man: Skin pigment is not an essential regulator. *Science, 211*, 590–593.

Hooton, E. A. (1926). Method of racial analysis. *Science, 63*, 75–81.

Hooton, E. A. (1931). *Up from ape*. New York: Macmillan.

Hooton, E. A. (1936). Plain statement about race. *Science, 83*, 511–513.

Hooton, E. A. (1939a). Should we ignore racial differences? Transcript from an NBC broadcast of *Town Hall*, 11/16/39. *Town Hall, 5*, 9–15.

Hooton, E. A. (1939b). *Twilight of man*. New York: G. P. Putnam.

Hooton, E. A. (1946). *Up from ape* (2nd ed.). New York: Macmillan.

Houshmand, M., Holme, E., Hanson, C., Wennerholm, U. B., & Hamberger, L. (1997). Is paternal mitochondrial DNA transferred to the offspring following intracytoplasmic sperm injection? *Journal of Assisted Reproduction and Genetics, 14*, 223–227.

Howells, W. W. (1942). Fossil man and the origin of races. *American Anthropologist, 44*, 182–193.

Howells, W. W. (1950). Origin of the human stock. Concluding remarks of the chairman: present outlook on human origins. *Cold Spring Harbor Symposia on Quantitative Biology, 15,* 79–86.

Howells, W. W. (1959). *Mankind in the making.* Garden City, NY: Doubleday.

Howells, W. W. (1973). Cranial variation in man: A study by multivariate analysis of patterns of difference among recent human populations. (Papers of the Peabody Museum of Archaeology and Ethnology). Cambridge, MA: Harvard University Press.

Howells, W. W. (1989). Skull shapes and the map: Craniometric analysis in the dispersion of modern *Homo.* (Papers of the Peabody Museum of Archaeology and Ethnology. Vol. 79). Cambridge, MA: Harvard University Press.

Howells, W. W. (1993). *Getting here. The story of human evolution.* Washington, DC: Compass Press.

Hrdlička, A. (1919). *Physical anthropology, its scope and aims; its history and present status in the United States.* Philadelphia: Wistar Institute of Anatomy and Biology Press.

Hrdlička, A. (1939). *Practical anthropometry.* Philadelphia: Wistar Institute of Anatomy and Biology.

Hudnutt, W. H., III. (1956). Samuel Stanhope Smith: Enlightened conservation. *Journal of the History of Ideas, 17,* 540–552.

Hulse, E. S. (1971). *The human species.* New York: Random House.

Huxley, J. S., & Haddon, A. C. (1935). *We Europeans: A survey of racial problems.* New York: Harper.

Ishida, H. (1992). Flatness of facial skeletons in Siberian and other circum-Pacific populations. *Zoological and Morphological Anthropology, 79,* 53–67.

Jablonski, N. G., & Chaplin, G. (2000). The evolution of human skin coloration. *Journal of Human Evolution, 39*, 57–106.

Jantz, R. L., & Moore-Jansen, P. (1988). A data base for forensic anthropology: Structure, content, and analysis. (Report of Investigations No. 47). Knoxville: Department of Anthropology, University of Tennessee.

Jantz, R. L., & Ousley, S. D. (2005). *Fordisc 3.0 personal computer forensic discriminant functions.* Knoxville: Department of Anthropology, University of Tennessee.

Jolly, C. J. (1993). Species, subspecies, and baboon systematics. In W. H. Kimbel & L. B. Martin (Eds.), *Species, species concepts, and primate evolution* (pp. 67–107). New York: Plenum Press.

Jordan, W. D. (1965). "Introduction." In Samuel Stanhope Smith, *An essay on the causes of the variety of complexion and figure in the human species* (pp. vii–lvii). Cambridge, MA: Belknap Press of Harvard University Press.

Jurmain, R., & Nelson, H. (1994). *Introduction to physical anthropology* (6th ed.). New York: West Publishing Company.

Katzmarzyk, P. T., & Leonard, W. R. (1998). Climatic influences on human body size and proportions: Ecological adaptations and secular trends. *American Journal of Physical Anthropology, 106*, 483–503.

Keith, A., Sir. (1931). *The place of prejudice in modern civilization (prejudice and politics). Rectorial address to the students of Aberdeen University.* London: Williams & Norgate.

Keith, A., Sir. (1936). Origins of modern races of mankind. *Nature, 138*, 194.

Keith, A., Sir. (1946). *Essays on human evolution.* London: Watts & Company.

Keith, A., Sir. (1950). *An autobiography.* London: Watts & Company.

Kevles, D. J. (1995). *In the name of eugenics: Genetics and the uses of human heredity.* New York: Alfred A. Knopf.

Kipling, R. (1907). *Collected verse of Rudyard Kipling*. New York: Doubleday, Page & Company.

Klag, M. J., Wheldon, P. K., Coresh, J., Grim, C. E., & Kuller, L. H. (1991). The association of skin color with blood pressure in U.S. blacks with low socioeconomic status. *Journal of American Medical Association, 265*, 599–602.

Klein, J. (1995, February 13). The end of affirmative action. *Newsweek, 125*, 36–37.

Komar, D. A., & Buikstra, J. E. (2008). *Forensic anthropology: Contemporary theory and practice*. New York: Oxford University Press.

Kottak, C. P. (2006). *Anthropology; The exploration of human diversity*. New York: McGraw-Hill.

Krieger, N. (1987). Shades of difference: Theoretical underpinnings of the medical controversy on black-white differences, 1830–1870. *International Journal of Health Services, 17*, 258–279.

Krieger, N., Rowley, D. L., Herman, A. A., Avery, B., & Phillips, M. T. (1993). Racism, sexism, and social class: Implications for studies of health, disease, and well-being. *American Journal of Preventative Medicine, 9* (Supplement), 82–122.

Krogman, W. M. (1939). A guide to the identification of human skeletal material. *FBI Law Enforcement Bulletin, 8*, 3–31.

Krogman, W. M. (1962). *The human skeleton in forensic medicine* (2nd ed.). Springfield, IL: Charles C. Thomas.

Krogman, W. M., & Işcan, M. Y. (1986). *The human skeleton in forensic medicine* (2nd ed.). Springfield, IL: Charles C. Thomas.

Kurzban, R., Tooby, J., & Cosmides, L. (2001). Can race be erased? Coalitional computation and social categorization. *Proceedings of the National Academy of Sciences, 98*, 15387–15392.

Larsen, C. P. (2008). *Our origins: Discovering physical anthropology*. New York: W. W. Norton.

Larson, J. L. (1971). *Reason and experience: The representation of natural order in the work of Carl von Linné*. Berkeley: University of California Press.

Lemann, N. (1999, September 6). Behind the SAT. *Newsweek, 134,* 52–57.

Leon, D. A., & Walt, G. (2001). Poverty, inequality, and health in international perspective. In D. A. Leon & G. Walt (Eds.), *Poverty, inequality, and health: An international perspective* (pp. 1–16). Oxford: Oxford University Press.

Lesly, M. (1988). *Subway gunman: A juror's account of the Bernhard Goetz trial*. Latham, NY: British American Publishing.

Lewin, R. (1993). *The origin of modern humans*. New York: Scientific American Library.

Lewontin, R. C. (1972). The apportionment of human diversity. In T. Dobzhansky, M. K. Hecht, & W. C. Steers (Eds.), *Evolutionary Biology* (Vol. 6) (pp. 381–398). New York: Appleton-Century-Crofts.

Lieberman, L., Kirk, R. C., & Littlefield, A. (2003). Exchange across difference: The status of the race concept—Perishing paradigm: Race—1931–99. *American Anthropologist, 105,* 110–113.

Lieberman, L., & Reynolds, L. T. (1996). Race: The deconstruction of a scientific concept. In L. T. Reynolds & L. Lieberman (Eds.), *Race and other misadventures: Essays in honor of Ashley Montagu in his ninetieth year* (pp. 142–173). New York: General Hall Publishers.

Lindroth, S. (1983). The two faces of Linnaeus. In T. Frängsmyr (Ed.), *Linnaeus: The man and his work* (pp. 1–62). Berkeley: University of California Press.

Linnaeus, C. (1956). *Caroli Linnaei, systema naturae per regna tria naturae, secundum classes, ordines, species, cum characteribus, differentiis, synonymis, locis* (10th revision of 1758, Vols. 1–2). Stockholm: Laurentii Salvii.

Little, M. A., & Baker, P. T. (1988). Migration and adaptation. In C. G. N. Mascie-Taylor & G. W. Lasker (Eds.), *Biological aspects of human migration* (pp. 167–215). Cambridge: Cambridge University Press.

Livingstone, D. N. (1987). *Nathaniel Southgate Shaler and the culture of American science.* Tuscaloosa: University of Alabama Press.

Livingstone, F. B. (1958). Anthropological implications of sickle cell gene distribution in West Africa. *American Anthropologist, 60,* 533–562.

Livingstone, F. B. (1962). On the non-existence of human races. *Current Anthropology, 3,* 279.

Livingstone, F. B. (1971). Malaria and human polymorphisms. *Annual Review of Genetics, 5,* 33–64.

Long, E. (1774). *The history of Jamaica, or general survey of the ancient and modern state of that island: With reflections on its situation, settlements, inhabitants, climate, products, laws and government* (Vols. 1–3). London: Lowndes.

Long, J. C., Williams, R. C., McAuley, J. E., Medis, R., Partel, R., Tregellas, W. M.,...Iwaniec, U. (1991). Genetic variation in Arizona Mexican Americans: Estimate and interpretation of admixture proportions. *American Journal of Physical Anthropology, 84,* 141–157.

Loomis, W. F. (1967). Skin-pigment regulation of vitamin-D biosynthesis in man. *Science, 157,* 501–506.

Lurie, E. (1960). *Louis Agassiz: A life in science.* Chicago: University of Chicago Press.

Lyell, C. (1830–1833). *Principles of geology.* London: Murray.

Mann, A. (2009). The origins of American physical anthropology in Philadelphia. *Yearbook of Physical Anthropology, 52,* 155–163.

Maples, W. R., & Browning, M. (1994). *Dead men do tell tales.* New York: Doubleday.

Marks, J. (1995). *Human biodiversity: Genes, race, and history*. New York: Aldine de Gruyter.

Mayr, E. (1963). *Animal species and evolution*. Cambridge, MA: Belknap Press of Harvard University Press.

Mayr, E. (1982). *The growth of biological thought: Diversity, evolution, and inheritance*. Cambridge, MA: Belknap Press of Harvard University Press.

Mayr, E. (1996). What is a species and what is not? *Philosophy of Science, 63*, 262–277.

McCullough, D. (1977). The American adventure of Louis Agassiz. *Audubon, 79*, 12–17.

McGrew, W. C. (2001). The nature of culture: Prospects and pitfalls of cultural primatology. In F. B. M. de Waal (Ed.), *Tree of origin: What primate behavior can tell us about human social evolution* (pp. 229–254). Cambridge, MA: Harvard University Press.

McPhee, J. (1982). *Basin and range*. New York: Farrar, Straus, and Giroux.

Meacham, J., Campo-Flores, A., Smith, V. E., Breslau, K., Samuels, A., & Clemetson, L. (2000, September 18). The new face of race. *Newsweek, 136*, 38–41.

Meier, B. (1994, September 7). Simpson team taking aim at DNA laboratory. *New York Times*. Retrieved December 12, 2008, from http://www.nytimes.com/1994/09/07/us/simpson-team-taking-aim-at-dna-laboratory.html

Meindl, R. S. (1987). Hypothesis: A selective advantage for cystic fibrosis. *American Journal of Physical Anthropology, 74*, 39–45.

Merriam-Webster's Collegiate Dictionary. (2003). (11th ed.). Springfield, MA: Merriam-Webster, Inc.

Michael, J. S. (1988). A new look at Morton's craniological research. *Current Anthropology, 29*, 349–354.

Molnar, S. (2002). *Human variation: Races, types, and ethnic groups* (5th ed.). Upper Saddle River, NJ: Prentice Hall.

Montagu, A. (1942). *Man's most dangerous myth: The fallacy of race.* New York: Columbia University Press.

Montagu, A. (1964). Discussion and criticism on the race concept. *Current Anthropology, 5,* 317.

Morison, S. E., Commager, H. E., & Leichtenburg, W. E. (1980). *The growth of the American Republic* (Vol. 2). New York: Oxford University Press.

Morning, A. (2003). New faces, old faces: Counting the multiracial population past and present. In L. I. Winters and H. L. DeBose (Eds.), *New faces in a changing America: Multiracial identity in the 21st century* (pp. 41–67). Thousand Oaks, CA: Sage Publications.

Morton, S. G. (1839). *Crania Americana; or, a comparative view of the skulls of various aboriginal nations of North and South America; to which is prefixed an essay on the varieties of the human species.* Philadelphia: J. Dobson.

Morton, S. G. (1844). *Crania Ægyptiaca; or observations on Egyptian ethnography derived from anatomy, history and the monuments.* Philadelphia: John Pennington.

Morton, S. G. (1847). Hybridity in animals, considered in reference to the question of the unity of the human species. *American Journal of Science and Arts, 3,* 203–212.

Morton, S. G. (1849). *Catalogue of skulls of man and the inferior animals in the collection of Samuel George Morton* (3rd ed.). Philadelphia: Merrihew & Thompson.

Morton, S. G. (1850). On the value of the word species in zoology. *American Journal of Science, 5,* 81–82.

Morton, S. G. (1851). Value of the word species in zoology. *American Journal of Science, 11,* 275–276.

Mourant, A. E., Kopec, A. C., & Domaniewska-Sobczak, K. (1978). *Blood groups and diseases*: *A study of associations of diseases with blood groups and other polymorphisms*. New York: Oxford University Press.

Muir, D. (1993). Race: The mythic roots of racism. *Sociological Inquiry*, *63*, 339–350.

Müller, F. M. (2004). *Biographies of words and the home of the Aryans* (Reprint of 1888). Whitefish, MT: Kessinger Publishing.

Murdock, Delroy. (2001, March 9). *The needed separation of race and state*. Retrieved October 24, 2007, from http://jewishworldreview.com/cols/murdock1.asp

Mydans, S. (1992, May 13). After the riots; 4 held in attack at riots' outset." *New York Times*. Retrieved April 9, 2008, from http://www.nytimes.com/1992/05/13/us/after-the-riots-4-held-in-attack-at-riots-outset.html

Nafte, M. (2000). *Flesh and bone*: *An introduction to forensic anthropology*. Durham, NC: Carolina Academic Press.

National Center for Health Statistics. (1993). *Vital statistics classification and coding instructions for live birth records*. Hyattsville, MD: National Center for Health.

Neuffer, C. H. (1960). John Bachman, a biography. In C. H. Neuffer (Ed.), *The Christian Happoldt journal*. *His European tour with John Bachman*. *Contributions from the Charleston Museum 13* (pp. 29–118). Charleston, SC: Charleston Museum.

Noll, M. A. (1989). *Princeton and the republic, 1768–1822*: *The search for a Christian Enlightenment in the era of Samuel Stanhope Smith*. Princeton, NJ: Princeton University Press.

Nystrom, P., & Ashmore, P. (2008). *The life of primates*. Upper Saddle River, NJ: Pearson Education.

Osborne, R. H., & DeGeorge, F. V. (1959). *Genetic basis of morphological variation*. Cambridge, MA: Harvard University Press.

Ousley, S., & Hefner, J. (2005). Morphoscopic traits and the statistical determination of ancestry. *Proceedings of the Annual Meeting of the American Academy of Forensic Sciences, 11*, 291–292.

Ousley, S. D., & Jantz, R. L. (1996). *Fordisc 2.0 personal computer forensic discriminant functions.* Knoxville: Department of Anthropology, University of Tennessee.

Oxford English Dictionary. (1989). (2nd ed.). New York: Oxford University Press.

Parra, E. J., Kittles, R. A., Argyropoulos, G., Pfaff, C. L., Heister, K., Bonilla, C.,…Shriver, M. D. (2001). Ancestral proportions and admixture dynamics in geographically defined African Americans living in South Carolina. *American Journal of Physical Anthropology, 114*, 18–29.

Patterson, O. (2001, May 8). Race by the numbers. *New York Times.* Retrieved February 12, 2008, from http://www.nytimes.com/ref/member-center/nytarchive.html

Post, P. W., Daniels, F., Jr., & Binford, R. T., Jr. (1975). Cold injury and the evolution of "white" skin. *Human Biology, 47*, 65–80.

Powell, A. (2004, February 5). *New categories cause confusion.* Retrieved October 24, 2007, from http://news.harvard.edu/gazette/print-gazette-archives/

Powell, J., & Rose, J. (2004, May). *Report on the osteological assessment of the "Kennewick Man" skeleton (CENWWW.97.Kennewick). Report prepared for the National Park Service, Department of the Interior, Washington, DC.* Retrieved September 2, 2005, from http://www.cr.nps.gov/aad/kennewick

Pruner-Bey, F. (1863). Obeservations sur le crane de Néanderthal. *Bulletins de la Société d'Anthropologie de Paris, 4*, 318–323.

Raven, P. H., & Johnson, G. B. (2002). *Biology* (6th ed.). New York: McGraw-Hill.

Relethford, J. H. (1997). Hemispheric difference in human skin color. *American Journal of Physical Anthropology, 104*, 449–457.

Relethford, J. H. (2005). *The human species: An introduction to biological anthropology* (6th ed.). New York: McGraw-Hill.

Relethford, J. H., & Harpending, H. C. (1994). Craniometric variation, genetic theory, and modern human origins. *American Journal of Physical Anthropology, 95,* 249–270.

Relethford, J. H., & Harpending, H. C. (1995). Ancient differences in population size can mimic a recent African origin of modern humans. *Current Anthropology, 36,* 667–674.

Renschler, E. S., & Monge, J. (2008). The Samuel George Morton Cranial Collection—Historical significance and new research. *Expedition, 50,* 30–38.

Rhine, S. (1990). Non-metric skull racing. In G. W. Gill & J. S. Rhine (Eds.), *Skeletal attribution of race: Methods for forensic anthropology* (pp. 9–20). (Anthropology Papers No. 4). Albuquerque, NM: Maxwell Museum of Anthropology.

Rhine, S. (1993). Skeletal criteria for racial attribution. In C. Gordon (Ed.), *Race, ethnicity, and applied bioanthropology* (pp. 54–67). (Bulletin No. 13). Arlington, VA: American Anthropological Association.

Rhine, S. (1998). *Bone voyage: A journey in forensic anthropology.* Albuquerque, NM: University of New Mexico Press.

Ripley, W. Z. (1899). *The races of Europe: A sociological study.* New York: D. Appleton & Company.

Roberts, D. F. (1978). *Climate and human variability* (2nd ed.). Menlo Park, CA: Cummings.

Robins, A. H. (1991). *Biological perspectives on human pigmentation.* Cambridge: Cambridge University Press.

Roitt, I. M. (1988). *Essential immunology* (6th ed.). Oxford: Blackwell Scientific Publications.

Romero, J. (1970). Dental mutilation, trephination, and cranial deformation. In T. D. Stewart (Ed.), *Handbook of Middle American Indians* (Vol. 9) (pp. 50–67). Austin: University of Texas Press.

Romualdi, C., Balding, D., Nasidze, I. S., Risch, G., Robichaux, M., Sherry, S. T.,...Barbujani, G. (2002). Patterns of human diversity, within and among continents, inferred from biallelic DNA polymorphisms. *Genome Research, 12*, 602–612.

Rosenberg, N. A., Pritchard, J. K., Weber, J. L., Cann, H. M., Kidd, K. K., Zhivotovsky, L. A., & Feldman, M. W. (2002). Genetic structure of human populations. *Science, 298*, 2381–2385.

Rudwick, M. J. (1972). *The meaning of fossils: Episodes in the history of palaeontology*. London: Macdonald.

Sarich, V., & Miele, F. (2004). *Race: The reality of human differences*. Boulder, CO: Westview Press.

Sauer, N. J. (1992). Forensic anthropology and the concept of race: If races don't exist, why are forensic anthropologists so good at identifying them? *Social Science and Medicine, 4*, 107–111.

Sauer, N. J. (1993). Applied anthropology and the concept of race: A legacy of Linnaeus. In C. Gordon (Ed.), *Race, ethnicity, and applied bioanthropology* (pp. 79–83). (Bulletin No. 13). Arlington, VA: American Anthropological Association.

Schiller, F. (1979). *Paul Broca: Founder of French anthropology, explorer of the brain*. Berkeley: University of California Press.

Schwartz, J. H. (1974). The human remains from Kition and Hala Sultan Tekke: A cultural interpretation. In V. Karageorghis (Ed.), *Excavations at Kition. The tombs* (Vol. 1) (pp. 151–162). Nicosia, Egypt: Cyprus Department of Antiquities.

Shapiro, H. L. (1981). Earnest A. Hooton, 1887–1954 *in memoriam cum amore. American Journal of Physical Anthropology, 56*, 431–434.

Shea, B. T., & Gomez, A. M. (1988). Tooth scaling and evolutionary dwarfism: An investigation of allometry in human pygmies. *American Journal of Physical Anthropology, 77*, 117–132.

Shipman, P. (1994). *The evolution of racism. Human differences and the use and abuse of science*. New York: Simon & Schuster.

Shreeve, J. (1994). Terms of estrangement. *Discover, 15*, 56–63.

Sirianni, J. (1993). Proceedings of the sixty-second meeting of the American Association of Physical Anthropologists. *American Journal of Physical Anthropology, 92*, 549–560.

Sollors, W. (2000). *Interracialism*: *Black-white intermarriage in American history, literature, and law*. Oxford: Oxford University Press.

Spencer, F. (1979). Aleš Hrdlička, M.D., 1869–1943. A chronicle of the life and work of an American physical anthropologist (Vols. 1–2). PhD diss.: University of Michigan, Ann Arbor.

Stern, C. (1973). *Principles of human genetics* (3rd ed.). San Francisco: W. H. Freeman.

Stewart, T. D. (1979). *Essentials of forensic anthropology, especially as developed in the United States*. Springfield, IL: Charles C. Thomas.

Stoddard, L. (1920). *The rising tide of color*: *Against white world supremacy*. New York: Charles Scribner's Sons.

Strier, K. B. (2007). *Primate behavioral ecology* (3rd ed.). New York: Allyn & Bacon.

Stringer, C.B., & Gamble, C. (1993). *In Search of the Neanderthals*. London: Thames and Hudson.

Tackett, R.L., Ergul, A., & Puett, D. (1995). Distribution of endothelin receptors in saphenous veins of African Americans: Implications of racial racial differences. *Journal of Cardiovascular Pharmacology, 34*, 327–332.

Tattersall, I. (1995). *The last Neanderthal*: *The rise, success, and mysterious extinction of our closest human relatives*. New York: Macmillan.

Taylor, R. E., Kirner, D., Southon, J., & Chatters, J. (1998). Radiocarbon dates of Kennewick Man. *Science, 280*, 1171.

Templeton, A. R. (1993). The "Eve" hypothesis: A genetic critique and reanalysis. *American Anthropologist, 95,* 51–72.

Templeton, A. R. (1994). "Eve": Hypothesis compatibility versus hypothesis testing. *American Anthropologist, 96,* 141–147.

Templeton, A. R. (1999). Human races: A genetic and evolutionary perspective. *American Anthropologists, 100,* 632–650.

Texeira, M. T. (2003). The new multiracialism: An affirmation of or an end to race as we know it? In L. I. Winters & H. L. DeBose (Eds.), *New faces in a changing America: Multiracial identity in the 21st century* (pp. 21–37). Thousand Oaks, CA: Sage Publications.

Thorne, A. G. (1981). The center and edge: The significance of Australasian hominids to African paleoanthropology. In R. E. Leakey and B. A. Ogot (Eds.), *Proceedings of the 8th Panafrican Congress of Prehistory and Quaternary Studies, Nairobi, September 1977* (pp. 180–181). Nairobi, Kenya: Tillmiap.

Thorne, A. G., & Wolpoff, M. H. (1992). The multiregional evolution of humans. *Scientific American, 266,* 76–83.

Tucker, W. H. (2002). *The funding of scientific racism: Wickliffe Draper and the Pioneer Fund.* Urbana: University of Illinois Press.

Tyson, N. (1999). Holy wars. *Natural History, 108,* 80–82.

Tyson, N. (2005). The perimeter of ignorance: A boundary where scientists face a choice, invoke a diety or continue the quest for knowledge. *Natural History, 114,* 28–34.

Ubelaker, D. H. (1951). *Human skeletal remains* (3rd ed.). Washington, DC: Taraxacum Press.

UNESCO. (1950). Statement on race. In A. Montagu (Ed.), *Statement on race* (p. 13). London: Oxford University Press.

UNESCO. (1951). *The concept of race: Results of an inquiry.* Paris: UNESCO.

University of Calgary. (2001). Population movements. The applied history group. Retrieved January 10, 2008, from http://www.ucalgary.ca/applied_history/tutor/migrations/home7.html

U.S. Census Bureau. (2000). Racial and ethnic classifications used in Census 2000 and beyond. Retrieved October 24, 2007, from http://www.census.gov/population/www/socdemo/race/racefactcb.html

U.S. Census Bureau. (2001). *The two or more races population: 2000 Census 2000 brief, November 2001*. Washington, DC: U.S. Census Bureau.

U.S. Census Office. (1872). *The statistics of the population of the United States*. Washington, DC: U.S. Government Printing Office.

U.S. Office of Management and Budget. (2000). *Provisional guidance on the implementation of the 1997 standards for the collection of federal data on race and ethnicity*. Washington, DC: U.S. Office of Management and Budget.

Vogel, F. (1975). ABO blood groups, the HL-A system and diseases. In F. M. Salzano (Ed.), *The role of natural selection in human evolution*. New York: American Elsevier.

Vogel, F., & Motulsky, A. G. (1986). *Human genetics: Problems and approaches* (2nd ed.). New York: Springer-Verlag.

Vogt, C. (1864). *Lectures on man: His place in creation and in the history of the earth*. London: Longman, Green, Longman and Roberts.

Von Koenigswald, G. H. R., & Weidenreich, F. (1939). The relationship between *Pithecanthropus* and *Sinanthropus*. *Nature, 144*, 926–929.

Walker, R. A. (1993). The impact of racial variation on human engineering design criteria. In B. Gordon (Ed.), *Race, ethnicity, and applied bioanthropology* (pp. 7–12). (Bulletin No. 13). Arlington, VA: American Anthropological Association.

Warren, J. (1911). Thomas Dwight, M.D., L.L.D. *Anatomical Record, 5*, 439–531.

Warren, J. W., & Twine, F. W. (1997). White Americans, the new minority? Non-blacks and the ever-expanding boundaries of whiteness. *Journal of Black Studies, 28*, 200–218.

Washburn, S. L. (1951). The new physical anthropology. *Transactions of the New York Academy of Sciences, 13*, 298–304.

Washburn, S. L. (1963). The study of race. *American Anthropologist, 65*, 521–532.

Watson, J. D., & Crick, F. H. C. (1953). A structure for deoxyribose nucleic acid. *Nature, 171*, 737.

Weidenreich, F. (1927). *Rasse und köperbau* [Race and body form]. Berlin: Springer.

Weidenreich, F. (1928). Entwicklungs-und Rassentypen des *Homo primigenius* [The evolution and racial types of *Homo primigenius*]. *Natur und Museum, 58*, 1–62.

Weidenreich, F. (1939). On the earliest representatives of modern mankind recovered on the soil of East Asia. *Peking Natural History Bulletin, 13*, 161–174.

Weidenreich, F. (1940). Some problems dealing with ancient man. *American Anthropologist, 42*, 375–383.

Weidenreich, F. (1943). The skull of *Sinanthropus pekinensis*: A comparative study of a primitive hominid skull. *Palaeontologia Sinica*, New Series D, No. 10 (whole series No. 127).

Weidenreich, F. (1946). Report on the latest discoveries of early man in the Far East. *Experienta, 2*, 265–272.

Weidenreich, F. (1947). Are human races in the taxonomic sense "races" or "species"? *American Journal of Physical Anthropology, 5*, 369–371.

Weeks, E. (1966). *The Lowells and their institute*. Boston: Little Brown.

Williams, B. J. (1979). *Evolution and human origins*. New York: Harper and Row.

Williams, D. R. (1999). Race, socioeconomic status, and health: The added effects of racism and discrimination. *Annal of New York Academy of Sciences, 896*, 173–188.

Williams, F. L. E., Belcher, R. L., & Armelagos, G. J. (2005). Forensic misclassification of ancient Nubian crania: Implications for assumptions about human variation. *Current Anthropology, 46*, 340–346.

Wills, C. (1994). The skin we're in. *Discover, 15*, 77–81.

Wilson, T. W. (1986). History of salt supplies in West Africa and blood pressures today. *Lancet, 1*, 784–786.

Wilson, A. C., & Cann, R. (1992). The recent African genesis of humans. *Scientific American, 266*, 593–607.

Wilson, J. F., Weale, M. E., Smith, A. C., Gratrix, F., Fletcher, B, Thomas, M. G.,…Goldstein, D. B. (2001). Population genetic structure of variable drug response. *Nature Genetics, 29*, 265–269.

Wolpoff, M. H., & Caspari, R. (1997). *Race and human evolution: A fatal attraction*. New York: Simon and Schuster.

Woo, T. L., & Morant, G. M. (1934). A biometric study of the "flatness" of the facial skeleton in man. *Biometrika, 26*, 196–250.

Wood, B. A. (1994). The problems of our origins. *Journal of Human Evolution, 27*, 519–529.

Wood, C. S. (1974). Preferential feeding of anopheles gambiae mosquitoes on human subjects of blood group O: A relationship between the ABO polymorphism and malaria vectors. *Human Biology, 46*, 385–404.

Wood, P. (Ed.). (2000). *The Scottish Enlightenment: Essays in reinterpretation*. Rochester, NY: University of Rochester Press.

Workman, P. L., Blumberg, B. S., & Cooper, A. J. (1963). Selection, gene migration, and polymorphic stability in a U.S. white and negro population. *American Journal of Human Genetics, 15*, 429–437.

Wright, L., & Hartman, C. (1994, November/December). Race/ethnic categories: Do they matter? Retrieved October 24, 2007, from http://www.prrac.org/index.php

Yamaguchi, B. (1973). Facial flatness measurements of the Ainu and Japanese crania. *Bulletin National Science Museum, 16*, 161–171.

TEXT AND ILLUSTRATION CREDITS

CHAPTER 1

Figure 1.1, p. 9, Code Network Media Group. Copyright ©2006; pp. 10, 12–14, *Human variation: Races, type, and ethnic groups* by Stephen Molnar, pp. 18–20. Copyright ©2002. Reprinted with the permission of Pearson Education, Inc.; pp. 15–17, *"Race" is a four-letter word: The genesis of the concept* by C. Loring Brace, pp. 24–26. Copyright ©2005. Reprinted with the permission of Oxford University Press; p. 7, From "The status of the race concept in physical anthropology" by Matt Cartmill, p. 651. Copyright ©1999. Reprinted with the permission of the author.

CHAPTER 2

pp. 30–32, 34, 38–39, 41, 43–44, 49, 53, *"Race" is a four-letter word: The genesis of the concept* by C. Loring Brace, pp. 40, 52–53, 80, 82–83, 90, 97, 101–102, 105, 109, 148, 152, 223, 235, 237. Copyright ©2005. Reprinted with the permission of Oxford University Press; p. 31, From "The geometer of race" by Stephen J. Gould, pp. 66, 68. Copyright ©1994. Reprinted with the permission of Rhonda Shearer.

CHAPTER 3

pp. 61–63, 65–66, 68–71, 78–79, *Race and human evolution: A fatal attraction* by Milford Wolpoff and Rachel Caspari, pp. 125–126, 134, 185, 194–195, 199, 262, and 357. Copyright ©1997. Reprinted with the permission of Simon & Schuster, Inc., and the authors; figure 3.1, p. 72, From *Race and human evolution: A fatal attraction* by Milford Wolpoff and Rachel Caspari, p. 201. Copyright ©1997. Reprinted with the permission of Simon & Schuster, Inc., and the authors; figure 3.2, p. 74,

CHAPTER 4

CHAPTER 5

Reprinted with the permission of the Maxwell Museum of Anthropology and Julie R. Angel; figure 5.3, p. 135, From "High resolution of human evolutionary trees with polymorphic microsatellites" by Anne Bowcock et al., p. 456. Copyright ©1994. Reprinted with the permission of Nature Publishing Group; figure 5.4, p. 138, From *The human species; An introduction to biological anthropology*, 6th ed., by John Relethford, p. 142. Copyright ©2005. Reprinted with the permission of McGraw-Hill Companies; p. 139, From "Race without color" by Jared Diamond, pp. 87–88. Copyright ©1994. Reprinted with the permission of the author; p. 57, From "Race, ethnicity, and human engineering: The impact of racial variation" by Robert Walker, p. 7. Copyright ©1993. Reprinted with the permission of the author.

Chapter 6

Table 3, p. 155, From "Selection, gene migration, and polymorphic stability in a U.S. white and negro population" by Workman et al., p. 430. Copyright ©1963. Reprinted with the permission of Elsevier.

Chapter 7

pp. 173–175, From "Are ethnic groups biological 'species' to the human brain? Essentialism in our cognition of some social categories" by Francisco Gil-White, pp. 517–519. Copyright ©2001. Reprinted with the permission of the University of Chicago Press; pp. 172–175, 177–179, 185, From *Us and them: The science of identity* by David Berreby, pp. xiii, xix, 69–70, 134–135, 168–169, 322. Copyright ©2005. Reprinted with the permission of Little, Brown & Company.

INDEX

population admixture, 2, 87,
140, 142–143, 150–151,
154–155, 157, 159. *See also*
African Americans; dihybrids;
Hispanics; hybrids; Latino;
multiracial; multiracialism; racial
classification; trihybrids
Principles of Geology, 35. *See also*
deep time; Lyell, Charles
Project RACE, 163–164, 194n49.
See also multiracialism; race
Pruner-Bey, Franz, 60. *See also*
Neanderthal; race
Putnam, Carleton, 55, 191n23.
See also Coon, Carelton S.;
race; *Race and Reason:
A Yankee View*

quadroon, 143, 160. *See also*
hybrids; mixed blood; mixed
race; mulattoes; multiracial

race, xiii–xvii, 1–3, 5, 7–16, 18–19,
22, 25, 27, 31–32, 34–36, 38–40,
42, 44–57, 59–106, 108–112, 114,
117, 119–121, 123–124, 126–129,
130–138, 140, 143–144, 146–148,
150–167, 170, 172–186, 187n1,
187n3, 187n5, 188n11, 189n16,
190nn18–19, 191n22, 191n25,
193n37, 193n40, 194nn45–46,
194n49
Race and Reason: A Yankee View,
55, 191n23. *See also* Coon,
Carleton S.; Putnam, Carleton;
race
Races of Europe, 46, 54, 64. *See also*
Coon, Carleton S.; race; Ripley,
William Z.

*Races of Europe: A Sociological
Study*, 46, 54, 134. *See also* Coon,
Carleton S.; Nordic; Ripley,
William Z.
racial admixture, 27. *See also* African
Americans; Hispanics; hybrid;
Latino; mixed blood; mixed
race; multiracial; multiracialsm;
octoroon; quadroon
racial classification, 150, 182. *See
also* anthropologists; forensic;
Hispanics; identity; Latino;
law enforcement
racial traits, 47, 134. *See also*
eyelid shape; facial angle; facial
prognathism; phenotype; shovel-
shaped incisors; skin color; skin
pigmentation; skull shapes
racialists, 9–10, 32, 93, 95, 98–103,
108, 126–127, 130–140, 150,
158–159, 163–167, 181–182,
187nn1–2
Relethford, John H., 75–76, 93–94,
100–107, 133, 137–138, 141, 152,
158, 193n40. *See also* skin color
Renschler, Emily, 37. *See also*
Morton, Samuel George
Retzius, Anders, 46, 112. *See also*
cephalic index; Ripley, William Z.;
skull shape
Ripley, William Z., 45–48, 54, 81,
112, 134, 146–147. *See also*
cephalic index; Nordic; race;
*Races of Europe: A Sociological
Study*; skull shape
*Rising Tide of Color Against White
World Supremacy*, 49. *See also*
Grant, Madison; mixed blood;
mixed race; race; Stoddard, Lothrop

social race, 2, 157, 167. *See also* identity; law enforcement; social label

Société d'Anthropologie de Paris, 45, 59. *See also* Broca, Paul

speciation, 38, 53. *See also* hybrids; Morton, Samuel George; race; species

species, 8–10, 13–14, 16–17, 19, 22–23, 25, 27, 30–32, 38, 40, 44, 52–53, 55–56, 59, 61–63, 67, 69–71, 73, 77–79, 84, 87, 92, 96–97, 107, 130, 143. *See also* hybrids; Morton, Samuel George; race

Stoddard, Lothrop, 49, 190n19. *See also* Grant, Madison; Nordic; race

Study of American Intelligence, 147. *See also* biological superiority; Brigham, Carl C.; immigration restriction laws; immigrants

Study of Race, 51. *See also* race; Washburn, Sherwood

subspecies, 8–11, 13–14, 130, 182. *See also* gorilla subspecies; race; taxonomic

Subway vigilante, 183. *See also* Goetz, Bernhard; race

Sutton, Walter, 85–86. *See also* genetics; inheritance

taxonomic, 8, 13–14, 32. *See also* Linnaeus, Carolus; race; species; subspecies

Tay-Sachs, 98–101, 131. *See also* Mendelian genetics; race; racial trait; simple inheritance

Templeton, Alan, 14, 75, 134. *See also* race

Teutonic, 46, 177, 189n15. *See also* Aryan; Aryan race; Gobineau, Joseph-Arthur; Nordic; Ripley, William Z.; Shaler, Nathaniel Southgate

thymine, 89, 95

Trial of the Century, 185. *See also* race; Simpson, O. J.

Trihybrid model, 155–156. *See also* admixed population; Hispanics; Mexican Americans; mixed race; multiracial; race

UNESCO Statement on Race, 56. *See also* Montagu, Ashley; race

unity of man, 19, 24, 41, 44, 55, 59, 72–73, 79, 161. *See also* ancestry; Blumenbach, Johann; Eve hypothesis; monogenism; Multiregional Evolution hypothesis; Out of Africa hypothesis; Smith, Samuel Stanhope

universal hybridization, 66, 71, 76. *See also* Multiregional Evolution hypothesis; polycentric; Weidenreich, Franz

Up from Ape, 50. *See also* biological superiority; Hooton, Earnest A.; race

valine, 95. *See also* hemoglobin S

variation, xiv–xvii, 2, 7–8, 14, 17, 20–22, 25, 34, 47, 68, 76, 78, 81–82, 84, 86, 88–90, 100, 103, 105, 109–110, 127–129, 137, 156, 158, 161, 180–182. *See also* Darwin, Charles; race; racial traits; skin color

ABOUT THE AUTHOR

Conrad Quintyn is an assistant professor of biological anthropology at Bloomsburg University. He holds a PhD and an MA from The University of Michigan and a BA from Baylor University. Dr. Quintyn's previous publications include *Human Origins: An Introduction* and *The Morphometric Affinities of the Qafzeh and Skhul Hominans*. He has published in several journals such as *Proceedings of the National Academy of Sciences* and the *Journal of Comparative Human Biology*.

www.ingramcontent.com/pod-product-compliance
Lightning Source LLC
Chambersburg PA
CBHW020342270326
41926CB00007B/288